A Gentleman's Bedside BOOK

TOM CUTLER

Constable · London

This book is dedicated to Jed,
an up-and-coming gentleman
of my acquaintance.

Constable & Robinson Ltd
3 The Lanchesters
162 Fulham Palace Road
London W6 9ER
www.constablerobinson.com

First published in the UK by Constable,
an imprint of Constable & Robinson Ltd., 2010

An extract of 'My Financial Career' by Stephen Leacock
reproduced by kind permission of the Leacock Estate.

A copy of the British Library Cataloguing in
Publication data is available from the British Library

ISBN: 978-1-84901-554-7

Printed and bound in the EU

5 7 9 10 8 6 4

PEFC
PEFC/16-33-111
CATG-PEFC-052
www.pefc.org

Acknowledgements

How lovely it would have been to sprawl on a silken divan with a cigar and watch slaves write this book for me as sultry nymphets fed me grapes. The reality was more pedestrian, though I did get help from some nice people, a few of the most assiduous of whom I should mention here. First, my parents, who, while having done what Philip Larkin said they would do, managed to mitigate the disaster during my formative years by putting plasters on grazed knees, leaving books all over the place and buying me the occasional Zoom (a form of austerity ice lolly). Second, I take my hat off to my editor, Leo Hollis, who did his best to shape this book, though I'm afraid it was rather like trying to put an avalanche into a cup. He seems to be drinking more. The task of copy-editing this broiling tohubohu devolved on the blandiloquent Howard Watson, who, with doughty hardiment, like Sherpa Tenzing amid the woozy ether of Everest's zenith, gamely scrimshawed kerfs, intrinsicate and Gordian of kidney, into every esker and moraine. But mainly he cut out sentences like that one. I am, as usual, grateful to my agent Laura Morris, who was always standing by with the crampons. The stylish drawings you will find sprinkled here and there – in a pathetic effort to disguise my inability to describe things with words – are the work of the sterling Carlos Castro, the E.H. Shepard *de nos jours*; my thanks go to him, also. Of those who aided me with research, I am grateful for help with languages to the reverberantly named Roberto García Blasco Guitiérrez San José, as well as to Lucy Cortey, Charles Neville-Smith, Fergus Anckorn and Elaine Rutledge. Martin Howells made helpful suggestions about various things, Douglas Stewart assisted with church matters, Terry Burrows told me about interesting guitarists, and Sarah Booker, Siobhan Collis, Rachel Cutler, Emma Hayward, Sarah McCarthy, Keri-Leigh Martin, Kadie Screech and Jo Uttley filled me in on the mysteries of female things. Finally, I especially thank Marianne and Jed – for the tea, and the sympathy, and everything else.

Contents

MAN ABOUT TOWN
Grooming, Dress and Gentlemanly Panache

Man Cooking

SPORT, SPEED, ACTION AND ADVENTURE
Mainly Aerobic

Mainly Isometric

Cars

Bikes

ARTS AND LETTERS

English Literature

English Language

Painting

Music Strangeness and the Problem of Noise

HOBBIES

Old-fashioned Activities in the Shed

House and Garden DIY

THE MEDIA

Famous Radio and Television Performances

Behind the TV Classics

Cinema

RELIGION FOR THE PRACTICAL MAN

Christianity Explored

FOREIGN AFFAIRS
Geography

Intercourse with Aliens

NUGACIOUS DEVIATION
Big Stuff

Potpourris

Oddball Gentlemen (and a Lady)

RELATIONSHIPS AND THAT

Love, Romance and 'Horizontal Refreshment'

New Man Skills

SCHOOL FOR SCOUNDRELS

Showmanship

Great Hoaxes and Swindles

Introduction

Next to my bed there is a pile of books. Unhappily, I haven't managed to get very far into any of them because, before you can say Mogadon, my eyes crash shut and *The Miss Marple Casebook* – as it might be – slides from my nerveless fingers on to the rug. Nor is the sedative lure of Morpheus the only problem: finding the proper bedtime reading matter is hard, too, because the brain is beginning to shut down. Let's face it, once you are between the sheets *Madame Bovary* is too heavy, magazines are too slippery and *The Guns of Navarone* too long. And if I've read the opening page of *Martin Chuzzlewit* once I've read it a hundred times. It puts you off, that book – it's got *864 pages*.

Fed up with this situation, I went to the shops, looking for something more suitable, but even after some superhuman rummaging I came away empty-handed, and decided I would jolly well have to write the thing myself.

There can be few chaps who haven't longed for a bedtime book written especially for the horizontal gentleman. What's wanted is a compendium of diverse pieces that are not only of interest to fellows but also short enough to finish before the snoring starts. *A Gentleman's Bedside Book* is my answer to this long-felt want, being both multifarious and concise. This is the Empire of Surprise, where unpredictable variety holds sway, where the quirky, serious and laugh-out-loud are in happy bedfellowship. No piece here is much longer than two or three pages either, so unless you suffer from narcolepsy you should make it to the end of even the longest of them. I have also aimed to provide frequent shots of intrigue and curiosity; and like *Ripley's Believe it or Not!* there's a good helping of 'Hey Pat!' moments – nuggets so remarkable that you just can't help poking the person dozing beside you.

A great deal of careful thought has gone into the arrangement of this literary car boot sale. Indeed, when my editor and I first sat down and looked at the heaving mass of material in front of us we almost cried. But, after several bottles of highly persuasive Balalaika-brand vodka, and some green pills which he told me had always worked for him, the two of us managed to force this gallimaufry into sections, in an attempt, possibly hopeless, to help you to find your way around.

Whatever you do, do not try reading the whole thing from start to finish, as you would *Tattooed Mountain Women and Spoon Boxes of Daghestan*. It would be like eating an entire *smörgåsbord* in one sitting. Instead, sample a zesty morsel here and another there, and then pay a visit to Snoresville. You'll discover that, in modest helpings, the material is easily digestible, with very little mastication required.

For some reason this reminds me to tell you that there is no pornography in this volume. If you are a gentleman of the five-fingered-widow persuasion, you will find plenty of that kind of thing in your local book emporium, probably somewhere between *Popular Astrology* and *Personal Growth*.

Nevertheless, this lucky dip of bedtime derring-do, humour, and rip-roaring oddity is pretty obviously of particular interest to gentlemen, if anyone knows what a 'gentleman' is these days. Recent research reveals that a woman's idea of the perfect gentleman is a man who can chop down a tree, play the Spanish guitar, cook a soufflé and then make love all night. Well, that might be OK in utopia but few of us can live up to this, because we are ordinary mortals whose bookshelves fall down, whose fingers hurt when we play B7, who burn the toast and who are often so blotto in the boudoir that all we can manage is a bit of world-class snoring. I think I'll stick to Harold Macmillan's definition of the gentleman as 'a fellow who knows how to play the accordion, but doesn't'. Anyway, in *A Gentleman's Bedside Book* you will discover everything from the art of sword-swallowing to all you ever wanted to know about breasts. What more could you ask for?

I hope that this fruitcake of unexpected curiosities will provide gentlemen – and others – with suitable entertainment for the last fifteen minutes of the day. Indeed, if I have done my job properly you should feel that I am actually there in bed beside you. Well, *you know what I mean.* If you're still awake, here we go . . .

SCIENCE

Health and the Body

1 Doctor slang

The abbreviations devised by doctors to say the unsayable about their patients appear less frequently on hospital records than once they did, owing to a rise in litigation. One doctor who had scribbled 'TTFO' on a patient's notes – roughly translatable as 'Told To Go Away' – was asked in court what the abbreviation meant. Thinking on his feet he replied brilliantly, '"To take fluids orally", M'Lud.' Here are some more.

- **CHANDELIER PROCEDURE**: any test requiring subsequent removal of patient from chandelier
- **CHEERIOMA**: life-threatening tumour
- **CODE BROWN**: incontinence emergency
- **CONCRETE POISONING**: fall or jump from great height
- **CRISPY CRITTER**: severe burns case
- **CTD (CIRCLING THE DRAIN)**: close to death
- **DEPARTURE LOUNGE**: geriatric ward
- **DIFFC**: Dropped In For Friendly Chat (i.e. no medical problem)
- **DILF (DOCTOR I'D LIKE TO KISS)**: nursing slang for cute medic (see VTMK)
- **DPS (DISAPPEARING PENIS SYNDROME)**: reaction to insertion of catheter (or anything)
- **GROLIES**: *Guardian* Reader Of Low Intelligence, In Ethnic Skirt
- **HANDBAG POSITIVE**: confused old lady on hospital bed, clutching handbag
- **HAPPY FEET**: epileptic seizure

- **HIBGIA**: Had It Before, Got It Again
- **HIVI**: Husband Is Village Idiot
- **HORRENDECTOMY**: hideously drawn-out and painful procedure
- **IFHS**: Informal Faecal Hardness Scale, ranging from CGTEN (Could Go Through the Eye of a Needle) to HAB (Hard As Bullets)
- **PANCAKE HOUSE**: stroke ward
- **IE**: Involuntary Euthanasia, a 'palliative' procedure for those annoying patients
- **LOBNH**: Lights On But Nobody Home
- **LOL**: Little Old Lady
- **NFN**: Normal For Norfolk
- **OBE**: Open Both Ends (diarrhoea and vomiting)
- **ORGAN RECITAL**: hypochondriac's medical history
- **PFO**: Pissed, Fell Over (A&E)
- **PGT**: Pissed, Got Thumped (A&E)
- **PHD**: Pakistani Healing Dance, useless procedure done to mollify patient's family
- **PUMPKIN POSITIVE**: light shone in mouth illuminates patient's whole head, owing to invisibly small brain
- **RAISIN FARM**: old people's home
- **REEKER**: smelly patient
- **ROSE COTTAGE**: STD clinic
- **RI**: Rothmans Index, i.e. tobacco-stained fingers, as in 'Patient denies smoking despite RI of 12'
- **SCRATCH & SNIFF**: STD test
- **SIG**: Self-Inflicted Gerbil (apocryphal)
- **SMURFOSIS**: patient turning blue
- **STREAM TEAM**: Urology Department
- **SVWI**: Something Very Wrong Inside (alarming undiagnosed condition)
- **SYB**: Save Your Breath (same as WNL)
- **TEETP**: Tried Everything Else, Try Prayer
- **TTR**: Tooth to Tattoo Ratio (higher is better)

- **TTFO**: Told To Go Away
- **TTJ**: Transfer To Jesus (dead)
- **TUBE**: Totally Unnecessary Breast Examination
- **TURN AND BASTE**: roll and clean patient after a Code Brown
- **VEGETABLE GARDEN**: Coma unit
- **VELCRO**: family accompanying patient everywhere
- **VTMK**: Voice To Melt Knickers (voice deliberately cultivated by some doctors)
- **WOFT**: Waste Of Blimmin' Time
- **WNL**: Will Not Listen
- **WHOPPER WITH CHEESE**: obese patient with genital thrush
- **YMRATFU**: Your Medical Records Are Totally Messed Up

2 Breasts: infrequently asked questions

A platypus is not a kind of cat, as you might imagine from the name; it's a so-called monotreme, which is a sort of egg-laying mammal. Marsupials such as kangaroos are mammals too, as are human beings and dolphins. To make sense of this strange melange it helps to remember that the term 'mammal' comes from the Latin *mamma*, meaning 'breast', like in that ABBA song, *Mamma Mia*, which presumably means 'My Breast' in Swedish. And what with the way those Swedes bounced up and down all the time, you can see where they got the idea from. Female mammals nourish their young with milk secreted by their mammary glands; therefore women's breasts tend to be larger than men's – sometimes enormously larger – as you will no doubt have spotted. Interestingly, though, few chaps know much about these mesmeric glands except from the point of view of what we might call 'art criticism'. So here are some infrequently asked questions, and answers, on this fascinating subject.

What are breasts?

Breasts are modified sweat glands which produce milk in women, and rarely also in men. Each breast has an exit pipe, called a nipple, surrounded by an areola. Most of a lactating woman's milk is stored in the back of the breast (no, not in the fridge) and delivered through ducts by the muscles of the internal mammary glands when the nipple is stimulated by suckling. The rest of the breast is made up of fat, ligaments and connective tissue.

What about the girl from Devizes, whose breasts were of different sizes?

Across the animal kingdom, breasts vary in size and shape from one creature to an udder. Likewise, human breasts vary pleasingly in size, shape and which political party they vote for. Their natural shape depends mainly on support provided by the 'suspensory ligaments of Cooper', on which they are hung from the collarbone.

At puberty, female sex hormones promote sexual development and a young woman's breasts start to become more prominent. It is common for the left breast to be slightly larger than the right, as you can demonstrate if you weigh the evidence carefully.

According to original research undertaken by this book's author, size variations are remarkable, with everything from the fried-egg look to the appearance of having been shot in the back by two torpedoes. At the top end of the bigness scale the names Marilyn Monroe, Jayne Mansfield and Dolly Parton spring immediately to mind but in 2009 *The Guinness Book of World Records* recognized fifty-year-old Norma Stitz, who has a non-standard bra size of 72ZZZ, as the unrivalled owner of the world's biggest unadulterated hooters. Each of Norma's breasts weighed in at some two stone and, what's more, they were the unenhanced genuine article – unlike her name.

Are they mainly for feeding babies, or what?

During pregnancy breasts become bigger and often firmer. Nipples may become larger and their pigmentation darker. All this generally goes back to normal after pregnancy. Nonetheless, as well as their function as infant-feeders, breasts play an obvious part in human sexual behaviour.

On sexual arousal, breast size increases and nipples harden. They may also become erect owing to muscular contraction in response to touch, cold, or someone fiddling about 'tuning the radio'. The result is the well-known 'peanut-smuggling' look.

According to reports, a groundbreaking German study has discovered that staring at women's breasts for ten minutes a day has the health-promoting benefits of a thirty-minute bike ride, adding five years to your life by exercising the heart and improving circulation. The study's authors say that this significantly reduces the risk of having a stroke but I wonder how many men have stared at a woman's breasts for ten minutes and then had a stroke. Probably more than you'd think.

Other recent research at Victoria University of Wellington, New Zealand, has uncovered the not very surprising fact that men often look longer and harder at a woman's breasts than at other parts of her body. The researchers observed that 'Men may be looking more often at the breasts because they are simply aesthetically pleasing, regardless of the size.' Rocket science it is not.

3 Human anatomy for the practical man

James Weldon Johnson (1871–1938) was a polymorph. Either that or he just couldn't decide what job he wanted to do. What do you mean, you've never heard of him? He was that African-American anthologist, author, civil rights activist, critic, diplomat, folklorist, journalist, lawyer, poet, politician, professor of New York University and songsmith who, one day when he had nothing else to do, wrote the tune for the song that goes, 'Toe bone connected to the foot bone, Foot bone connected to the leg bone, Leg bone connected to the knee bone', etc., which has been used to teach anatomy to children for years, even though it is obviously anatomical rubbish.

Perhaps this accounts for the recent findings by a team from King's College London that the British public are useless at basic anatomy, with many people having little idea even where their major organs are. Fewer than half of the 700-plus people the researchers spoke to knew where their heart was, even though it was beating away right there. Surely if you can't feel your heart beating you must be dead and should ring for an ambulance at once. Fewer than a third got their lungs in the correct place, even though you can feel them when you cough or breathe in cold air, but for some weird reason well over three-quarters got their intestines right, as you can see from the accompanying chart.

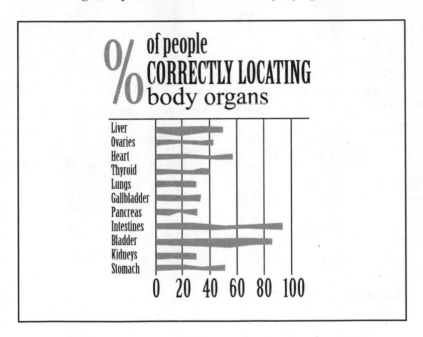

% of people CORRECTLY LOCATING body organs

Liver
Ovaries
Heart
Thyroid
Lungs
Gallbladder
Pancreas
Intestines
Bladder
Kidneys
Stomach

0 20 40 60 80 100

Many of these ignoramuses – I mean 'subjects' – didn't even know the basic shape of bodily organs. They were asked to identify the lungs, the pancreas and so on from shaded forms inside the outline of a body, but, even when they were being treated for problems in a particular organ they were trying to identify, they did badly. More than half those being treated for kidney problems, for example, couldn't recognize the blimmin' things from their shape.

1 Where is the heart?

2 Where are the kidneys?

3 Where is the pancreas?

Why not have a go yourself? The diagrams on page 12 show particular organs in a variety of positions, only one of which is right in each picture. There are no prizes except a lovely warm smug feeling when you get them right.

4 Strain versus stress, or how to be happy tomorrow

I recently came across an article in the backwoods of Cyberville headlined, 'The Ten Secrets of Happy, Can-Do People'. This told me that no amount of wealth would lead to my happiness and that it was better to be content with what I have and to value the beauty of nature than to hanker after material things. Now it might be true that looking at the flowers and smiling like an idiot will make me happy, I don't know, but the theory was rendered a bit suspect by the surrounding welter of adverts touting hair-raisingly expensive cars and some kind of yoghurt that makes you thin. Besides, I'd rather live in a house with a roof on (that I had to pay money for) than squat in a filthy ditch, admiring the rain.

Among the bits of advice based on the ten secrets of these happy, can-do people was the following: 'Paint your room in colours that cheer you up. The best colour is blue, which is associated with nature.' Hang on a minute, what about green, or brown, or all the colours of the rainbow? Surely they are associated with nature, too. The next piece of advice was no better: 'Pretend every day is your birthday.' Can you imagine? You'd be 10,950 years old by the time you were thirty. The trouble with advice columns of this kind is that the authors don't know what they are talking about. I once saw one called something like 'Overcoming Shyness' that said, 'If you find social situations difficult, introduce yourself to a few strangers the next time you are at a party and watch your confidence soar.' How many shy people even *go* to parties, let alone clap strangers on the back? And how many shrinking violets do you know whose confidence is any higher than a snake's armpits, no matter what they do?

No, this isn't good enough. So here's some advice on a simple thing you can do to lift your mood if your job or something else is stressing you out. It won't cure clinical depression or psychosis but it does work, and instead of being based on whimsy it is based on science.

Not so long ago, scientists from Nottingham Trent University identified a naturally produced chemical, phenylethylamine, which is linked to the regulation of physical energy and mood, and seems to act as an anti-depressant. An enzyme in the body changes phenylethylamine into phenylacetic acid, the chemical structure of which is very like that of amphetamines. Since you produce a lot more phenylacetic acid after exercise, doctors have supposed that this chemical might have more than a little to do with the so-called 'jogger's high', which you can get also from mountain climbing, tug-of-war, cycling, tennis, swimming, running up stairs, chopping wood and vigorous car-washing.

It not only looks as if *stress* can be beaten by *strain*, it also seems that even moderate exercise produces phenylacetic acid. So it doesn't have to be the London Marathon: a walk in the park or a quick mow of the lawn will make you feel happier, too. Maybe shining a pair of boots will also do it – anyway it's cheaper than joining a gym.

But in case you are unconvinced by this idea, or just love being miserable, you might like to know that a recent university study that listed Denmark as the 'happiest' country in the world didn't have an explanation for its also being lumbered with the second highest suicide rate in Europe. Perhaps not enough Danes were painting their rooms blue.

Abnormal Science

5 Making a stink: the world's smelliest chemical

One warm summer's day when I was working in an office near St Paul's Cathedral in London the main sewer under Ludgate Hill developed a fault. The resultant perfume, which began to engulf the area around the Bank of England, is hard to put into words but I remember seeing serious pinstriped gentlemen grimacing as they caught the miasma full in the chest before dipping their wan heads into rubbish bins to dilute the stench.

The military have long recognized the potential of a disabling stink bomb and during the Second World War they developed a startlingly unpleasant pong in a secret lab up a hill somewhere. Dubbed 'Who, Me?' by some waggish scientist, the astonishingly niffy chemical has been characterized as powerfully fart-like, with a smell akin to bad eggs and rotting garbage. It was put into atomizers with the aim of spraying it at Nazis but it was never used, having got all over the volunteers from the French Resistance who were testing it and made them smell horrid.

The history of stink-research continued during the 1960s, when scientists, who were aiming to develop an alternative to policemen hitting people with truncheons, came up with the eye-wateringly smelly 'Go Home'. This product was designed to break up assemblies of bra-burning feminists and pot-frazzled peaceniks by making them too woozy to agitate – if they weren't so already. Nothing much came of it, overtaken as it was by lachrymatory agents such as tear gas, which had first been used in 1915.

The dean of smelly research must surely be Dr Pamela Dalton, a psychologist with long experience of, and unrivalled expertise in, horrible smells. Together with her team at Monell Chemical Senses Center in Philadelphia she has spent years trying to concoct an olfactory agent so malodorous that it will induce paralyzing fear in the smeller. This work, unsurprisingly, is funded largely by the military as part of their 'non-lethal weapons development' programme.

In the early stages Dalton and her team experimented with substances like butyric acid – the stuff that makes strong cheese and vomit smell the way they do; skatole – a chemical component of faeces; and triethylamine – a fish odour. Ultimately, she developed two usable weapons-grade 'malodorants':

1   US Government Standard Bathroom Malodor: an especially nasty substance with a strongly faecal smell, Bathroom Malodor is also said to possess 'an undertone of rotting rodent' and is used commercially by deodorant manufacturers to challenge the effectiveness of their products. In 'sniff tests' on a variety of ethnic and national groups, victims recruited through newspaper advertisements described Bathroom Malodor as the most repellent stink they had ever come across. 'We got cursed in a lot of different languages,' said Dalton. As one person who encountered the product put it, 'It smells like shit, but much, much stronger. *It fills your head.*'

2   Stench Soup: Dalton's masterpiece combines the cheerful excesses of Bathroom Malodor and Who, Me? with t-butyl mercaptan, the unpleasant-smelling chemical that is added to household gas to give it a detectable pong. The reek of Stench Soup is generally agreed to be the most disgusting smell ever created by a human being. In addition to the perfumes mentioned above, it contains delightful hints of decomposing flesh and rotting mushrooms, and is so revolting that just one sniff stops many victims in their tracks, causing retching, watering of the eyes and mental confusion.

Pam Dalton points out that the power of smells as weapons lies in their propensity to cause an emotional response. The limbic system is a set of brain structures that deal with smell, emotion, memory and behaviour, and it is this system that triggers the response to smells. The more revolting the odour, the stronger the reaction of the limbic system and the greater the revulsion, disgust and fear. Disgust is a reaction to things that might make us ill, such as rotting food, sewage and dead bodies. The power of Stink Soup is that it causes no harm to human health, only a feeling in the smeller that harm is likely, or is actually happening. This, together with the smeller's inability to identify the source of the odour, causes anxiety, fear and confusion, renders him vulnerable to attack and encourages him to run away as fast as he can.

6 The weirdness of earthquakes

There is a terror among some television journalists that unless they insert a superlative into every utterance, the audience will find what they are saying insufficiently interesting and turn over. A man on the news the other night said that Keswick had long been the epicentre of pencil manufacture in England, believing, I suppose, that 'epicentre' means the most central centre, as if there could be such a thing. In fact, an epicentre is the point on the earth's surface directly above the focus, or 'hypocentre', of an earthquake, so unless the pencils he was talking about were being mined beneath Keswick Moot Hall or carved underground he had goofed.

This led me to wonder what happens in an earthquake so I looked it up in my book of earthquakes. An earthquake is usually the result of volcanic activity, or of the big sheets of rock that float about on the surface of the planet (tectonic plates) banging into each other, scraping against each other, or sliding one under another. They try to do this sliding and scraping smoothly but all the ragged bits at the edge catch on to things and they get stuck, locked into position. The plates are still trying to move, and with terrific force, but they are jammed tight, until one day or night the thing gives way under the gigantic forces and all the stored up energy is suddenly released. This stop–start process is known as 'sticking and slipping' and while the sticking part can last lifetimes, the slipping is often over in seconds.

When the earthquake finally happens it creates undulations which travel across the surface (seismic waves), shaking things from side to side and up and down. With a big quake soil can sometimes be shaken so much that water-saturated granular material (such as sand) will turn temporarily from a solid into a liquid. So-called soil liquefaction can cause buildings to list like the Leaning Tower of Pisa or sink weirdly into the ground.

The energy released by an earthquake is recorded with a seismometer or seismograph (same thing) and once upon a time a given number on the Richter scale would indicate the amount of energy an earthquake had released. This scale has now been superseded by the moment magnitude scale, which, like Richter, is logarithmic. This means that an increase of one step on the scale corresponds to a quake in which 31.6 times more energy is released than the previous step. Likewise, an increase of two steps corresponds to the release of 1,000 times more energy. So while you are unlikely to notice a quake of less than magnitude 3, a magnitude 7 will topple buildings and tear everything up. The actual intensity of shaking at a given spot depends on everything from soil type to the way a building has been put up, and it is measured on a different scale that you needn't worry about.

When the epicentre of a large earthquake is under the sea it can cause water displacement enough to generate a tsunami. Tsunamis can travel at almost 500 miles per hour (800 km per hour), depending on water depth, but they are often not noticed by people on the ocean, owing to an increase of wave height of less than a foot. The distance between wave crests can be more than 60 miles (100 km), and the wave periods may be up to an hour apart. Once the tsunami approaches land, though, these measurements are concertinaed such that the wave becomes much higher and the forces much more concentrated. On 1 April 1946, a huge earthquake near the Aleutian Islands, where the Pacific Ocean floor is being pushed under Alaska, generated a tsunami which swamped Hilo on Hawaii's Big Island with a 46 ft (14 m) high surge. That's taller than a big house. The tremendous force of all this water – which is heavy – coming at you faster than you can run means that if you are caught in its path you are more likely to be bashed to death than drown.

The most famous earthquake of recent times was the San Francisco earthquake of 1906, which struck just after 5 a.m. on Wednesday, 18 April. This scored an estimated 7.8 on the moment magnitude scale, but might have been even bigger. The epicentre was about 2 miles (3.2 km) offshore, near Mussel Rock. A 296-mile (477 km) long rupture split the San Andreas Fault north and south, and the quake was felt as far as central Nevada. The 1906 earthquake and subsequent fire are together regarded as the worst natural disaster in the recorded history of the United States. Some 3,000 people died.

7 Ball lightning

On the Banks of Plum Creek by Laura Ingalls Wilder describes her childhood experience of a terrifying Minnesota blizzard in the days of the American pioneers, before central heating and proper windows. Wilder says how, during this storm, as the family sheltered from the biting cold in their windswept prairie house, the stovepipe began to rattle loudly. This was followed by a ball of fire 'bigger than Ma's big ball of yarn' rolling down the stovepipe, across the stove, and on to the floor where Wilder's mother, lifting her skirts, tried to stamp on it. It seemed to jump through her foot so she attempted to brush it into the ashpan, whereupon it doubled back, attracted by her knitting needles. More fireballs then came down the stovepipe, and rolled around her knitting before vanishing.

Unlikely though all this sounds, it is a classic description of ball lightning, which is not a dietary technique for gentlemen with heavy testicles but an infrequently reported electro-atmospheric event. Although recognized as a real phenomenon, 'unconventional plasmas' are yet to be properly understood by science. To this end the International Symposium on Ball Lightning meets regularly. It beats working for a living, I suppose.

Though rare, ball lightning is witnessed often enough for it to have appeared on YouTube, with some 5 per cent of Americans saying they have seen the real thing. But as 22 per cent of them also claim to have seen a ghost, I'm not sure how much store should be set by that figure. One of the earliest reports was written down after a huge thunderstorm at a church in Widecombe-in-the-Moor, Devon, on 21 October 1638, when an 8 ft (2.5 m) ball of fire hit the church, came in and split in two, filling the building with foul smoke. One ball smashed its way out again through a window. Large parts of the church wall were hurled to the ground, pews splintered and some sixty people injured, four of whom died.

Another deadly sighting occurred in 1809 when three 'balls of fire' injured the crew of HMS *Warren Hastings*. The first ball killed a crewman on deck and then set fire to the main mast. A sailor who went out to attend to his colleague's body was struck by a second ball which, though knocking him sideways, left him with only minor burns. A third man was killed by a final ball.

Further nautical incidents were recorded during the Second World War, when submarine crews reported the frequent appearance of small, explosive floating balls of lightning in the confined quarters of their subs. Coming from sailors as they were, it is not clear whether these complaints about glowing balls floating in front of their faces were taken seriously by the Admiralty.

Nikola Tesla, an Austro-American electrical engineer and inventor, made an attempt to explain ball lightning in 1904 but there is still no scientific agreement about what exactly it is. Several theories have been proposed, including the vaporized silicon hypothesis, the nanobattery hypothesis, which suggests that ball lighting is made up of tiny batteries(!), and the black hole hypothesis. Take your pick.

For those who remain sceptical, perhaps the most scientifically reliable report of recent times comes from August 1994, when a ball of lightning was seen by residents of Uppsala, Sweden, to pass through a closed window, leaving a circular hole two inches across. Authority was added to the report by a lightning strike tracking system at Uppsala University, which recorded the event. No wonder Ma Ingalls thought ball lightning was 'the strangest thing I ever saw', though one has to remember that she had never seen Black Rod opening Parliament.

8 'Canals' on Mars

American businessman and astronomer Percival Lowell (1855–1916) spent much of his life trying to prove that there was intelligent life on Mars. He was particularly interested in the 'canals' on the surface of the planet, having seen detailed depictions of them criss-crossing some of the Martian maps drawn by the director of the Milan Observatory, Giovanni Schiaparelli (1835–1910). Schiaparelli had first observed this network of what he took to be straight lines in 1877, calling them *'canali'*, which means channels or grooves in Italian, and naming them after rivers, real and imaginary. His work was influential for many years and the names he used for bits of the planet remain today. Schiaparelli was cautious about deciding exactly how these channels might have formed and was inclined to believe them to be the product of the planet's natural evolution, but he did allow that their peculiar 'geometrical precision' looked as though they might be the work of intelligent beings.

Somewhat unhelpfully, whether by carelessness or for some devious purpose, Schiaparelli's term *'canali'* was translated into the ambiguous English word 'canals'. This messy translation now fertilized the imaginative soil, allowing the sprouting of fast-growing wrong ideas and dodgy guesswork about the likelihood of intelligent life on Mars and what the Martians might be up to with those huge canals.

In 1894, Percival Lowell set up a new observatory at an altitude of more than 7,000 ft, (2,100 m) in Flagstaff, Arizona Territory, where skies were uncommonly clear and clouds few and far between. Over the next fifteen years he made a study of Mars, recording his observations in a series of highly detailed drawings, and published several books on the subject, including *Mars and Its Canals* in 1906. Lowell speculated that a race of intelligent Martians had built the canals in a desperate attempt to draw water from the ice caps as the planet dried out, a theory that was a mixture of the known and the highly improbable.

Many astronomers remained properly sceptical of Lowell's intelligent Martians idea, largely on the grounds that they couldn't see through their telescopes anything that resembled the things he had put in his drawings. In 1909 the 60 in. (1.5 m) Mount Wilson Observatory telescope in southern California got a closer and much better look at the supposedly straight 'canals', revealing them to be meandering natural features. Scientists concluded that what Lowell had been seeing were either optical illusions or optimistic extrapolations of blurry surface features that he had wishfully mistaken for, or imagined to be, canals, rather in the way people see 'the face of Jesus' on biscuits.

Despite the scientific scepticism, the idea of Martian canals gripped the public imagination for much of the twentieth century and produced some terrific science fiction, from H.G. Wells' – not to mention Orson Welles' – *War of the Worlds* to Steven Spielberg's *Close Encounters of the Third Kind*. The public's wild imaginings were only quieted in 1965, when the *Mariner 4* spacecraft got close enough to take pictures of the surface of Mars with a television camera, revealing only a lot of sand and lumps of rock. No canals.

But, in case you feel like relaunching the Martian science-fiction craze, you might like to think about the idea that, as the Sun gets hotter towards the end of its life, the ice on Mars may melt and transform the planet into a place fit for human life. Don't forget, though, that the gravity on Mars is only 3.8 per cent of the gravity on Earth. So, if you weigh 10 stone on Earth, you'll weigh 3.8 stone on Mars (great – you can forget all about that diet) and you'll be able to jump three times as high as you can down here.

The World of Numbers

9 Orders of magnitude explained

Big numbers can be a bit scary. Take eternity, for example: an eternity of seconds. Just imagine a planet made of steel, with the diameter of our galaxy, where every thousand years a fly lands, walks around for a bit and then takes off again. When that fly has worn away the planet by the friction of its feet not a blink of an eye will have passed in eternity. Or, to use numbers with which you are more familiar, how many days does 1 million seconds add up to? It's about 11 days – give or take. Fair enough, you say, but how about 1 billion seconds? Don't look, have a guess. It's a shade more than 31½ *years*. Are you surprised? And what about 1 trillion seconds? That is some 31,000 years, or more accurately, 31,709.791983 years, or, if you are keener on words than figures, 3 myriads, 7 centuries, 1 lustrum, 1 olympiad, 41 weeks, 2 days, 1 hour, 46 minutes, 12 seconds. Those relative differences between million, billion, and trillion are large, and that leads me on to the subject for today's lesson: orders of magnitude, which are a useful way to get a sense of the relative scale of things.

'Magnitude' just means 'size', and orders of magnitude are used to compare two or more objects of the same kind. Most often differences in order of magnitude are measured on the logarithmic scale in 'factors' or 'powers' of ten, so-called 'decades'. Two numbers of the same order of magnitude are pretty roughly the same size – the larger being less than ten times bigger than the smaller. With a difference of one order of magnitude, the larger thing is about *ten times* larger than the smaller thing. If the numbers differ by two orders of magnitude, the difference is a factor of about 100. Just count the zeros.

IN WORDS	(SHORT SCALE)	PREFIX	SYMBOL	DECIMAL	POWER OF TEN	ORDER OF MAGNITUDE
quadrillionth	septillionth	yocto	-y	0.000000000000000000000001	10^{-24}	-24
trilliardth	sextillionth	zepto	-z	0.000000000000000000001	10^{-21}	-21
trillionth	quintillionth	atto	-a	0.000000000000000001	10^{-18}	-18
billiardth	quadrillionth	femto	-f	0.000000000000001	10^{-15}	-15
billionth	trillionth	pico	-p	0.000000000001	10^{-12}	-12
milliardth	billionth	nano	-n	0.000000001	10^{-9}	-9
millionth	millionth	micro-	μ	0.000001	10^{-6}	-6
thousandth	thousandth	milli-	m	0.001	10^{-3}	-3
hundredth	hundredth	centi	-c	0.01	10^{-2}	-2
tenth	tenth	deci	-d	0.1	10^{-1}	-1
one	one	-	-	1	10^{0}	0
ten	ten	deca	-da	10	10^{1}	1
hundred	hundred	hecto	-h	100	10^{2}	2
thousand	thousand	kilo	-k	1,000	10^{3}	3
million	million	mega	-M	1,000,000	10^{6}	6
milliard	billion	giga	-G	1,000,000,000	10^{9}	9
billion	trillion	tera	-T	1,000,000,000,000	10^{12}	12
billiard	quadrillion	peta	-P	1,000,000,000,000,000	10^{15}	15
trillion	quintillion	exa	-E	1,000,000,000,000,000,000	10^{18}	18
trilliard	sextillion	zeta	-Z	1,000,000,000,000,000,000,000	10^{21}	21
quadrillion	septillion	yotta	-Y	1,000,000,000,000,000,000,000,000	10^{24}	24

Above is a table showing different ways of describing orders of magnitude ascending from −24 to 24. I bet you didn't know there was such a word as 'billiardth'.

10 A spoonful of pi

π (or pi) is an infinite number, the value of which is the ratio of a circle's circumference to its diameter. The first person to use the Greek character 'π' to stand for this ratio was Welsh mathematician William Jones, in 1706. Leonhard Euler (pronounced 'oiler') took it up in 1737 and 'π' quickly became the recognized symbol.

In 1897, T.I. Record introduced House Bill #246 in the Indiana House of Representatives based on the work of *amateur* mathematician Edward J. Goodwin, which suggested three different estimates for pi, including 4 (the most inaccurate estimate ever). The true value of pi is roughly 3.141593, or, more precisely,

3.14159265358979323846264338327950288419716939937510582097494459230781640628620899862803482534211706798214808651328230664709384460955058223172535940812848111745028410270193852110555964462294895493038196442881097566593344612847564823378678316527120190914564856692346034861045432664821339360726024914127372458700660631558817488152092096282925409171536436789259036001133053054882046652138414695194151160943305727036575959195309218611738193261179310511854807446237996274956735188575272489122793818301194912983367336244065664308602139494639522473719070217986094370277053921717629317675238467481846766940513200056812714526356082778577134275778960917363717872146844090122495343014654958537105079227968925892354201995611212902196086403441815981362977477130996051870721134999999 . . .

and so on, forever. I only stopped because of that interesting row of nines, which is to be expected in an infinite sequence of utterly random digits. Pi never repeats itself.

You can easily estimate the value of pi for yourself by drawing a big circle and carefully measuring both its diameter and its circumference. If you then divide the circumference by the diameter you will get pi. And you don't need hundreds of decimal places to be accurate. A value of pi to just thirty-nine decimal places is enough to work out the circumference of any circle you can squash inside the observable universe, to within the value of the radius of a hydrogen atom – if that's precise enough for you.

Many mathematical and physical formulae involve pi, and mathematicians have long been held in its thrall, straining to add digits to the end of its known value. The Ancient Greeks, Indians, Ancient Egyptians and Babylonians all knew it was more than 3 and by 1900 BCE the Babylonians and Egyptians both had it right to within 1 per cent of its actual value.

Ptolemy worked it out correctly to 4 decimal places (3.1416) in about 150 CE, and, for those who believe the Bible to be literally true, it's worth pointing out that chapter 7, verse 23–26, of the first Book of Kings (600 BCE), estimates the value of pi to be 3, which is quite a bit worse than the older estimates. Accuracy has come quite a way with the advent of the computer, and Professor Yasumasa Kanada of Tokyo University has now calculated pi to 1.2411 trillion places. Silly sausage. Just imagine having to memorize that for your Maths GCSE.

11 'My Financial Career' by Stephen Leacock

Stephen Leacock (1869–1944) was an internationally popular Canadian humorist and writer. In 1911 more people were said to have heard of him than had heard of Canada, and he was admired by readers and fellow humorists alike. John Cleese acknowledges his influence and Groucho Marx was a fan. This piece is typical of his work.

'My Financial Career'

When I go into a bank I get rattled. The clerks rattle me; the wickets rattle me; the sight of the money rattles me; everything rattles me.

The moment I cross the threshold of a bank and attempt to transact business there, I become an irresponsible idiot.

I knew this beforehand, but my salary had been raised to fifty dollars a month and I felt that the bank was the only place for it.

So I shambled in and looked timidly round at the clerks. I had an idea that a person about to open an account must needs consult the manager.

I went up to the wicket marked 'Accountant'. The accountant was a tall, cool devil. The very sight of him rattled me. My voice was sepulchral.

'Can I see the manager?' I said, and added solemnly, 'alone.' I don't know why I said 'alone.'

'Certainly,' said the accountant, and fetched him.

The manager was a grave, calm man. I held my fifty-six dollars clutched in a crumpled ball in my pocket.

'Are you the manager?' I said. God knows, I didn't doubt it.

'Yes,' he said.

'Can I see you,' I asked, 'alone?' I didn't want to say 'alone' again, but without it the thing seemed self-evident.

The manager looked at me in some alarm. He felt I had an awful secret to reveal.

'Come in here,' he said, and led the way to a private room. He turned the key in the lock.

'We are safe from interruption here,' he said. 'Sit down.'

We both sat down and looked at each other. I found no voice to speak.

'You are one of Pinkerton's men, I presume,' he said.

He had gathered from my mysterious manner that I was a detective. I knew what he was thinking, and it made me worse.

'No, not from Pinkerton's,' I said, seeming to imply that I came from a rival agency.

'To tell the truth,' I went on, as if I had been prompted to lie about it, 'I am not a detective at all. I have come to open an account. I intend to keep all my money in this bank.'

The manager looked relieved but still serious; he concluded now that I was a son of Baron Rothschild or a young Gould.

'A large account, I suppose,' he said.

'Fairly large,' I whispered. 'I propose to deposit fifty-six dollars now and fifty dollars a month regularly.'

The manager got up and opened the door. He called to the accountant.

'Mr. Montgomery,' he said unkindly loud, 'this gentleman is opening an account, he will deposit fifty-six dollars. Good morning.'

I rose.

A big iron door stood open at the side of the room.

'Good morning,' I said, and stepped into the safe.

'Come out,' said the manager coldly, and showed me the other way.

I went up to the accountant's wicket and poked the ball of money at him with a quick convulsive movement as if I were doing a conjuring trick.

My face was ghastly pale.

'Here,' I said, 'deposit it.' The tone of the words seemed to mean, 'Let us do this painful thing while the fit is on us.'

He took the money and gave it to another clerk.

He made me write the sum on a slip and sign my name in a book. I no longer knew what I was doing. The bank swam before my eyes.

'Is it deposited?' I asked in a hollow, vibrating voice.

'It is,' said the accountant.

'Then I want to draw a cheque.'

My idea was to draw out six dollars of it for present use. Someone gave me a cheque-book through a wicket and someone else began telling me how to write it out. The people in the bank had the impression that I was an invalid millionaire. I wrote something on the cheque and thrust it in at the clerk. He looked at it.

'What! Are you drawing it all out again?' he asked in surprise. Then I realized that I had written fifty-six instead of six. I was too far gone to reason now. I had a feeling that it was impossible to explain the thing. All the clerks had stopped writing to look at me.

Reckless with misery, I made the plunge.

'Yes, the whole thing.'

'You withdraw your money from the bank?'

'Every cent of it.'

'Are you not going to deposit any more?' said the clerk, astonished.

'Never.'

A idiot hope struck me that they might think something had insulted me while I was writing the cheque and that I had changed my mind. I made a wretched attempt to look like a man with a fearfully quick temper.

The clerk prepared to pay the money.

'How will you have it?' he said.

'What?'

'How will you have it?

'Oh' – I caught his meaning and answered without even trying to think – 'in fifties.'

He gave me a fifty-dollar bill.

'And the six?' he asked dryly.

'In sixes,' I said.

He gave it to me and I rushed out.

As the big door swung behind me I caught the echo of a roar of laughter that went up to the ceiling of the bank. Since then I bank no more. I keep my money in cash in my trousers pocket and my savings in silver dollars in a sock.

12 Fibonacci numbers and the golden mean

Bertrand Russell maintained that *number* holds sway above the flux of life, and who can disagree with him. Wherever you look, whether at the careful proportions of a Georgian house or the stately Parthenon, the branching of blood vessels or the swirl of a distant galaxy, you see number at work.

But some numbers have greater majesty than others and the Fibonacci series is about as wonderful and surprising a row of digits as you could find. Fibonacci numbers are a sequence, beginning with 0, then 1, and proceeding by the simple process of adding each succeeding number to its predecessor to produce the next in the row. So the Fibonacci sequence looks like this: 0, 1, 1, 2, 3, 5, 8, 13, 21, 34, 55, 89, 144, 233, 377 . . .

The Fibonacci sequence is named after Italian mathematician Leonardo of Pisa (*c*.1170–*c*.1250), who is also known as Leonardo Pisano, Leonardo Pisano Bogollo, Leonardo Bonacci and Leonardo Fibonacci ('son of Bonacci'). Fibonacci was one of the West's finest Middle Age mathematicians, by which I don't mean that he was middle-aged, I mean that he was working during the Middle Ages. He popularized the Hindu-Arabic system of numerals in his book *Liber Abaci* (1202) and it was in this volume that he mentioned the sequence of numbers that came to be known by his name. The use to which he put this series in his book was the calculation of the top speed at which rabbits could fornicate.

The prevalence of the Fibonacci sequence in nature had long been recognized. For example, the number of petals on many flowers is a Fibonacci number. Lilies have 3 petals, buttercups have 5, some delphiniums have 8, and so it goes on, with some daisies having 34, 55 or 89 petals.

The characteristic pattern of seeds in the head of a sunflower is a result of the Fibonacci series, too, and is related to a mathematical constant called the golden mean, golden ratio or golden number. Here's how it works.

If you divide the larger of two successive Fibonacci numbers by the smaller, you get this sequence:

$^1/_1 = 1$, $^2/_1 = 2$, $^3/_2 = 1\cdot5$, $^5/_3 = 1\cdot666...$, $^8/_5 = 1\cdot6$, $^{13}/_8 = 1\cdot625$, $^{21}/_{13} = 1\cdot61538$ ...

After a bit, the ratio settles down to a value of approximately 1.618034. This is the golden ratio, golden number or golden mean. Its mathematical symbol is the Greek letter phi (φ).

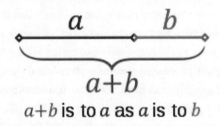

a+b is to *a* as *a* is to *b*

The golden section (Latin: *sectio aurea*) is the point on a line divided according to the golden mean. The total length *a + b* is to the longer part *a* as *a* is to the shorter part *b*.

To demonstrate how these numbers create patterns that we are used to seeing, here's a way to draw the recognizable spiral of the nautilus shell, using Fibonacci numbers.

Begin with two adjacent 1-unit squares. Below them draw a 2-unit square (*see diagram*). Now draw a 3-unit square in the position shown.

Next draw a 5-unit square, followed by an 8-unit square. The diagram goes up to a 55-unit square and you could go on drawing till you drew your pension, but you might like to stop at 8. The long side of each (Fibonacci) rectangle in this group of squares is the length of two successive Fibonacci numbers; and each square has sides whose lengths are Fibonacci numbers.

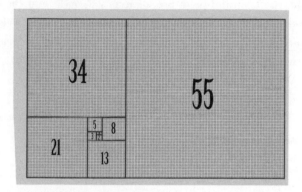

Now, by using a pair of compasses to draw in each square a quarter of a circle, whose centre is the corner of each square and whose radius is the length of each square (in the way shown below), you get a distinctive spiral that you will find all over the place in nature, from shells to the growth pattern of broccoli florets.

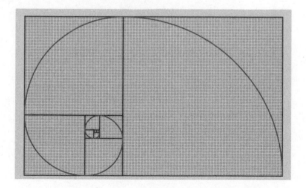

The golden ratio or 'divine proportion' was used widely in Renaissance sculpture, architecture and painting, in which artists often made use of the golden section in their compositions. Painters commonly used a Fibonacci rectangle for their canvases, and still do.

All kinds of design make use of Fibonacci numbers and the golden mean, including book design. According to the great book designer Jan Tschichold, the beautiful page proportions 2:3, 1:√3, and the golden section were once commonplace. Many books produced between 1550 and 1770 are designed precisely to these proportions. The modernization of paper sizes has rather put the boot into this – unfortunately.

The World of Dreams

13 The most frequent dream subjects

In the wonderful *Diary of a Nobody* (1892), Charles Pooter recounts to his wife and his best friend Gowing a dream he has had: 'I dreamt I saw some huge blocks of ice in a shop with a bright glare behind them. I walked into the shop and the heat was overpowering. I found that the blocks of ice were on fire . . . Gowing said there was nothing so completely uninteresting as other people's dreams . . . Carrie, who had hitherto been quiet, said: "He tells me his stupid dreams every morning, nearly."' That's the way it is with dreams, they seem so meaningful to the dreamer and so yawnworthy to everyone else. Perhaps the dreams that we can best sympathize with are those that resemble the dreams we have ourselves dreamt, and there's no shortage of common recurrent subjects. Whether it's worthwhile trying to analyse the symbolism of these dreams – if there is any – is debatable but it is interesting to note how many of these subjects are familiar.

1 Falling: this is one of the most common dream subjects. Often it causes the dreamer to wake up with a jerk. I don't mean that in the vulgar sense of waking up next to someone who is a jerk; I mean waking with a twitch, glad that you are not plummeting to your death from a great height.

2 Being chased: this is another unsettling, sometimes frankly frightening dream. Often the chaser is a powerful dog, some sort of monster, a terrifying figure with a masked face or the man from Her Majesty's Revenue and Customs.

3 Teeth – breaking, loosening, or falling out: it has been suggested that this one reflects a feeling of vulnerability in waking life. Who knows?

4 Inability to run: we've all had those dreams where you can't run at any speed. Sometimes they are part of the 'being chased' scenario and sometimes they are just a sort of slow-motion experience. Not very nice.

5 Flying: sometimes the dreamer dreams he is in a plane, helicopter or hang-glider, sometimes he is soaring over the earth rather like that flying sequence in *The Snowman*, which it appears the broadcasting people are obliged to transmit every blimmin' Christmas.

6 Ex-girlfriend: an unsettling one this. Sometimes combined with the 'sexual activity dream' (see no. 23). Nuff said.

7 Finding something: there's an old saying that goes, 'See a pin and pick it up, and all the day you'll have good luck.' In dreams it's more like, 'See a pin and pick it up, and all the day you'll have a pin.' I once dreamt I found an artificial leg. That was when I was, briefly, a theatre usher in London and between shows we found everything you can imagine, including a duffel bag full of grapes, several bunches of keys, cigarette lighters, some wigs and, once, a microwave oven.

8 Parts of the body: huge feet, tiny hands, bad skin, hair, nails and belly buttons (usually your own) are all fairly common dream subjects.

9 Being lost: another insecurity dream, I suppose.

10 Missing the train: another unpleasant one.

11 Being naked or partially dressed in public: we've all found ourselves walking down the high street in our pyjama jacket, haven't we? In dreams, I mean.

12 Looking ridiculous: not much different to ordinary life, this one. For me, anyway.

13 Being unprepared for a public duty: got to give a speech, go on parade, show the Queen round, and you're not ready? You're not the only one.

14 Being unable to drive a car or fly a plane: I used to dream that I was

in charge of a huge jet and had to reach over from the back seat to fly it. But I didn't know how.

15 The dead – family, friends: unsolved psychological business to attend to, according to 'experts'.

16 Snakes: usually poorly disguised penis symbols.

17 Guns: same again.

18 Knives: same again. Are you having a lot of these penis dreams? Could be something going on there.

19 Hair falling out: real life again.

20 Tests or examinations: how irksome to get so many dreams like this and so few no. 23s.

21 People you haven't seen or thought of for years: these can stay in your head all day. Very weird.

22 Being back at school: oh gawd!

23 Sexual activity: my favourite, but woefully uncommon. I once dreamt I was surrounded by young ladies dressed in nothing but plastic see-through raincoats, jostling me provocatively in a rainstorm. How unlike real life was this dream. And anyway I woke up before I could get much going. Rats!

24 Lifts: don't ask me.

25 Technology that won't work: real life, yet again.

26 Huge body of water: this can be terrifying – deadly car-splitting tumultuous rapids, huge blank oceans in which you are adrift, gigantic dark waves towering over you . . .

27 Gargantuan tornadoes: often one is looking up into the giant swirling centre.

Ooer!

14 Freud and his hang-ups

When the American physicist Richard Feynman (1918–88) was a student, a friend told him that there was a theory that dreams have symbolic significance and might be interpreted psychoanalytically. Feynman was sceptical.

The same night he dreamt he was playing a game called 'Titsies' with three billiard balls. While he found it easy in his dream to get the green and white balls into the pockets of the billiard table, he couldn't manage it with the grey ball.

When he woke up, it was immediately clear to him that the balls represented women – the name of the game gave it away. The white ball corresponded, he realized, to a girl he was seeing who worked in a white uniform, the green ball represented a girl he had just been out with who'd been wearing a green outfit, but the grey ball he couldn't place. A while later, Feynman remembered saying goodbye to a girl he liked who had just gone abroad, and he recognized that she was the character represented in his dream by the grey ball.

When he told his friend that he thought there was something to psychoanalysis after all, he found his dream analysis being rebuffed as 'too perfect – too cut and dried'. This is what happens with psychoanalysis; it is a persuasive theory in many ways but is full of holes and get-out clauses.

Born in 1856, Sigmund Freud was an Austrian Jewish neurologist who invented psychiatric psychoanalysis as a treatment chiefly for neurosis. Freud came up with a number of theories about the unconscious mind, focusing on sexual desire as the chief human motivation (no brain surgery required there). He also developed the idea that the interpretation of dreams can unlock unconscious human desires.

Interestingly, Freud himself suffered several psychosomatic disorders as well as a neurotic fear of dying and a classic 'addictive personality'. In a self-analysis he said of his childhood, 'I found in myself a constant love for my mother and jealousy of my father. I now consider this to be a universal event in childhood.' Like many of his pronouncements, the idea that his own peculiar childhood experience was the same for all children seems unlikely, though Freud appears to have built the whole notion of the Oedipus complex upon it.

Freud's father was extremely hardworking, a trait he seems to have inherited, while his mother was doting. Being a very bright child, Sigmund was favoured by his parents over his siblings and, like many spoilt children, became convinced that the sun shone out of his ego.

Training as a doctor at the University of Vienna, he had access to the whole pharmacopeial cupboard, and became an early user of cocaine. His chief addiction, however, was nicotine, in the form of cigars, and he was never seen without a fat one between his lips. On one occasion, while Freud was giving a talk on oral fixation, some wag asked him if he was aware of the phallic obviousness of the thing he was sucking. He allegedly replied, 'Sometimes a cigar is just a cigar', which is another of those Freudian get-out clauses.

Freud spent his entire life rationalizing his addiction. He smoked from the moment he got up until he went to bed, well past midnight. Those who worked closely with him found themselves expected to take up cigars if they did not already smoke. Hans Sachs, a close colleague, said that Freud was 'somewhat irritated when men around him did not smoke'.

In 1923, after some forty years of non-stop sucking, Freud's cigar chickens came home to roost when he developed oral cancer and was told to stop smoking. He wrote to his doctor, 'I have not smoked for seven weeks since the day of your injunction . . . I felt, as expected, outrageously bad. Cardiac symptoms accompanied by mild depression, as well as the horrible misery of abstinence.' So it isn't the smoking that is making him ill, Freud rationalizes, it is the *not smoking*. The non-Freudian term for this is 'childishness'. As clinical psychologist Evan J. Elkin says in his lovely essay on Freud and smoking, 'When it came to cigars, Freud's capacity for self-knowledge broke down.' At one point he did begin to muse that his addiction to smoking might have relieved him of 'withdrawal symptoms' from addictive masturbation in childhood. He said, 'I owe to the cigar a great intensification of my capacity to work *and a facilitation of my self-control*' [Author's italics]. What exactly he had in mind when he mentioned 'self-control' you might guess at. He did not pursue this idea.

In September 1939, after sixteen years of cancer and more than thirty operations, Freud asked his doctor and friend Max Schur to overdose him with morphine. He died on 23 September, leaving his cigars to his brother.

15 Famous dreams

Even after the development of feminism, new-man-ism, equality of the sexes and so on, I challenge anyone to persuade me that men are now any better at sewing than they were in the past. They aren't. Women have always been better at it than men – it's as obvious as Jewish rabbis, big mountains, yellow dusters and alcoholic whisky. Even the sewing machine hasn't helped.

The sewing machine was invented in 1845 by a chap with a huge beard called Elias Howe (*he* was called Elias Howe, not his beard – *do keep up*). Howe had the idea for a needle-machine before he had properly worked out its mechanics and his first experiments were not a success. For example, he tried a needle that was sharp at both ends with an eye in the middle. This failed for obvious reasons. Then, one night, he dreamt that he was the prisoner of a tribe of spear-wielding savages – this was before the caricature had become politically incorrect. As the natives danced around him he noticed that their spears had holes near their points. When he woke up he moved the hole in his needle to the tip, and Bob was his uncle. Mr Singer took over from there. As Leonardo da Vinci wondered, 'Why does the eye see a thing more clearly in dreams than the imagination does when awake?' Good question. Here are some famous dreams that led to more or less important realities, artistic and scientific.

In 1816, nineteen-year-old Mary Shelley (1797–1851) was visiting the sybaritic poet Lord Byron at his villa on Lake Geneva, with her future husband, another poet, Percy Bysshe Shelley (so she was actually still Mary Wollstonecraft Godwin, but never mind that). One evening, there being no telly then, Byron challenged them each to write a ghost story. Mary retired to bed where, she remembered, 'I saw the hideous phantasm of a man stretched out, and then, on the working of some powerful engine, show signs of life, and stir with an uneasy, half-vital motion.' She put her dream into words and it became the gothic novel, *Frankenstein*. In fact, she'd never actually nodded off, so it wasn't really a dream, but Mary Shelley herself called it a 'waking dream', so I think it definitely counts.

Like Mary Shelley, Robert Louis Stevenson (1850–94) wrote a classic Gothic horror story, *The Strange Case of Dr Jekyll and Mr Hyde* (1886). Stevenson, who described how 'that small theatre of the brain which we keep brightly lighted all night long' was a useful germinator of plots, remembered how he'd come up with the conception of what he called his 'shilling shocker' and 'fine bogey-tale': 'For two days I went about racking my brains for a plot of any sort; and on the second night I dreamed the scene at the window, and a scene afterward split in two, in which Hyde, pursued for some crime, took the powder and underwent the change in the presence of his pursuers.' The story not only became a huge hit; 'Jekyll and Hyde' entered the language as the shorthand for a kind of divided personality which switches exaggeratedly between good and bad.

President Abraham Lincoln, whose good attributes included the writing of short speeches and whose bad attributes included having a foul temper, is said to have mentioned a dream to his wife shortly before his dramatic assassination at the theatre. This is what he recalled: 'I could not have been long in bed when I fell into a slumber, for I was weary . . . Before me was a catafalque, on which rested a corpse wrapped in funeral vestments . . . "Who is dead in the White House?" I demanded of one of the soldiers. "The President" was his answer. "He was killed by an assassin!" Then came a loud burst of grief from the crowd, which awoke me from my dream.'

Srinivasa Ramanujan (1887–1920) was a self-taught Indian mathematical prodigy of enormous creative ability. He worked with G.H. Hardy at Cambridge and made significant contributions to number theory and mathematical analysis, amongst other things. Ramanujan was unusual in his mathematical approaches, being steeped in the traditions of Indian religion. 'An equation means nothing to me', he said, 'unless it expresses a thought of God.' His mathematical ideas frequently came to him in dreams and he described one of these: 'While asleep I had an unusual experience. There was a red screen formed by flowing blood as it were. I was observing it. Suddenly a hand began to write on the screen. I became all attention. That hand wrote a number of results in elliptic integrals. They stuck to my mind. As soon as I woke up, I committed them to writing.'

As well as numbers, you can dream colours, smells, the sensation of touch, and music, too. In 1965, when the Beatles were filming *Help!*, Paul McCartney dreamt the tune to 'Yesterday'. He was sleeping in an attic room in Wimpole Street when, he remembered, 'I woke up with a lovely tune in my head.' He got out of bed, sat down at the piano (in an attic?) and transposed his dream to the keyboard. 'I liked the melody a lot,' he said, 'but because I'd dreamed it I couldn't believe I'd written it.'

Dreams certainly seem to be a back door to creative ideas. The author Stephen King says he regards them as a mirror that reflects the subconscious, while Henry Thoreau believed them to be 'the touchstone of character'. For me, they are the inevitable result of too much Stilton before bed.

Drugs and Poisons

16 Arsenic and old Luce

Clare Boothe Luce (1903–87) was an American writer, editor, Congress-woman and socialite with a waspish tongue and an interesting past. Born Ann Boothe, she was the second illegitimate child of a dancer and a patent-medicine salesman who was married to another woman. Her parents separated in 1912 and to support herself she worked as a call girl. In 1935, Boothe married Henry Luce, the publisher of *Time* and *Life*. During the 1952 presidential election she campaigned on behalf of Republican Dwight Eisenhower, being rewarded with the ambas-sadorship to Italy in March 1953.

When Clare Boothe Luce arrived in Rome she wasn't exactly flavour of the month. She was the guest of a country with a strong Communist party, unused perhaps to a forthright Republican, anti-Communist, American *woman* telling them what to do.

The American ambassador's official residence, the Villa Taverna, is a fancy place, famous for its formal gardens and beautiful Renaissance interior, and Clare Boothe Luce lost no time in rearranging her apartment. She began by turning what had been an upstairs study into a bedroom-study. This room was renowned for its beautiful stucco ceiling, decorated with white roses and painted a soothing green. It seemed that Luce was going to have everything just the way she wanted, but, noticing the speed with which the new ambassador had also replaced her press attaché, embassy staff may well have become anxious for their jobs.

Clare Boothe Luce began each day with breakfast in bed at 8 a.m., engagements at the embassy beginning at 10 a.m. There were lunch and meetings back at the residence from 1.30 p.m., followed by the afternoon's work at the embassy before the ambassador returned to the residence at 7 p.m. to dress for what was often more than one party.

Seldom in bed before midnight, she had already complained about being awoken each morning at the crack of dawn by the rattling and shaking of the washing machine in the laundry room immediately above her. Despite her undoubted dedication and hard work, she was already ruffling feathers among the staff.

And it wasn't long before she began to tread on Italian corns too. In one speech she referred to Communism as a cancerous growth on the country's body politic, arousing open hostility in many quarters. It was starting to look to some as if she was going to make enemies everywhere.

At this time Italian politics were febrile and fragile and after an uncertain summer election the coalition government collapsed, leaving the ambassador in the lurch. But this wasn't her only problem, for Clare Boothe Luce was feeling decidedly unwell, with chronic stomach upsets. Her occasional nausea made it hard for her to eat the food at the endless round of embassy dinners or prepared for her in the kitchen at the residence. She complained that her morning coffee tasted unnaturally bitter.

Arriving in August to visit his wife, Henry Luce was shocked to see her so gaunt after just three months in the job and took her away for an immediate holiday. Just as her health was beginning to improve she was recalled to Rome because of the Trieste crisis, a serious incident involving Yugoslavia, Italy, Britain and the United States. She did her best to intercede but without success. She was again feeling desperately fatigued and nauseous, and there was now a new symptom: loss of sensation in her leg, which she found she had to drag.

So she decided to take a long break in the US, where once again she began to feel better.

When Clare Boothe Luce returned to Rome, the Trieste crisis had finally been resolved, due in no small part to her own hard work. But her symptoms now returned with a vengeance. Her fingernails had begun to break, her teeth were becoming loose, and she was starting to behave weirdly at functions, complaining, on one occasion, of flying saucers on the roof. Finally, she went for tests at a US naval hospital and, on advice, returned to America for Christmas.

Over the holiday, she received an urgent handwritten letter. It informed her that traces of arsenic had been discovered in one of her urine samples. The CIA explained that she had probably been receiving small doses over a long period. It looked as though she was being regularly poisoned in Rome, possibly at the embassy or the residence, or at the many functions she attended. Was someone putting something in her coffee? There were many possible grudge-bearers.

Everyone at the embassy and the residence now fell under suspicion as a gigantic operation was set in motion to investigate the political backgrounds of likely suspects inside and outside the ambassador's circle. Clare Boothe Luce was told to stay in the United States while it was explained to staff that work was being planned on the buildings and that technicians would be looking around. Agents arrived in Rome and began surreptitiously investigating the staff.

Colourless and tasteless, arsenic is an ideal poison to administer in food or drink and it was realized that the poisoner must have had close access to the ambassador's meals. So chefs and servants were watched closely. But since the ambassador was not there to be poisoned they drew a blank, until, one day in the private apartments, an observant agent noticed a grey dust on a Linguaphone disc. He found further deposits in drapes, on surfaces, and in the ambassador's makeup. On analysis the dust was found to contain minute paint flakes containing lead arsenate. Attention turned at once to the ornate ceiling, agitated every morning by the washing machine upstairs. A decorator who had worked on the room said that he had not done the ceiling, which had been painted years before with what was found to be an arsenic-rich green paint. This flaking paint, shaken off by the shuddering washing machine, had been falling for months into Clare Boothe Luce's food and drink.

The ceiling was stripped and redecorated, but the ambassador, exhausted, had decided to retire from the job. Back in the United States she recovered her health and continued to work and be rude about people. She died in Washington in 1987 at the age of 84.

17 The story of heroin

John Mortimer's wonderful creation, Rumpole of the Bailey, was always going on about the way his red wine habit kept him astonishingly 'regular'. It's certainly better in this respect than a heroin habit, which, as Mortimer's dad warned him, renders you a 'stranger to the lavatory'. Heroin is a wonderfully useful drug that is used daily in British medicine to improve the life of people in terrible pain. It is made from morphine, a derivative of the opium poppy, and doctors call it diamorphine (diacetylmorphine).

As a 'recreational' narcotic, heroin is presented in news bulletins as a deadly menace and there is no doubt that on the street it is the cause of less happiness than down the hospital, mainly due to its addictive properties when taken regularly, its adulteration by salespeople and a lack of hygiene among street users. There's truly little romance attached to crouching in a drain trying to inject something that is half heroin, half Ajax into your last remaining vein with a filthy second-hand syringe.

Though the opium poppy has been cultivated in Mesopotamia (Iraq) since 3400 BCE, heroin itself was synthesized only in 1874, by an English chemist, C.R. Alder Wright. It really took off years later, after Felix Hoffmann, a chemist working for the German drugs company that would soon become Bayer, produced it by accident.

The men at Bayer were delighted with their new drug, naming it 'heroin' in 1895, and selling it as a cough suppressant and cure for morphine addiction. But they soon discovered that their over-the-counter morphine-addiction cure rapidly metabolized *into* morphine, and it wasn't long before people realized that, in its narcotic capacities, heroin was an improvement on morphine. Before you could say 'collapsed veins' it was being traded on the streets.

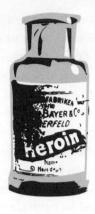

The heroin 'high' is a kind of euphoric relaxation, or as I read on a website somewhere: 'It feels like you're floatin' to Marrrrsss, dude' [Author's punctuation, spelling corrections and capitals].

Illicit intravenous injection is called 'slamming' or 'shooting up'. In the US the drug is available in its hydrochloride salt, which is already water-soluble, but in the UK the heroin base must be dissolved in water, mixed with an acid – such as citric acid powder or lemon juice – and then heated, before injection.

Heroin can also be 'snorted' or inhaled in a roll-up. 'Chasing the dragon' – another way of smoking it – involves reducing the powder to a liquid by heating it on a piece of foil. When rolled across the foil, it produces smoke, which is then inhaled through a tube. Intravenous injection provides the fastest and most intense 'rush', within eight seconds, with intra-muscular injection slower, at about eight minutes. Snorting or smoking produces an effect in about twice that time and swallowing is slowest of all, with a 'rush-free' onset in about half an hour.

Among the many undesirable short-term effects of heroin are low blood pressure, protracted vomiting, eye-watering constipation, itching, pinpoint pupils and shallow breathing. Frequent, regular heroin users develop tolerance, followed by moderate physical dependence and severe psychological dependence. I have a friend who took up heroin in California, seriously messing himself up, until, finally, he managed to come off the stuff. 'I was in this den,' he told me, 'crying out to these terrifying yardies, "Feed me, feed me . . . "' So not exactly tea at the Ritz, then.

Heroin overdose is a well-recognized hazard, causing fatal respiratory depression, while deaths from the interaction of heroin with other depressant drugs such as alcohol or benzodiazepines are not uncommon. The drug has been used for committing suicide and famously also for murder. Dr John Bodkin Adams used it as a murder weapon, as did the charming Dr Harold Shipman.

Coming off heroin is no picnic, either. The withdrawal syndrome usually begins within a day of stopping. Symptoms include: sweating, anxiety, nausea, vomiting and diarrhoea, yawning, sneezing, streaming eyes, runny nose, insomnia, severe aches, pains, cramps, fever and priapism (persistent erection of the penis – not fun, a medical emergency).

A glass of Horlicks for me, please.

18 The discovery of insulin

In 2009, an American called Gerald Cleveland died, at the age of ninety-three. These days that great age isn't so surprising; what is surprising is that Gerald Cleveland had been a lifelong diabetic, who had been kept alive on daily insulin injections for seventy-seven years. Just as surprising is that Gerald's younger brother Bob had been on insulin for more than eighty years, having been one of the first patients ever to be given this wonder-hormone, which was discovered in 1921.

Severe (type-1) diabetes is largely an illness of children, in which the pancreas suddenly and completely loses its ability to regulate the metab -

olism of carbohydrates. As a result, glucose builds up in the blood and is excreted in the urine, while the body starts to consume itself in search of energy.

The Ancient Greeks knew the symptoms of diabetes: great thirst, incessant urination, gnawing fatigue, weight loss, and finally coma and death. They believed that the bodies of the youngsters who got it were turning into urine. By the seventeenth century, diagnosis of 'the pissing evil' remained a death sentence, with no reprieve. All that parents could do was watch helplessly as their child melted away.

It was not until 1869 that a glimmer of hope began to be visible, when a German medical student, Paul Langerhans, identified some previously unnoticed 'islands of clear cells' sprinkled about the pancreas. Might the function of these 'islets of Langerhans' be the production of secretions that regulated digestion?

It was another twenty years before a definite relationship between the pancreas and diabetes was established, when Polish-German Oskar Minkowski and German Joseph von Mering removed the pancreas from a healthy dog. Days later flies were reportedly seen buzzing around the dog's urine, which, on testing, was found to contain sugar.

For the next two decades work to develop a treatment for diabetes with a pancreatic extract was slow and stumbling. The first person to isolate an active substance from the islets of Langerhans – one that regulated blood-glucose – was Romanian Nicolae Paulescu, a professor of physiology at the University of Medicine and Pharmacy in Bucharest. He called his discovery pancreine, publishing his animal-research results in 1921 and patenting his method. Pancreine, though, was never used on human patients and he was overtaken by the work of a young Canadian doctor, Frederick Banting.

Banting believed that researchers were contaminating the islet extract with digestive products. He thought it could be purified if the bulk of the pancreas was removed. In his notes he wrote, 'Try to isolate internal secretion . . . and relieve glycosurea [sugar in the urine].' Banting was always a rotten speller and got 'glycosuria' wrong. Neither could he spell 'diabetes', spelling it 'diabetus', but his idea that you could isolate the secretion of the islets by disabling most of the rest of the pancreas, then purify it and treat diabetes with it, was novel.

Banting explained his theory to the Professor of Physiology at the University of Toronto, J.J.R. Macleod, and Macleod lent him a laboratory and some dogs. Two medical students, Charles Best and Clark Noble, flipped a coin for the position of lab assistant. Best won the toss. The result of this flip was to change his life, turning him rapidly into one of the most famous people in the world.

Over a period of weeks Banting and Best tied off part of the dogs' pancreases until the digestive cells died, leaving thousands of islets. They made a crude extract from these islets, which they called 'isletin'. (The language of diabetes is the language of islands.) They then injected isletin into dogs whose pancreases had been removed so as to make them severely diabetic.

Though Banting and Best worked extremely hard, they were often rather unsystematic and occasionally slapdash. Their notes were not always properly kept, dogs died of infection and Banting's volcanic temper once almost resulted in his doing physical harm to his assistant.

Nonetheless, after much failure, they finally managed to keep alive a de-pancreatized dog by lowering its blood-sugar with injections of isletin.

Professor Macleod suggested improved methodology, and gave helpful advice, and as results continued to be positive he used his influence to publish them in Toronto. But Banting, whose relationship with Macleod was for some odd reason one-sidedly hostile, believed that the professor was trying to muscle in on his ideas and complained about it to anyone who would listen.

The pancreatic extract was still by no means pure, containing a lot of unwanted matter, so in December 1921, Macleod asked a biochemist called James Collip to join the team to work on purification. Collip worked hard to refine what he called 'this mysterious something' and make it safe for use in human patients.

Finally Collip produced a clear extract, and announced his results to Banting. Banting was an unpolished, volatile, foul-mouthed man who made enemies easily, and when Collip hinted that he might patent the technique, Banting threatened to smash his face in. Nobody doubted that he seriously meant to give Collip a thrashing.

At this time, few diabetic children lived longer than a year even on an aggressive almost zero-carbohydrate diet – about as interesting as charcoal and water. Those who were in the final stages of the illness, many of them comatose, were looked after in specialist wards, often with hopeless parents at the bedside, awaiting the inevitable. The desperate situation had been a spur to produce an effective extract as quickly as possible, and so it was that on 11 January 1922 the team decided to try their still impure bovine extract on a fourteen-year-old diabetic boy, Leonard Thompson, who was dying in Toronto General Hospital. Thompson was given an injection, becoming the first human being to receive 'insulin'.

But it was not a success. Thompson suffered a severe reaction to the impurities in the extract and the treatment was stopped. Over the next fortnight Collip worked like a slave to purify the hormone sufficiently and on 23 January Thompson received his second dose. As the team held their breaths, Thompson's urine began to clear of sugar, with no visible side effects.

Realizing the immense significance of this result, Banting, Best and Collip toured the diabetes ward with their new extract, injecting comatose children one bed at a time. As they were reaching the last patient, the first few children were already waking from their sleeping death. Amazed and jubilant parents shed tears of gratitude.

Techniques were rapidly improved, to the point where insulin could be made in large quantities from beef pancreases harvested from slaughterhouses. Drug firm Eli Lilly and Company was given the job of making large volumes of the highly refined hormone, which it soon did. The product, now officially called 'insulin', went on sale soon afterwards, turning Eli Lilly into a huge player in the pharmaceuticals market.

For five decades, diabetics around the world successfully managed their own treatment on daily injections of cow and/or pig insulin, but in 1977 the first genetically engineered, biosynthetic 'human' insulin was produced, becoming available in 1982.

Banting and Macleod were awarded the Nobel Prize in 1923 for their work on insulin but – of course – Banting blew his top, furious that Macleod had, as he saw it, usurped his assistant Best. Banting publicly shared the prize money with Best and Macleod likewise split his prize money with Collip. They were all strong personalities and it is little wonder that some referred to Banting as 'the prick with the needle'.

MAN ABOUT TOWN

Grooming, Dress and
Gentlemanly Panache

19 How to iron a shirt

I used to know a man who ironed his socks. He also claimed to iron his underpants but I was never given the opportunity to verify this startling assertion, thank goodness. Unlike crocheting those things that people put over their toilet rolls, ironing is one of the things that men seem capable of doing as well as women; it's just that we aren't all that interested. Certainly, no chap in his right mind would want to iron his pants. On the other hand there are times (weddings, interviews, blind dates) when you need to look a bit presentable and an ironed shirt makes a noticeable impression. Nobody is going to be much persuaded by polished shoes and combed hair if your shirt looks like the corner of some pirate's Jolly Roger.

There's nothing to it really, so here are the basics.

First you need an ironing board. Set it up at about waist height – this is another subject in itself. Don't iron beside cans of paint or the dog's dish because the sleeves will end up in there, sure as eggs is eggs. And don't try doing it on the table either; you are likely to impregnate your garment with yesterday's ingrained dinner residue. Make sure the blunt end of the board is on your dominant side and that there's a plug socket nearby.

I'm going to assume that your shirt is cotton. The manoeuvres are the same for silk or polyester but the heat setting is different. Using a spray bottle or a nailbrush, spray the shirt lightly all over with water. Have a cup of tea or something while it becomes evenly damp. If yours is a steam iron, now's the time to fill it with water. It shouldn't take you more than half an hour to find out where it is supposed to go.

Plug in the iron and set the temperature with the little wheel-thing. Cotton is safe on the hottest setting but be careful if your shirt is nylon or you'll get a sort of mozzarella cheese effect when you lift it off the material. While it's heating up leave the iron sharp-end up on the little square of asbestos at the fat end of the ironing board. You can use this useful pad for the iron whenever you need a rest.

Next, do the wet-finger-hiss test. This is related to the gobbing-sizzle-fat test I saw once in an unlovely chippy in Scarborough, whereby the proprietor gobbed intermittently into the fat, waiting for that optimal moment when it was hot enough to bounce out his ball of saliva with a little hiss. Once it's hot get the shirt by the collar and spread it out on the ironing board, underside of the collar uppermost. You'll notice that much of the time the shirt will want to slide off the board on to the floor. It's gravity and there's damn all you can do about it except hold tight. Iron the collar from the sharp ends into the middle then turn it over and do the same to the other side.

Next pull the shirt so that the sharp end of the ironing board pokes slightly into the fat end of a sleeve, with most of the part of the shirt that goes on top of your shoulders lying flat on the surface. Iron this bit and then repeat the process with the leftover portion on the opposite side.

I was discussing with a friend recently whether one should do sleeves first or last. I think it's a matter of personal choice. The trick is to remember that if the sleeves are going to be inside a jacket and nobody will be able to see them, a quick squish with the iron is fine. But if the sleeves are going to be visible it's all a bit fiddlier. First of all, choose a cuff and iron it thoroughly. If it's a double-cuff, iron it open, not folded. This is one of those moments, incidentally, when the shirt will try to slide on to the floor as soon as you take your hands off it.

Next put the entire sleeve flat on the ironing board, creases opposite each other, and, starting at the shoulder, iron right down to the cuff. It's awkward and this is often where you burn your fingers. Once you've finished swearing turn the sleeve over and do the other side. When you've done this I'm afraid it's the same palaver all over again with the other sleeve.

It's now time for the front. Hooray! The end is in sight. With the sharp end of the ironing board tucked into the collar end of the shirt, get the buttonhole side flat on the board. Apply a bit of tension by pulling against it and iron this side. Going round those buttonholes is a bit of a nuisance so attack it from all angles with the tip of the iron. Rotation of the garment will help, especially at the shoulder end. You can now go over the side seam and on to the back. If you keep going like this the button side will eventually come around. Iron this bit in the same way as the buttonhole side. Those buttons will get in your way, so use the tip of the iron again. If you are a fingers-and-thumbs sort of chap, the air will probably be blue with your language by this time. But, guess what, you've finished, so hang it up quick before your nephew comes in with some skateboard wheels and decides to wipe them with your shirt.

If you are using a steam iron, don't forget to empty it. Do this while it's still hot and it won't dribble when you put it away. By the way, never leave the iron on the material while you get a can of beer or check your mobile or you'll burn an iron-shaped hole in your shirt. Unless very pressed for time, don't iron a shirt while you are wearing it, and, just as important, never be tempted to answer the phone while you are ironing; it's very easy to get your instruments confused and iron your ear.

20 Shaving: top tips from the pros

I remember an old buffer once telling me that he objected to men with long hair because it was 'unnatural'. I pointed out that, actually, his short hair was the more unnatural, as was his having just landed from Scotland in an aeroplane. Trying to change the subject, he said that he didn't like men with beards either because that was unnatural. I said that, actually, shaving was the unnatural thing. We were getting nowhere because what I meant by 'unnatural' was something that didn't accord with nature, while what he meant by 'unnatural' was something he didn't like.

It is undoubtedly true that a well-trimmed beard or moustache is a sign of good breeding (see various members of the royal family), but it is also true that a bogie-covered tash or a beard full of last week's goulash is not. So-called designer stubble is possibly all right if you are young and handsome but on many people it just looks as if the community nurse has forgotten to come in and shave you.

Regular shaving is vital for the man about town and, although electric shavers are all very well, their work is revealed under the microscope to be of the slash and burn school. A traditional wet shave is the proper way to do it and is the closest possible, apart from those creams that disable your follicles – and no man wants his follicles messed with.

Manual razors are of two sorts: so-called open, cutthroat or straight razors, which are drop-forged and hardened, and the sort most men use, safety razors. Gentlemen of taste still use straight razors, as do more and more barbers, but using one takes a lot of practice and, like teapots and loose tea, the open razor has fallen victim to its perceived inconvenience.

The main advantage of the safety razor, of course, is that you don't have to get in a strop sharpening the thing on a piece of leather, because technology has made replacement blades superbly efficient. A friend of mine who was a prisoner of war said that he used the same safety razor blade for three years, sharpening it daily on a stone, and they're even better today.

There are several rather nice handles you can pick up that will fit these modern replacement blades, but avoid at all costs the cheaper, plastic, all-in-one razors, which are often blunt and hideous to look at, too. It's like trying to shave with a woodworker's plane.

Before a wet shave you must soften your bristles with water. Getting the water to stay on there for long enough that the hairs absorb enough to become softer and larger is the point of shaving soap. The soap also lubricates the face, helping to prevent razor burn. A bonus of lather is that you can easily see the bits you've missed.

The only proper way to get the lather on there is to use a good long-bristled shaving brush. Avoid aerosol cans. They may be quicker but they don't do such a good job. You need to spend a couple of minutes lathering the face, and just squirting the stuff on and hoping for the best won't give you the closest shave. Soap comes in the shape of a shaving stick or in a shaving mug that you can really lather up with a brush.

There are some mind-bogglingly expensive badger shaving brushes and though you needn't spend millions, a decent one is worth investing in, like a good saucepan or a good chair. These are things you use every day – it's worth getting the best you can afford. There are three grades of badger hair, called 'Pure', which is dark medium-to-short hair, 'Best', which is soft, long-to-medium hair with a pale tip, and 'Super', which is long with a white tip. Super brushes are the expensive ones, because they are handmade from these rarer badger bristles.

If you want to use an open razor, it is recommended that you take it along to a barber and get him to teach you. There's nothing like a hands-on lesson. But I am assuming that you are going to be using a safety razor.

Wet shaving may be done in one pass, along the grain, or in two passes, first with and then against the grain. If you do it this way, be careful to avoid razor burn, which is a mild but unpleasant skin irritation. Preparation is important, and having a shower or bath first will help. A good lather and plenty of water are also vital to success.

Start the shave wherever you like, sliding the razor lightly over the face, while holding the skin taut with your free hand – mind that pink thing sticking out, that's your nose. Keep the razor very well rinsed to avoid clogging the blade. Dip every stroke if you like. Too much water is impossible – if you've washed the soap off, just apply more.

Once you've finished shaving, splash cold water on your face. Yes, it makes you jump but it seals things up. Pat – don't rub – dry. Cuts, if you have any, should be treated with a styptic pencil. Some people like to put on a balm, but you should avoid alcoholic aftershaves and perfumes, which can irritate the face something rotten.

Rinse and flick your brush and razor to get most of the water off. The brush should be put somewhere warm and dry to allow the water to evaporate. Sunshine works well. Rest it in a stand, bristles pointing down so that water doesn't seep into the brush handle. Fresh air is important to avoid starting a fungus factory.

Now put on your dinner jacket and it's off to the debutantes' ball.

21 Improve that pronunciation

A student photographer called Rokas once took my picture for his degree show. It was a good picture and it later went into an exhibition in his native Lithuania. Then, one day, an extraordinarily tall and pretty young lady – as it turned out, a Lithuanian model – approached me in a London pub. I thought my luck was in but I'm afraid all she wanted was to say that she recognized my face from this exhibition. Shortly thereafter a man with a thick accent telephoned me. I thought I might be being recruited to some foreign spy agency, but no, he just wished to tell me that he also had seen my picture, and wanted to fly me to Vilnius for two days to model as a farmer examining an ear of barley for a Lithuanian beer ad. Hotel, flights and fee would all be paid, but I asked for too much money and was turned down. Pity – it would have been fun.

During these conversations I couldn't understand a blimmin' word these people were saying to me, though they seemed to have no trouble with my accent, and it led me to wonder about the Queen's English and the way it is now pronounced.

English, Scottish, Welsh, Northern Irish and all the other British micro-accents have always been divisible into subgroups, often along class lines. Once upon a time you could tell straightaway whether a person was posh, middle class or a member of the great unwashed just by hearing him speak. But things are changing, partly as a result of the international melting pot that British cities have become, partly as the result of Australian and American soap operas on the telly, and partly because posh people increasingly try to talk like everyone else. As one newspaper put it: "Er Maj. don't talk so posh no more.'

If you wish to talk with a more refined accent, there are a number to choose from. None has a rolled 'R' except those of the West Country,

Liverpool, Northumbria, Northern Ireland and parts of Scotland. So don't bother with that unless you want to sound like Noël Coward. The posher accents are bolstered by standard grammar but also tend to require the taking of pains with enunciation and the careful separation of elements, such that 'Prime Minister' is not pronounced 'Pry Minister' and 'What is that?' is never 'Wassat?'

In some regions a collocation of vowels is spoken with an extra syllable. In Wales, for example, 'road' sounds more like 'row-ad', but this is to be avoided if you wish to sound posher. The 'glottal stop', a hallmark of the cockney accent, may be commendably apt when used by a Petticoat Lane barrow boy, but it should be avoided if you wish to blend in at a table where there are more than three lots of knives and forks set for dinner.

Also to be avoided is the growing tendency to employ a rising inflexion at the end of a sentence, which makes the statement, 'It's my birthday', sound as if you're surprised. Rising inflexions sound doubtful and therefore lack authority. Do not use them.

You should avoid the mannered top-end accents. To listen to Nancy Mitford or Brian Sewell is to wonder what exactly happened to them in the nursery. Nonetheless, if you wish waiters in expensive hotels to snap to attention you might try cultivating the County accent (see below). For most of us, though, ordinary Received Pronunciation is generally good enough.

In this fast-changing field it is rash to try to pin down distinct pronunciation differences too emphatically, so this somewhat fuzzy classification list will have to do.

- Royal: a weird posh accent spoken by nobody but the monarch and her very close family. Don't try this one – you're getting ideas above your station.
- Brian Sewell: a sort of unclassifiable posh accent, full of elastic swoops and an uncommon 'spelling out' of longer words, such as 'parl-i-a-ment-*a*' instead of 'parlamnt', and the painstaking emphasis

of usually relaxed internal consonants, such as '*tiss*-ue' instead of 'tishoo'. Kingsley Amis said the word 'tissue' was a good 'wanker detector'. I couldn't possibly comment.

- County (rhymes with ninety): a plum *and* a silver spoon in the mouth. No wonder they talk like that. The 'huntin', shootin', end fishin'' accent. County speakers do not cut the grass with a 'mower' but have a man do it with a 'myrrh'. When Lord Harris once committed the sin of wearing a brown bowler to Ascot, Edward VII is said to have joshed: 'Goin' rettin', 'Erris?'. That's County. A lot less common nowadays.

- Hyperlect: there's an overlap these days between County and Hyperlect (a variety of language associated with the upper strata of society), which is plum-in-mouth but not quite County. Slightly posher than ordinary RP, contemporary Hyperlect is to be found among some characters in Radio 4's *The Archers*, and it's here that you'll find people wearing brine trisers, while still fishing rather than fishin'.

- Sloane: named after London's expensive Sloane Square. Monied but not County. For the 'Yaah' brigade, a crèche is a road accident. It is cut-glass with urban slang and pints of lager, with some self-conscious Estuary influence.

- Received Pronunciation (RP): Radio 4 English/Standard regional.

- London Educated: Received Pronunciation with an urban flavour and some Estuary elements (see below). Self-aware glottal-stopism but not too much. Cool, and with it.

- Cockney: a demotic language of delightful richness and rhyming slangery. The 'I' sound is pronounced 'oi', so 'Blimey!' becomes 'Bloimey!' Strong use of the glottal stop, inni'! For example, in the word 'battle' the glottal stop is used to stop the air abruptly at the back of the tongue/top of the chest after the first syllable, before being expelled with a staccato puff in the second syllable. This causes it to come out as an 'oo' sound. Grammatical quirks: when asked if he and his wife hadn't been planning to go to Disneyland Paris, one cockney speaker replied, 'We was bu' we never!' To be avoided unless you were born within the sound of Bow bells.

- Estuary: a kind of half-cockney 'electrician's language' that is spreading beyond the Isle of Thanet or 'Planni' 'Fanni" (Planet Thanet), as Estuary speakers call it, to areas around London. To be heard among educated – younger – TV and radio presenters. 'Waw-ah' instead of 'water' and use of so-called 'yod-coalescence', which just means that 'Tuesday' sounds like 'choose day' and 'sand dunes' are 'san junes'. Avoid.

In case you think all this is unimportant, you should recall that, at a dinner to celebrate her husband's retirement as President of France, Mme de Gaulle was asked by her English host what she was most looking forward to in the years ahead. A huge smile broke out on her face and she announced loudly, 'A penis!' After an embarrassed hush, General de Gaulle leaned over to his wife and murmured, 'Darling, I think the English pronounce it "happiness".'

22 Turn-ups for the book

I used to work in a gentlemen's outfitters, where, one day, I sold a pair of trousers to 'Captain Birdseye'. They had no turn-ups, I remember. Turn-up or not turn-up, that is the question, and has been for ages because, let's be honest, the fellow who turns up turned out in turn-ups when turn-ups are down not up the dress-code scale is considered a bounder of the lowest water and the club's membership secretary is likely to give him the turn-down and turn him out. So what are the rules, then, and where did turn-ups come from?

Trousers themselves have not been around all that long, becoming relatively common only in the sixteenth century, when they were popularized by a foolish old character from the *commedia dell'arte*, named Pantalone (Italian for 'trousers'). 'Pantaloon' became the Anglicized word for men's close-fitting breeches fastened below the calf or at the foot, and it was soon shortened to the now familiar 'pants'.

By the final decade of the nineteenth century the gentlemen of inclement northern Europe frequently had to turn up their trouser bottoms in filthy weather, to protect them from the mud, but it wasn't until the 1890s that the Prince of Wales (later King Edward VII) had the bright idea of having his trousers turned up all the time. Of course, if it was good enough for the sovereign's heir it was good enough for Joe Bloggs, and by the turn of the century, turn-up wearing had begun to take off. Turn-ups or 'roll-ups' became an increasingly common sight in the kingdom and its colonies, and tailors, having their eye on sales figures, began to stitch permanent turn-ups into the bottom of gents trousers. Indeed, the Savile Row term for turn-ups is PTUs (Permanent Turn-Ups).

The British government put a stop to turn-ups during the Second World War to save cloth. The same fate befell ladies' silk and nylon stockings, which were transmogrified into parachutes, tents and tyres. But, turning trouble into triumph, the man about town simply began wearing un-turned-up trousers again and the turn-up-free trouser has remained the usual thing until the present day, when turn-ups are a charming rarity at the bottom of a gentleman's leg. (No good dinner suit ever has turn-ups, by the way.)

As anyone who has worn turn-ups will tell you, the things are magnets for coins and dust, but there are several (accidental) advantages to them, too. They add weight to the trouser leg, keeping it anchored, allowing pleats to drape well, and promoting crispness of crease. Unless you are artistic or Jon Snow you don't want to draw attention to your socks, and turn-ups will help to keep your ankles covered as you walk.

23 The man who wore brown shoes in the City

Some of those old cockney songs have great charm. There's 'With Her Head Tucked Underneath Her Arm', for example, about Anne Boleyn, or 'Knees Up Mother Brown', about Mother Brown getting her knees up, and, 'I'm Henery the Eighth, I Am', about Henry the Eighth telling us what number Henry he is. These songs were all co-written by R.P. Weston and Bert Lee, except for the last, which Weston wrote with Fred Murray.

Western and Lee wrote a song a day and in 1940 they produced 'Brahn Boots', a sentimental elegy about a chap who is shunned at a funeral because he's come wearing brown boots. It turns out he has given away his black boots to a man who has no boots at all. The song is guaranteed to bring a tear to even the most jaded duct.

People are very sensitive about clothes and there are strict unwritten rules. Who could take seriously a nun in a mini skirt, a dustman in a frock coat, or the Queen opening Parliament in trainers? An acquaintance of mine once turned up for a meeting at the Bank of England in a sober business suit and – horror! – knocked-about brown brogues. 'I'd come up in the dark from a weekend in the country,' he told me, 'and it wasn't till I got out of the cab in Threadneedle Street that I realized my faux pas. There was no time to do anything, and though nobody said anything, I felt like a complete cad.'

Somebody once wrote off Sir Anthony Eden with this terse put-down: 'Not a gentleman; dresses too well.' This not-dressing-too-well business is a good rule of thumb, especially now that dress code things are much more relaxed and tieless gentlemen are a commonplace sight in offices where once it would have been a hanging offence. The man about town should be careful to avoid being sucked into the world of fashion of course, so here are a few dress tips for the gentleman of taste. Break any of these rules if you can carry it off with panache.

- Fibres: natural always, except for waterproof footwear and umbrellas. Always get your clothes from the best supplier you can afford.
- In town: sober, single-breasted suits with a white or pale shirt. Wear double-breasted only if you have the personality to carry it off. Same for pin or chalk stripes. Jacket always darker than the shirt, tie darker than the jacket. Avoid black suits as they are likely to threaten your boss or client. Black is the colour of authority and should be reserved for priests and the top banana. (You can ignore this one if you are top banana.) In business situations, always look better

dressed than your client. Same is true if you are being interviewed for a job. Favour the formal. Your clients may dress like slobs if they please, and often will; it's their way of showing who's in charge. No brown suits or shoes, no, no, no.

- Trousers: good corduroy or tweed favoured in the country. Tartan trews OK only if you are Scots. Jeans? Not really, chaps. Turn-ups or not? See the turn-ups section on pp. 60–1.

- Sweaters: wool, obviously; avoid loud patterns, which are only fit for the likes of Val Doonican. Remember him? No? Oh, never mind.

- Socks: dark in town. Always short. No 'proper man' wears socks above the mid-calf region and then only if he's old or has knickerbockers on. In the country there is a whole variety to choose from; green and brown are always safe bets, but the rules for sock height etc. are too complex to go into here. Avoid words and pictures on your socks unless you want to look like a berk. Bright colours must be carefully handled. If you are not a dandy, avoid. White socks? Don't waste my time.

- Ties: silk always. In the office, patterns should be small, un-loud, geometric and repeating, and the hairy tartan ones are for the weekend only. Military or club ties are allowed an emblem. Bow ties may be spotted or paisley but not too bright, chaps. Those revolving ones are for the children's entertainer. Tie the thing properly, for gawd's sake. And remember – no gentleman wears a made-up bow tie.

- Belt or braces: never both. The most important thing about a fellow's belt is that it matches his shoes. Leather, of course. Loud braces are fine in the country but should be worn in town only if you are a dandy or brash entrepreneur. Vulgar otherwise – that's the problem.

- Hats: should have brims – all the way round, unless it's a Russian job, deerstalker or a tweed cap. Avoid anything that doesn't, especially baseball caps and those almost ubiquitous clingy things that look like ribbed tea cosies. Smoking caps are all right, of course, and de rigueur when doing crumpets on your toasting fork.

- Scarves: quality again, wool or cotton. Avoid tying a scarf in that special looped way that seems to have come from somewhere. The proper way to wear a scarf is to let it just hang there, to wind it around the neck like a snake, or to tie a simple overhand knot at the front.
- Handkerchiefs: white in town. In the country, large, colourful snuff hankies are useful and attractive. Spots are best.
- Pocket square: silk always, plain or patterned. Best omitted in the office these days, unless you are a flamboyant type.
- Cufflinks: best quality gold or silver preferred. Unostentatious, always.
- Finger rings: oh, if you must. Gold or silver, and small.
- Leather elbow patches: not even if you are a teacher. Sorry. However, brown-leather repairs to the cuffs of a favourite jacket are permitted for casualwear or fiddling with the jalopy.
- Watches: get as good a watch as you can afford but avoid showiness – it's so vulgar. Nothing wrong with a leather strap.
- Footwear: proper leather always. Black shoes or boots at the office. Never brown in town. In the country, of course, there are waders, wellies, brogues and who knows what else. No socks with sandals: never, never. Shoes should always be shiny enough to reflect the knickers of the girl you are dancing with.

24 How to grow a dashing moustache

If asked who was the more stylish, Hitler or Stalin, you would have to go for Stalin because of the moustache. That's not to say you'd want him round for dinner, but his mo' had undeniable dash. Hitler's 'toothbrush' moustache was about as dashing as a hernia operation and looked as though he had simply cut the ends off a proper one, which is exactly what he did do when, as one of the Kaiser's hairy privates, he was ordered to trim the long points of his full handlebar to fit under the First World War mustard-gas respirator.

There's really nothing to growing a tash so long as you have the right genes. Some gentlemen have trouble growing hair on the upper lip, or what I have heard called more precisely the 'ergotrid' (the bit between your upper lip and your nose). For them it is often a case of stylish sideburns, instead. But if you have a detectable amount of stubble there and the desire to grow a dashing tash comes upon you, here are some tips from the pros.

The first thing to do is to stop shaving altogether and grow a full (temporary) beard. This has several advantages over trying to grow just a moustache, among which are that you will be able to monitor the character and strength of your overall facial hair growth and check colour distribution. The moustaches and/or beards of some men are of a different colour than the hair on their noggins, while others find patches where the hair fails to grow at all, or there are aberrant white spots among the dark. By growing a full beard you will be able to see whether the style of moustache you favour is going to work for you. Furthermore, trying to grow a moustache on its own is more likely to result in your girlfriend leaving you in disgust, and street urchins flinging orange peel and contumely in your direction.

Human hair grows at about 6 in. (15 cm) a year or roughly 0.000000011 miles an hour. Once you have a decent length, depending on how long you want the tash, you can carefully cut, clip and shave off the unwanted hair, leaving your new smasher in place. A pencil moustache is going to be ready in short order, while a walrus is going to take you longer. Then it's just a case of maintaining the styling and keeping it trim. The Handlebar (Moustache) Club of Great Britain has some excellent advice on growing one of that kind, and on using wax.

Being the proud owner of a 'soup-strainer' myself, I maintain that you don't really grow a moustache – a moustache grows *you*. But unless you want to look like the vicar's knitting after the cat's got at it, good maintenance is important. When the Handlebar Club was criticized by the Beard Liberation Front for forbidding beards and encouraging good grooming, the most dashing man about town I know, Michael 'Atters' Attree said, 'I'd rather be shot by a moustachioed fascist than bored to

Natural

English

Hungarian or
Wild West

Dalí

Imperial

Freestyle

Freestyle

Chevron

Pencil

| Toothbrush | Walrus | Zapata |

death by the BLF.' Quite! Here are a few moustache styles you might try – handlebar and otherwise – that will lend your face undeniable éclat.

- Handlebar: a broad range here, with everything from Salvador Dalí to Wild West. Consult the illustrations.
- Chevron: Tom Selleck wore this type in *Magnum P.I.*
- Pencil: simple and stylish. Errol Flynn, Vincent Price and Clark Gable wore this type.
- Toothbrush: Hitler, Charlie Chaplin and Oliver Hardy had these. Not dashing – sorry. Don't know why I put it in.
- Walrus: Friedrich Nietzsche had the most enormous one of these hummers. Difficult to carry off. Requires intensive grooming to prevent you looking like an old tramp. Avoid soup.
- Zapata: the ends extend downwards towards the chin. As seen on the face of Jason King. Blimey, Jason King, I haven't thought of him for decades.

Good luck.

Man Cooking

25 How to slaughter and bleed a pig

Ever slaughtered a pig? No? Then you should acquaint yourself with the method. What do you mean, 'Yuck!'? Are you a real man or what? If you've done this before you can skip this one – everyone else, let's get the rubber aprons on and off we go.

First get your pig. You can slaughter pigs at different ages, from piglets to young pigs of between four months and one year old, which will provide most of your pork and bacon. Older pigs will be good sausage-makers. (Boars – uncastrated males – are usually de-testiculated a month before they are slaughtered.) I hope my own retirement is a bit more fun than this.

In olden times you would starve the pig for a day before slaughter and then give him a breakfast of coal to clean the intestines, which can be cooked as food (chitterlings) or used for sausage skins. It would then be quickly upended and dispatched with a very sharp knife to the jugular vein and carotid artery. These days you must first stun the animal. One way is to make it watch *The Jeremy Kyle Show*, but the more usual methods are to zap it with an electric current, stun it with a 'captive bolt pistol', a sort of compressed-air gun that fires a retractable rod at its forehead, or make it breathe in carbon dioxide (CO_2).

■ Stunning electrodes: should deliver at least 1.3 amps at a voltage of at least 260 volts under a load of impedance equal to a pig's head. Test them on your mother-in-law. Hold the electrodes halfway between the eye and the ear, so that they span the brain. Hold them tight and switch on for three seconds. Your pig, or mother-in-law, should collapse and become rigid, before relaxing.

- Captive bolt: either of the other methods is preferable to the bolt, but here's how. Place the gun centrally an inch above the pig's eyes, aiming towards the tail. Fire and it should immediately fall down, stop breathing rhythmically and look as if it's been to a stag party.
- CO_2 inhalation: put the pig in an enclosed space (such as a caravan) full of CO_2 at a concentration of between 70 per cent and 90 per cent. Don't breathe this stuff in yourself. The CO_2 load changes the blood chemistry, causing the pig to expire. Leave it there for two minutes and then test it by pricking its nose with a needle. If it responds to the prick, re-stun.

It is vital that you exsanguinate (bleed) your pig within fifteen seconds of stunning, so that he does not begin to come round. By the time he is putting on his shoes to go shopping or filling his pipe it is too late. Bleeding also helps in the preservation of the meat. So take a very sharp knife to the carotid artery and the jugular vein. Do not do this in your sitting room. The blood can be collected, by people standing by with pans and things, for use in the making of black pudding.

Once bled, put the carcass in a pig scalder (a sort of trough) and drench in boiling water to assist in the removal of the hair. I suppose the bath will do. Shave the pig and rewash with boiling water. If you still have a stubble problem use a blowtorch (*on the pig*).

Eviscerate the animal using the *Collins Guide to Pig Evisceration*, or something, then cut off the head and divide the carcass into halves, and wash. If all this seems like too much work, you can buy half a pig from your butcher.

Put the bits of pig in the fridge (I don't know how, perhaps you need a bigger fridge) as this will help with the cutting and boning process later.

If you prefer to salt your pork, bung it in a barrel and fill with salt, then store in a cellar for ten days. Remove after this time and squeeze out the remaining blood. Then put it back into storage for a few months. You can produce salted buttocks (ham), bacon and sausages from the minced bits and bobs squeezed into the intestines. Anything left over, including the head, can be used to make brawn. Everything of the pig is used except the squeak. Traditionally, the eyes are included in the brawn, although I must say I don't like to be looked at while I'm eating.

26 The perfect hamburger in a twinkling

German snacks such as the frankfurter are often named after their place of origin. The origin of the name 'hamburger' is, unsurprisingly, Hamburg, where minced meat was traditionally served in a bread roll, called a *Brötchen*.

However, the origin of the hamburger we know today is contentious, with the American burghers of Connecticut, Texas and Missouri all claiming first-burger status. The supposed date of introduction hovers very roughly around the turn of the nineteenth to the twentieth century.

Hamburgers are now a staple of the Western diet but those you get in a fast-food restaurant differ in important respects from the kind you barbecue yourself in the garden. One leading burger is reported to contain, in addition to meat, the following yummy ingredients: calcium lactate, benzoic acid, dextrose, mono- and diacetyltartaric acid esters of glycerides of fatty acids, water, mono- and diglycerides of fatty acids, soy, saccharose, sodium stearoyl-2-lactylate, calcium sulphate, ascorbic acid, sodium acetates (i) sodium acetate (ii) sodium hydrogen acetate (sodium diacetate), powdered bones and teeth, and salt. If you'd rather make your own hamburger next time, here is the last word on the subject.

1   Choose the right meat. Coarse ground is what to look out for. Finely ground meat can become mushy and hard to work. High fat is the key to yumminess (but not necessarily to heart health). Lean beef, like sirloin makes a dry burger. The more fat there is, the more succulent the meat – but the more it will shrink during cooking, with 30 per cent fat beef dwindling by as much as 25 per cent. Try mince with about 20

per cent fat, but make the burgers a bit wider than your buns to allow for shrinkage.

2 Mix the meat with black or white pepper, a little olive oil and some minced garlic. But no salt yet because it has a deliquescent effect, sucking the moisture out of the meat and producing burgers as dry as crumbled plaster. Instead, sprinkle salt on the burgers just before you put them on the grill. You need plenty of it – sorry about your blood pressure.

3 Form into burger shapes, pressing your thumb into the centre of each so that you have a ring-shaped thing with a dent, a bit like a blood cell. This will stop the burgers becoming almost entirely spherical as they cook. You aren't doing meatballs.

4 Heat an oiled barbecue rack until it's too hot to hold your hand over. Position the burgers on the rack, salt them and smartly close the lid (if you have one).

5 Wait for a couple of minutes.

6 Try lifting a burger with a spatula. If it sticks, keep cooking until the moment it comes free, then flip all the burgers.

7 Close the lid and cook for another couple of minutes.

8 Check, and as soon as the burgers come free of the rack, flip once more.

9 Cook until the juices run clear and the burgers feel firm.

10 Remove from the barbecue and make sure they're done by piercing with a fork. If they are too pink for you, cook for another minute or so.

11 Serve on good buns with fried onions, horseradish, condiments and whatnot to taste.

27 How to open a champagne bottle with a sword

I was at once at a posh reception in Belgravia where an oleaginous man with a made-up bow tie offered to open the champagne for our hesitant hostess. He wrenched off the foil, tore away the wire cage and began pushing violently at the cork with his thumbs. He then thrust the thing between his thighs and doubled himself over in a most unattractive posture, grimacing as if in agony. At length he began an undignified low cursing, causing dismayed guests to put down their empty flutes and wander away. In a fit of reactive rage he gave the bottle a final violent shake as if wringing its neck. All at once there was a crack like a rifle, followed by a sickening tinkle as the speeding cork struck the face of an ormolou mantel clock. Our man shot backwards in a jet of froth, upsetting a vase of orchids and banging his head against an unsmiling iron bust of Lord Brabazon. 'Funny fellow,' muttered a distinguished-looking gentleman in a cummerbund.

It really needn't be this difficult and to prove it I have included here this wonderfully exhibitionistic procedure that will not only get the cork out in double-quick time but will also wow the crowd.

The opening of a bottle by means of your sword is what the French call *le sabrage*. Napoleon's Hussards were always at it, yelling '*sabrer la bouteille*' ('sabre the bottle'), when they should have been practising chopping the enemy's heads off. Maybe that's why we were able to give them such a thrashing at Waterloo.

In essence, *le sabrage* involves using the back (blunt) edge of your sabre to break the neck off the bottle. Beheading a bottle in this showy fashion is not difficult but does require diligent practice and the sacrifice of half a case or more of low-grade bubbly. You need to be prepared to invest up to £20 (say, up to a dozen bottles of sparkling 'hobo's wine').

Method

1   Using a linen napkin, dry an unshaken bottle of chilled champagne, and remove the foil and wire.
2   Locate the hemispherical seam that marks the vertical join created during the bottle's manufacture. This is known as the crease. The bottle is weakest at the point where the crease meets the lip (the round bump your finger encounters if you run it down the neck from the fat end), and it is here that you will strike.
3   Hold the bottle firmly and point it upwards (away from living creatures, e.g. your grandma) at an angle of about 45 degrees.
4   Lay your sword against the bottle with the blunt edge facing the cork.

72

Look, I don't know where you are going to get a hussar's sabre from. Use your imagination; I have my own problems. (Specialist 'champagne swords' are available on the internet, *Ed.*)

5   In a swift, firm, masculine movement, slide the sword impressively down the seam, toward the lip (a bit like a slow, backhand tennis stroke). Hit at just the right speed, and with the proper amount of force, the lip will be knocked clean off the bottle, taking the cork with it, and will fly off in a pleasing and most satisfactory fashion.

Safety

1   Unless you know what you are doing with sharp swords, use a metal ruler instead.
2   The edge of the neck will be sharp, so wear leather gauntlets and a welder's facemask, and a full suit of armour.
3   Don't rehearse in your living room. The back garden is the best place, but be careful not to mow the lawn before you've picked up all those corks.
4   Discard incorrectly decapitated bottles and do not drink from any without a clean break.
5   Or you could just open a can of beer.

28 Eponymous nosh: dishes named after people

If you ever find yourself hanging around the Melbourne docks you will probably see a hideous metal statue of a woman with hair sculpted like the torch on the Statue of Liberty. This is alleged to be a likeness of Australian singer and prima donna Dame Nellie Melba (1861–1931), who took her stage name from her hometown and had several foods named after her. These included Melba sauce, a sort of raspberry and current purée, Melba toast and Melba Garniture, which is chicken, truffles and mushrooms stuffed into tomatoes, with stock. Sounds rather rich to me – a bit like its namesake. Like Ronald McDonald, you need to be famous to have a food named after you. Here are a few.

- Fillet of Beef Prince Albert: Queen Victoria's consort had several dishes named after him, including this beef dish, a white sauce, a soup containing brussel sprouts and smoked bacon (blimey!), and Albert Pudding, which sounds like a character from Dickens.

- Gâteau Alexandra: Edward VII's missus, Alexandra of Denmark (1844–1925), was Princess of Wales and later, of course, Queen. As well as the chocolate gâteau, there is Alexandra consommé and various fish, chicken, quail and other meat dishes.

- Consommé Princess Alice: not to be outdone, Princess Alice (1883–1981), granddaughter of Queen Victoria, had a consommé, too. It's got artichoke hearts and lettuce in it. Crazy name, crazy soup!

- Amundsen's Dessert: some American friends invented this pudding for the Norwegian explorer. I don't know if there was any ice in the recipe.

- Omelette Arnold Bennett: the Savoy Hotel invented an open omelette with smoked haddock for northern writer Arnold Bennett. Somehow the very French 'omelette' crashes gears a bit with the very English 'Arnold Bennett'. I'm sure it's delicious, though.

- Battenberg Cake: this long square cake has a marzipan wrapping and yellow-and-pink quarters when you cut it. It's named after the Battenberg family, who changed their German name during the First World War to Mountbatten. It's a literal translation.

- Eggs Benedict: New York stockbroker Lemuel Benedict said he had a hangover one day in 1894 so he went to the Waldorf Hotel and asked for a light breakfast that wouldn't nauseate him: bacon, poached eggs, toast and hollandaise sauce. Personally, I would have called that 'Eggs Emetic'.

- Eggs in a Mould Bizet: the French composer of *Carmen*, Georges Bizet (1838–75), had named after him a dish consisting of eggs cooked in moulds lined with minced pickled tongue, and served on artichoke hearts. Sounds worse than that disgusting Eggs Benedict.

- Caesar Salad: this famous salad was named after the chef who invented it: Caesar Cardini (1896–1956). Contains eggs, croutons and Worcestershire sauce among other crazy ingredients.

- Chateaubriand: steak recipe named after Vicomte François René de Chateaubriand (1768–1848), French writer and ambassador to England.
- Clementine: Père Clément Rodier, a French monk, created this hybrid of the mandarin and Seville oranges in the twentieth century. Or maybe he just found it growing on a tree, the history is unclear. If it was the latter story, the fruit might just well be called 'Everybodyines'.
- Veuve Clicquot: veuve is French for 'widow'. This champagne was named after Barbe-Nicole Ponsardin, the widow of François Clicquot. I wonder if she had a bubbly personality.
- Cox's Orange Pippin: Richard Cox (1777–1845) created this best of English apples in Buckinghamshire.
- Cumberland Sauce: unlike the curly sausage, this was not named after the county but the man – Ernst August of Hanover, third Duke of Cumberland.
- Veal Pie à la Dickens: Charles Ranhofer created this tasty-sounding if unlikely dish to cash in on Charles Dickens' visits to the US. He also did Beet Fritters à la Dickens, which is like Beet Fritters à la J.K. Rowling – ludicrous.
- Garibaldi Biscuits: delicious flat 'squashed fly' biscuits, containing currants, named after Giuseppe Garibaldi (1807–82), the Italian political figure who visited England in 1864 to much cheering. They don't dunk well, these.
- Earl Grey Tea: named after Earl Grey – who did you think? He was Charles Grey, Second Earl Grey, Viscount Howick and Prime Minister, 1830–34. Amazing he had time for tea.
- Jésus Sausage: if Jesus can't have a food named after him who can? But did it have to be a small French Basque/Savoy sausage?
- Lamingtons: a sponge cake named after Charles Cochrane-Baillie, Second Baron Lamington, Governor of Queensland, 1896–1901. One of Australia's national dishes.
- Leibniz-Keks: delicious high-quality German chocolate biscuit, and surely the only food to be named after a philosopher (Gottfried Leibniz, 1646–1716).

- Pizza Margherita: the story is that this is the patriotic pizza, in the colours of the Italian flag, that was presented to Queen Margherita of Savoy (1851–1926) when she visited Naples. It's like Pizza Hut doing a 'Windsor Pizza' with the Union Jack on it.
- Peach Melba: I mentioned Nellie Melba earlier. The famous Savoy hotel chef Auguste Escoffier is said to have heard her sing at Covent Garden and decided to invent a pudding in her name. Fair enough.
- Napoleon Brandy: Napoleon Bonaparte. Who else?
- Lobster Newberg: good story to this one – Captain Ben Wenberg is said to have brought the recipe he'd found in his travels to chef Charles Ranhofer, who put the meal on his restaurant menu, calling it Lobster Wenberg. Then they argued and, in revenge, Ranhofer twisted the name.
- Bath Olivers: these are like Lucozade and cornflakes, in the sense that they were invented as a medicinal foodstuff. In this case it was Dr William Oliver (1695–1764) who had opened a bath in Bath and gave his fat and gouty patients this unspeakably uninteresting cracker as a digestive treatment. Or maybe as a punishment.
- Pavlova: fruity meringue desert named after the Russian ballerina, Anna Pavlova (1881–1931).
- Dom Pérignon: Dom Pérignon (1638–1715), a blind French Benedictine monk, had a lot of time to think. He helped to develop the first champagne.
- Queen Mother's Cake: Elizabeth, the Queen Mother (1901–2002), was having tea with her friend the Polish pianist Jan Smeterlin (1892–1967) when he served her this chocolate cake. She became an instant fan.
- Salisbury Steak: this bunless burger was the invention of another health-food nut, American, Dr James H. Salisbury (1823–1905). It's a sort of early Atkins-type meal.
- Sandwich: John Montagu, 4th Earl of Sandwich (1718–1792), often wanted to eat while playing cards. The kitchen conjured up the cutlery-free meal and it caught on.

- Beef Stroganoff: Russian, this one – how did you guess? A nineteenth-century meal of sautéd beef with sour-cream sauce, it was named after Count Pavel Alexandrovich Stroganov. Or maybe it was Count Grigory Dmitriyevich Stroganov. These food-naming stories seem to be 85 per cent embroidery and 5 per cent fibs.
- Crêpe Suzette: in 1896, the Prince of Wales was with this bird, Suzette somebody or another, at the Café de Paris in Monte Carlo. When pudding came up it was a flambéd crêpe with a caramelized sauce, orange zest and liqueur. Apparently, he dedicated it to his lady-friend. I understand that the current Queen likes pancakes.
- Victoria Sponge: named after an Egyptian pharaoh. Only joking; it's the Queen again.
- Beef Wellington: like the boot, this beef dish covered in pastry is named after Arthur Wellesley, First Duke of Wellington (1769–1852). He's the Waterloo man.
- Woolton Pie: a wartime staple and a delicious meal – I've made it myself. Frederick Marquis, 1st Earl of Woolton, was the Minister of Food during the Second World War and he asked chefs at the Savoy Hotel to invent a root vegetable pie that could persuade people to cut back a bit on meat and tuck into vegetables, which were the one item available in decent quantities. It worked.

29 Novel dishes for the jaded palate

Among the delicious recipes included by Prosper Montagne in his *Larousse Gastronomique* is one for a dish named *Entrecote à la Bordelaise*. This sounds delicious until you realize it is 'grilled rats Bordeaux style'. This speciality requires the catching, skinning and gutting of a few alcoholic rats of the type that live in French wine cellars (I'm not making this up). The boozy rodents are then brushed with a viscous dressing of olive oil and crushed spring onions, before being grilled over a fire of broken wine barrels.

Both brown rats and roof rats have been enthusiastically eaten by hungry Parisians over the years, while the ancient Romans particularly enjoyed sewn-up fish-and-nut-stuffed dormice, baked in the oven. The litany of quirky nosebag down the ages also includes horse, witchetty grubs, pig's nose and mashed brains, as well as the now rather commonplace frogs and snails. So, for those who have had enough of roast beef, bangers and mash, and spotted dick, here are a few novelty meals that will make your guests sit up and pay attention.

Souris à la crème

Mice in cream is a pretty good one to start off with. It's accompanied by an interesting salad and followed by a novel dessert, so you could serve the whole lot as a three-course meal, maybe with a liquidized spam and anchovy shake as a palate cleanser. Here's what you need for the mousey element:

- A few fat mice
- A hunk of salted belly of pork
- A bottle of industrial-strength vodka
- 3 oz Grand Marnier
- A few cloves
- ½ lb plain flour
- Salt and pepper

1 Skin, eviscerate and wash the mice but leave the heads on. If you don't like the reproachful look in their eyes, tie an old sock over their faces.
2 Marinate in vodka for two hours (*the mice*, not you).
3 While you wait, dice the pork belly and render the fat by cooking slowly for several hours.
4 Drain the mice (be careful – that vodka is flammable).
5 Cover them thoroughly in the flour, seasoned well with salt and pepper.
6 Sauté in the pork fat for five minutes.
7 Add ¼ pint vodka, the Grand Marnier and a pinch of cloves.

8   Simmer covered for fifteen minutes.
9   Prepare a béchamel cream sauce (your mum's cookbook will show you how if you don't know) and transfer the hot, succulent and orangey mice into it.
10 Warm for about ten minutes.
11 Serve.

Spider side salad

You should include spiders of as many different kinds as you can find. Big ones are best.

1   Steam your spiders live, like crab, to maintain crispness.
2   Amputate the legs from larger specimens and quarter them.
3   Make a bed of sweet cos lettuce, parsley, chopped portobello mushrooms, radishes and spring onions. Toss in one cup of chopped spiders and a goodly squirt of extra virgin olive oil, vinegar, lemon juice and fresh ground pepper. Sliced jalapeño pepper adds an extra kick. Well, you won't get one from the spider legs.

Cow udder eclairs

■   12 fresh cow udders
■   1 pt double cream
■   1 tin artichoke hearts
■   1 filleted smelt (small)
■   6 oz brown sugar
■   2 oz lump of butter
■   Food mixer
■   Frying pan
■   1 can depilatory cream (such as Nair)

1   Soak the udders in depilatory cream to remove the hair. Repeat as necessary until bald (until the *udders* are bald). Shaving won't do it; it leaves a nasty stubble.

2   To remove milk traces, soak the udders in lukewarm water for 2–4 hours while you go and make a periscope or something.

3   Rinse.

4   Melt the butter in a warm frying pan and add the udders. Fry until golden.

5   Finely chop the artichoke hearts and smelt.

6   In a mixer, gently whip the cream, sugar, artichokes and smelt. Remove the udders from the pan when creamy and slit down the side of each. Spread the gunge into the slits and serve cold. A majestic dessert.

30 Bloody hot chilli

There are two sorts of food: the kind a chap can make and the kind he can't. Spun sugar, tiny marzipan roses and soufflé are the sort of things that tend to crash and burn if a man is attempting them, while steak, hamburgers and hot dogs are all on the man-can-do-this list. What's more, chilli is on the list, too, which is good because chilli is a pretty universal man-food.

In 1828 J.C. Clopper noticed people in San Antonio chopping the little meat they had and stewing it together with an equal amount of chilli to stretch the meal. The chilli certainly helps tenderize and disguise inferior meat. Garlic and beans seem to be twentieth-century additions to this staple and nowadays there's plenty of good meat and a range of chillies from the mildest and sweetest to tiny innocuous-looking things that blow your eardrums out and melt your clothes. Choose the sort that suit you but don't forget that other people have to eat the stuff, too.

This recipe will easily provide enough chilli for sixteen people, so it's a good rugby club meal. If you suddenly find there are more people than you think you can feed, stir in some more chopped jalapeño. That will slow them down a bit. Or if you are on your own, just eat one portion, freeze fifteen, and live on the rest for the next fortnight.

■   4 tbsp olive oil

- 4 medium onions (chopped)
- 2 medium green peppers (chopped)
- 8 lb best mince
- About 6 oz tomato puree
- 2 lb tinned tomatoes
- 2 tbsp tomato sauce
- 6 cloves garlic (crushed)
- 6 oz chilli powder
- 4 jalapeño peppers (seeded, de-veined and chopped. Do not touch your eyes!)
- 2 tbsp salt
- 1 tbsp oregano
- 2 tbsp garlic powder (or as much as your friends will put up with)
- 1 tbsp ground black pepper

1 Fry the meat in large pan. There's a lot of it so it may take two goes. Once it's browned, drain the juice.
2 Heat the oil in a huge pot over a medium heat. Sauté the onions, peppers and crushed garlic until soft. Do not burn.
3 Add the meat, tomato puree, stewed tomatoes and tomato sauce. (This is not a good meal if you are allergic to tomatoes.)
4 Stir in the garlic powder, salt, pepper, oregano, chilli powder and jalapeño.
5 Turn down to low and simmer for three hours, stirring every fifteen minutes. Yes, it's boring.
6 Halfway through cooking (stir number 6) season with salt and pepper, and add more chilli if underperforming. This can be a skin-peelingly hot chilli, depending on the quality of your chillies. Serve with grated cheese, onions and tortilla chips for dipping.

Vegetarian chilli

You might wonder why a vegetarian would wish to eat a meal of chilli. After all, it's basically a meat dish. But I have this friend who says he's a vegetarian not because he respects animals but because he hates plants. For a person like him substitute kidney beans, extra onions and more tomato puree for the meat (weight for weight). A little butter is sometimes required to replace the meat fats. It is amazingly good and even unreconstructed carnivores will dig in.

SPORT, SPEED, ACTION
AND ADVENTURE

Mainly Aerobic

31 How to go over Niagara Falls in a barrel

You know that feeling you sometimes get when life is driving you crazy with its boring tediousness and the weekend prospect is a barren one of joyless food shopping, car washing and bill paying? Well the French have a word for this, *ennui*, and we've had enough of it, haven't we?! The time has come to strike back, to kick against this oppressive monotony, to reclaim those thrills and excitements that are our birthright. Yes, it's time to go over Niagara Falls in a barrel.

The first person to go over Niagara Falls in a barrel was a woman, sixty-three-year-old retired school teacher Annie Edson Taylor, who claimed (unpersuasively) to be only forty-three. This was 1901 and Annie, at something of a loose end, thought that this stunt would make her rich and famous. So she got hold of a long, thin pickle barrel, put in an anvil for ballast, and on 24 October, her birthday, she strapped herself to pillows and climbed inside (with her cat). Then, watched from the bank by a doubtful audience, she went over the Falls.

Annie was pulled from her barrel minutes later with only a small cut to her head. She never made any money from her amazing feat, but she'd invented an idea. Ten years later a fellow called Bobby Leach went over in a steel barrel and also survived the plunge, dying, in a very boring way, many years later after slipping on an orange peel.

But there have been noteworthy failures, too. In 1920, an Englishman, Charles G. Stephens, tied himself to an anvil inside his barrel. All that remained of him after his plunge were a few wood staves and his tattooed right arm. In 1930 a Greek waiter named George L. Statakis became trapped for many hours and suffocated behind the Falls. His three-hours of air supply were enough, though, for his good-luck pet turtle to survive. Using a more modern approach, in 1995 the stupendously named Robert Overacker put on a parachute and rode a jet-ski over the edge to publicize the cause of the homeless. Unfortunately, his chute failed to open and, as he plummeted to his death, he found himself instead promoting the benefits of better parachutes.

Instructions

Naturally, you want to succeed in your attempt so you need to understand a few things first. The Niagara Falls are actually three falls and the only survivable one is the so-called Horseshoe Falls. The plunge itself, variously described as 'a skydiver's free fall' or 'dropping in an elevator without a cable', is, of course, the safe part of the exercise. It's the landing that's dangerous. The Niagara River pours hundreds of thousands of gallons over the Horseshoe Falls every second and it's a 170-foot (52 m) drop to the water below.

Even though more than half the daredevils who go over the Falls in a barrel survive, the chances are pretty high that you will hurt yourself. You are, for example, likely to receive a brain injury from the rapid deceleration when you land. There is also the obvious danger of being smashed to pieces on the rocks and/or being pummelled to death by the water. There's drowning, of course, and suffocation, if you find yourself trapped in your barrel behind the falling water. So how do you survive?

There are various theories including obvious ones about having a stout, water-resistant container that will absorb energy instead of transmitting it to your body. Some people have used giant ball-like contraptions; others have protected their barrels with solid foam. There are four main survival ideas, but I'm not sure how good the evidence is for any of them.

1   Use the 'water cone'. This 'protective cushion' is supposed to exist at the foot of the Falls and is said to soften the blow as you land. Hmmm.

2   Body-surf. This is for those people who wish to have a practice first without a barrel. 'Riding' the water like a body surfer is said to allow you to 'slide' down the Falls rather than falling straight down and splattering on the concrete-hard water surface. Let me know how you get on with this one.

3   Be put in near the brink. The idea behind this one is that if your barrel goes in the water upstream you will accelerate as you approach the edge, making the exercise more hazardous. There's no evidence I could find that this is true. You'll just have to try it.

4   Be lucky. This is the best one in my view. Prayer, crossing your fingers, and being kind to animals are all said to improve your chances.

Finally, I should point out that going over the Niagara Falls on purpose is not only likely to introduce you to your maker fairly quickly; it is also illegal. So don't try it. As if you would.

32 Coming out on top in a pub brawl

I remember I was in this pub near Dulwich College in London once, with a couple of guys from the English department. As we minded our own business the door slammed open and a bald giant with a mouth full of gums stepped over the threshold. He pointed at a little man with a spider web tattooed on his face and boomed, 'I'm gonna fockin' do you!' 'Oh, dear,' whispered one of my friends. 'He's split the infinitive there.' My friends then had a chat about whether that infinitive could be un-split, while four large barmen encouraged the donkey-jacketed ogre to leave, which he did.

Had this all turned nasty I'm not sure I would have been able to defend myself from a thorough glassing-up, so I thought I'd look into the business of coming out on top in a pub brawl.

Anyone can come out on top in a brawl by biting ears off or shooting people, but a gentleman is at the mercy of good manners. So, my first port of call was the Marquess of Queensberry rules, which seemed to offer an excellent guide to looking after yourself politely in a punch-up.

They are named after John Douglas, 9th Marquess of Queensberry, who, being eccentric, is said to have instructed his executors to bury him vertically. They apparently did so, but, quirky themselves, put him in upside-down. Anyway, before snuffing it he endorsed the Marquess of Queensberry rules. These are they, with my own interpolated comments in brackets.

The Queensberry rules for the sport of boxing

1   To be a fair stand-up boxing match in a 24-ft ring, or as near that size as practicable. (Most pubs have rooms smaller than this. You'll just have to make do.)
2   No wrestling or hugging allowed. (Hitting people with chairs is OK though.)
3   The rounds to be of three minutes' duration, and one minute's time between rounds. (This one doesn't really apply.)
4   If either man falls through weakness or otherwise, he must get up unassisted, ten seconds to be allowed him to do so, the other man meanwhile to return to his corner, and when the fallen man is on his legs the round is to be resumed and continued until the three minutes have expired. If one man fails to come to the scratch in the 10 seconds allowed, it shall be in the power of the referee to give his award in favour of the other man. (Not really, you should stamp on a man once he's down. He'd do the same to you.)
5   A man hanging on the ropes in a helpless state, with his toes off the ground, shall be considered down. (Or pissed.)
6   No seconds or any other person to be allowed in the ring during the rounds. (But girlfriends screeching things such as 'Leave it Darren!' are permitted.)
7   Should the contest be stopped by any unavoidable interference (such as the arrival of the police), the referee to name the time and place as soon as possible for finishing the contest; so that the match must be won and lost, unless the backers of both men agree to draw the stakes.

8 The gloves to be fair-sized boxing gloves of the best quality and new. (This is no time for niceties – get in there with your knuckledusters.)

9 Should a glove burst, or come off, it must be replaced to the referee's satisfaction. (You can forget about this one.)

10 A man on one knee is considered down and if struck is entitled to the stakes. (Rubbish, kick him hard.)

11 That no shoes or boots with spikes or sprigs be allowed. (Those are the best kind.)

12 The contest in all other respects to be governed by revised London Prize Ring Rules. (You've got to be joking.)

On second thoughts, you will probably emerge with more teeth if you simply run away.

33 How to smash paving slabs with your bare hands

There are some things in life that just seem impossible, such as getting a simple yes or no from a politician or eating spaghetti bolognese in a white shirt without finishing up looking like the victim of a drive-by shooting. Perhaps the most impossible-looking thing is the one that those black-belt experts of what my grandma used to call the 'marital arts' do with a pile of concrete blocks, namely, smash them in half with a single blow of the hand. Can their bones really be stronger than concrete? The answer is yes and no, as we will learn.

In case you haven't seen this performed, here's a quick run-down. A number of 'concrete blocks' or 'paving slabs' – anything from one to half a dozen or more – are laid flat, with the bottom slab supported at each end by a breeze block on its side. Each additional paving slab is supported an inch or so above the one below it by a narrow strip of something hard, so that there is a gap between each slab.

Next, a fellow dressed in karate-style gear approaches the pile of blocks and does a bit of oriental-type concentrating, sometimes with noises. He then does one, two or several mini karate chops over the middle of the top slab, without making contact, so as to get his hand into the optimal position. Finally, he raises his arm high and brings it down with a staccato wallop on to the top slab, often with a cry of '*Kiai!*' (pronounced 'key-eye' by experts and 'hi-yah!' by schoolboys), or words to that effect. Sometimes he will yell, 'Ouch!' This usually happens when the blocks fail to break. In this case he will thrust his hand under his armpit, going, 'Ow oow owa,' and swaying from side to side in pain. After a bit of this overacting, he will generally get the thing to work at the second attempt, with all the blocks breaking in the middle and collapsing one on another. It's dead impressive.

But there's more to this than meets the eye – a mixture of sound science and wily showmanship. For a start, those so-called 'paving slabs' are not the things you are used to walking about on. Often they are cinder blocks, heavy but brittle. And then there are those gaps. Why leave a gap between each block? The point here is that if the slabs were directly on top of each other they would effectively form a single, much thicker, much stronger block. The gaps allow the energy from the hand to be transmitted into the first block, which breaks and falls hard on to the next, and so on in a cascade.

Another part of the science is the well-understood law that objects with momentum transmit a greater force to a stationary object than objects without momentum. This is why punching a fellow who has just called your sister a fat cow is preferable to resting your fist against his cheek and pushing. You won't knock many teeth out that way. When a karate chop hits that top slab it will typically be going at more than 20 miles an hour (32 km/h), exerting a force of thousands of newtons. This is like dropping a 48-stone man on the slabs. And with all that force concentrated into an area as small as the edge of the hand you can understand why the blocks break. Just be glad that it wasn't your nose under there.

But it is also true that animal – including human – bones are very strong. How could an elephant support itself if they weren't? Bone is lighter and more flexible than concrete, and can resist something like forty times the stress. If an elephant's leg bones were made of concrete they would collapse.

In addition to all this, the soft tissue of the human hand provides a cushion that absorbs and distributes the energy of the blow. But you need to know what you are doing or you might well damage yourself. This is not the place to learn – go to an expert. He will train you to position your strike so that your hand is at optimum speed and in just the right position when it reaches the slab, hitting it bang in the centre, at its weakest point.

What a ridiculous way to make a living.

Mainly Isometric

34 Edward Ciderhands: a game for real men

Have you seen the film *Edward Scissorhands* (1990), starring Johnny Depp as a bloke with scissors for hands – enormous great long blades on all his fingers? Goodness knows what palaver he must have gone through to avoid inadvertent amputation when tucking his shirt in. The game of Edward Ciderhands is named after that film. The rules are simple and the entertainment is suitable for home, office or stag night. It might, for all I know, even be apropos during a lull between courses at a banquet with the Queen. Anyway, here's what's involved.

Equipment

- 2 big bottles of rough cider or superstrength scrumpy
- A roll of gaffer tape
- Two or more players not younger than drinking age

Method

1 Grasp an unopened bottle of cold cider in each hand.
2 Have the bottles securely taped to your palms.
3 Ask an assistant to remove the bottle tops.
4 On the command *'Legg mi am Åsch!'* (a Bavarian exclamation roughly translatable as 'Well, what a surprise!'), drink both bottles.
5 The first player to finish is the winner.

Rules

1 You must not remove the tape or either bottle until both are finished.
2 You may do anything while playing, so long as you do it with the

bottles taped to your hands. If you need to brush your teeth or 'water your horse', you'll just have to ask one of the ladies in waiting to assist with your zip.

3　If you remove tape or bottles before finishing, you lose and must, as a forfeit, immediately drink both bottles.

Straight from the fridge, those big bottles of cider are freezing cold and heavy when full. It is entertaining to watch players having to answer the phone with their teeth or help fellow competitors light cigarettes with their elbows.

Among the delightful variants of Edward Ciderhands are Edward Winehands (self-explanatory) and the French Edouard Champagnemains (black belt).

35　How to build a snowman

My uncle Bob used to ask me every Christmas, 'What's the difference between a snowman and a snow-woman?' Before I could breathe in to answer, he would shout, 'Snow balls!' Judging by the ten-minute wheezing paroxysm that would result, he thought this the funniest riposte in the history of crap jokes. But he made a great snowman – he had the magic touch and was full of good advice, such as never eat yellow snow. Here's Uncle Bob's perfect-snowman procedure.

1　Look out of the window to check it has snowed sufficiently. It must be the right kind of snow, too, not the dry powdery stuff that immobilizes the railways every winter, but the soft compactable kind.

2　Get some warm gear on.

3　Go out and immediately take off your gloves. You can't make a proper snowman with gloves on because they absorb water and stick to the snowman's trunk.

4　Begin by rolling a ball large enough to form the main part of the body. Keep going, leaving that characteristic brown/green trail behind you.

5　Change direction frequently to maintain a sphere or you'll end up with a sort of squat sausage.

6 Time for a stiff scotch. Probably best to have a hipflask with you.

7 As the snowman's body becomes heavier it may begin to pick up a lot of mud. Once this starts happening, it's too big. Be on the lookout for this and stop before it happens.

8 Once you have a body of sufficient size, roll it where you want it and begin rolling the head in the same way. If you are doing this in a small garden make sure to leave enough snow for the head.

9 The head shouldn't take you long, although you may be crying with cold by this time. Pain thresholds are customarily measured using a test that involves holding your forearm in a tank of almost freezing water, and *it hurts*.

10 Put the head on the body and secure it as firmly as you can by wiggling and pushing.

11 Arms can be made with stout sticks or you can mould snow artistically on to the body. Moulded is more professional looking, but sticks have an amateur charm.

12 Eyes and mouth are traditionally made with lumps of coal. The mouth should be smiling. A straight line makes your snowman look like a doctor who is about to tell you that you've got Hansen's disease. Your granddad's biggest old pipe stuck in the gob area will add a touch of authenticity, as will a long scarf tied around the neck. University scarves are nice and long. For God's sake, ask permission first or you might find you've used your brother-in-law's new £400 Matthew Williamson silk. Bad karma, man.

13 The only proper nose is a long carrot, positioned thin end out. Are snowmen haunted by the smell of carrots, do you think?

14 Top hats are nice if you are Lord Fancypants, otherwise a bobble hat will do (*on the snowman*).

15 A vertical row of coals for buttons creates a nice impression of a coat.

16 You're done. Stand back and admire. Time for another stiff one. And then wait till nightfall and you and the snowman can fly round the world singing that Aled Jones song.

Cars

36 The Mini story

Recently, I was due to visit the weirdly named Bucklers Hard, in the New Forest, so I put 'bucklers hard on beaulieu river' into my computer. The unexpected pictures that sprang into view made my hair prick up. Bucklers Hard is a riverside hamlet that was once home to a historic shipworks; Lord Nelson's *Agamemnon* was built here, and if you've ever wondered why the New Forest is a treeless, pony-sprinkled scrub, it's because they chopped all the trees down to make the ships. The National Motor Museum, which is nearby, is run by Edward John Barrington Douglas-Scott-Montagu, 3rd Baron Montagu of Beaulieu, as a tribute to his father, who was the first person to drive a car into the yard of the Houses of Parliament. Lord Montagu is an interesting fellow who has, during his active life – how shall I put this? – tried 'driving in both lanes'. You can learn more from his fascinating autobiography, *Wheels within Wheels*. Which brings me – by the scenic route – to the story of the Mini.

You could say that Gamal Abdel Nasser was responsible for the development of the Mini because, following the Suez Crisis of 1955, petrol was rationed in Britain and nobody was buying big cars. Moreover, the German 'bubble car' was becoming a common sight on British roads. Leonard Lord, boss of the British Motor Corporation (BMC), is said to have remarked in his mild way, 'God damn these bloody awful Bubble Cars. We must drive them off the road by designing a proper miniature car.' And so it happened.

The design job was given to Alec 'the Greek god' Issigonis and Lord gave him the maximum measurements he would allow for his new two-door vehicle: a box 10 ft x 4 ft x 4 ft (3 m x 1.2 m x 1.2 m). He said that, of the car's 10 ft length, the passenger compartment was to occupy 6 ft (1.8 m). Eighty per cent of the available space would be available for people and luggage.

By October 1957, Issigonis and his small team had designed and built the prototype. They had saved space by making the new car front-wheel drive, putting the wheels on the corners, and replacing suspension springs with compact rubber cones. These novelties gave the Mini the nippy go-kart handling for which it would become famous, but also made the ride bumpy. The Mini used an existing BMC four-cylinder water-cooled engine, but Issigonis mounted it crosswise and fitted the radiator on the left side, thus saving on length. The unwanted effect of this was, though, to allow rainwater coming through the grille to interfere with the ignition system, a problem which any driver of vintage Minis (such as myself) will tell you about until you wish he was dead. The team specified new 10 in. (254 mm) wheels, which required Dunlop to develop new tyres.

Space was saved wherever it could be. Sliding windows allowed Issigonis to design pockets in the doors that would just fit a bottle of Gordon's gin. Sensible! To increase luggage capacity in the small boot, the team hinged the lid at the bottom to allow the Mini to be driven with the door open.

The British Motor Corporation produced the Mini in a variety of models, including a van, a high-performance rally car and a pickup, from 1959 until 2000. It quickly saw off the bubble car and gained a reputation similar to that of Hitler's 'People's Car', the Volkswagen Beetle. Like the VW Beetle, the utilitarian design was attractive, and the car quickly became a fashion item, even starring in *The Italian Job* (1966), in which a load of the cars are driven down Italian stone stairs, through drains and into a coach. Famous Mini owners included Peter Sellers, Ringo Starr, John Lennon, George Harrison, Marianne Faithfull and Monkee Michael Nesmith.

Over the past thirty years the Mini has found new popularity on the crowded roads of Japan's cities but as an indirect result of conglomerations in the car market the last Mini was built on 4 October 2000. Sir Alec Issigonis died in 1988, and today BMW sell a new so-called 'MINI', which under the bonnet is a different car altogether. From the kerb, though, it does retain a shadow of its pugnacious profile of yesteryear.

37 Famous car crash victims

In 2006 the UK had 5.4 road deaths per 100,000 population, one of the lowest rates in the European Union. This figure was also lower than that of the US (14.3 per 100,000 population), Australia (7.8 per 100,000 population), and Japan (5.7 per 100,000 population). Though there has been a marked decline in road deaths in recent years, people still do die. Here is a list of some of the internal combustion engine's most famous victims.

- Marc Bolan (1947–77): born Mark Feld, Bolan was a rock star with English glam band T. Rex. He died on 16 September 1977 when Gloria Jones, who was driving him in a purple Mini, hit a tree in Barnes, London. He wasn't wearing a seatbelt.
- Albert Camus (1913–60): this Nobel Prize-winning French-Algerian writer and philosopher died on 4 January 1960 in a car crash in Villeblevin, France. He had planned to travel by train and the unused ticket was found in his pocket.
- Roger Delgado (1918 –73): Roger Caesar Marius Bernard de Delgado Torres Castillo Roberto (!) was best known for his role as the first Master in *Doctor Who*. He died after being chauffeur-driven into a ravine in Turkey, where he was shooting a film.
- James Dean (1931–55): actor James Byron Dean died on 30 September 1955 when his Porsche 550 Spyder, in which he was travelling with his mechanic Rolf Wütherich, hit a 1950 Ford Custom Tudor Coupe head-on near Cholame, California. Dean's last words were allegedly, 'That guy's got to stop. He'll see us.' Wütherich died in a different car crash twenty-six years later (1981), after several suicide attempts.

- Princess Diana (1961–97): Diana Frances née Spencer, Princess of Wales, famously died in a crash in the Pont de l'Alma tunnel in Paris on 31 August 1997. She, Dodi Fayed, their bodyguard, and their driver, Henri Paul, were being pursued by paparazzi. All but the bodyguard died. She was not wearing a seatbelt.

- Isadora Duncan (1877–1927): American dancer Isadora Duncan died in an unusual car accident in Nice, on 14 September 1927. She was travelling in an open-top car when her long silk scarf suddenly wound around one of the spoked wheels and the rear axle, flinging her from the vehicle. Depending on which report you believe, she either died instantly 'by the force of her fall to the stone pavement', or was strangled and almost beheaded by the tightening of the scarf around her neck.

- Princess Grace of Monaco (1929–82): Grace Kelly was a gorgeous American actress and later Princess consort of Monaco. On 13 September 1982 she drove herself and her daughter off a winding mountain road in Monaco after reportedly suffering a stroke. She died the following day.

- Jayne Mansfield (1933–67): on 29 June 1967 at about 2.30 a.m. the car in which this bathykolpian (great word – look it up) blonde was being driven went into and under the back of a tractor-trailer that had slowed for a truck spraying mosquito fogger, in Biloxi, Mississippi. The three adults in the front, including Mansfield, were killed. Her three children, sleeping in the back, survived.

- T.E. Lawrence (1888–1935): Lieutenant Colonel Thomas Edward Lawrence, CB, DSO, was a British Army officer and writer, who was immortalized on screen as Lawrence of Arabia. At the age of 46, a few weeks after leaving the military, Lawrence was thrown over the handlebars of his motorbike, near his cottage in Dorset. He died six days later.

- Desmond Llewelyn (1914–99): this Welsh actor played Q in most of the James Bond films. On 19 December 1999, Llewelyn crashed his un-Bondish Renault Mégane head-on into a car on the A27, near the village of Berwick in East Sussex. He was eighty-five.

- Linda Lovelace (1949–2002): Linda Susan Boreman was a porn actress who, under the name 'Linda Lovelace', demonstrated the art of high-end salami swallowing in the 1972 film *Deep Throat*. On 3 April 2002 she mangled herself so badly in a car crash that she had to be put on to a life support system. She died later the same month. She was fifty-three.
- Jackson Pollock (1912–56): on 11 August 1956 alcoholic Abstract Expressionist painter Jackson Pollock died while driving his Oldsmobile convertible. He was on his own and, as usual, boozed up.
- Karen Silkwood (1946–74): American union activist Karen Silkwood was a technician at the Kerr-McGee chemical plant near Crescent, Oklahoma, where she made plutonium pellets for the fuel rods of nuclear reactors. She died in contentious circumstances on her way to a meeting with a journalist to discuss 'irregularities' at the plant. Her body was discovered in her 1974 Honda Civic, having apparently run off the road. The crash was described as a 'classic, one-car sleeping-driver accident'. Her documents were not in the car. *Dramatic chord.*

38 How to wash a car: Luton, Croydon and Belgravia methods

I have a friend who lives in Brighton, and he tells me that the seagulls that inhabit that raffish conurbation live off a diet of discarded hamburgers, chips, and leftover beer, which, as twilight falls, they siphon out of smeared glasses abandoned on the tables of the promenade cafés. This gaudy diet has turned these birds into truculent monsters the size of eagles and causes them to excrete pints of a filthy alcoholic guano, as potent as plutonium in its corrosive virulence. My friend says they fly over his house in reeking eventide flocks, dive-bombing his car with unspeakable gobbets of their poisonous shit. Unless this is cleaned straight off, he says, the paint just peels away like a scab.

Luckily, washing a car is not generally as challenging or chronic a problem as this. Methods vary, so I thought I would describe three of the main kinds, which I have observed over the years.

Luton method

The Luton car-wash is a bucket rather than hose method and relies on high volumes of very wet water and a good deal of Fairy Liquid. Typically, it takes place on a Sunday and is done by a young lady in alligator cowboy boots, hot pants and a straw hat. Generally speaking, she also has on a white T-shirt, which becomes clingier the wetter it gets. The Luton method is usually accomplished by the lady saturating a large yellow sponge with soapy Luton tap water from a shiny plastic bucket and then vermiculating the contours of an elderly Ford Corsair, by writhing about all over the hot bodywork, and sopping the windscreen under a broiling sun. Generally, she does as much leaning across the bonnet as the limits of human anatomy will permit. A fine spectator sport.

Croydon method

There's a good deal of vacuuming done before the Croydon car-wash proper can get under way. Often this is achieved by the use of five miles of extension cord from the first-floor flat. Once the Murray Mint wrappers and pieces of cardigan fluff have been sucked from the interstices, the wet bit can get going. The man doing the Croydon car-wash will more often than not be sporting a heroic comb-over. When the wind is blowing, this will be lifted into an 18in. flapping vertical enormity, rather like the silk 'flames' one finds inside electric-coal fires. Much chamois-leathering goes on in the Croydon method and the washer always wears sensible shoe-protection and pink Marigolds, sometimes an apron. Rinsing is a three-stage process, and a thorough dry is done with J Cloths. The cars in question can be anything from Morris Minors to mobility scooters. The dangling deodorant in the shape of a fir tree will be regularly replaced. Afterwards the man is likely to have a small bottle of pale ale or a medium sherry, followed by his wife-cooked roast-beef dinner, which will be pronounced 'very tasty, dear'.

Belgravia method

A Polish, Latvian or Filipino maid will tell the man playing cards in the underground garage that the Rolls-Royce with the registration number 'B1G C4R' or the red Triumph with the registration 'FUN C4R' must be valeted by 7 p.m. The man will then drive the car up to a fellow he knows in Pimlico, who tells his assistant to vacuum, wash and dry the car, 'So I can see me face in the door and eat me breakfast off the dashboard.' This is done with a hose by three cigarette-sucking men with squeegees. The gleaming car is returned by reversing the complicated outbound route. At each handover a 'bung' will change hands, resulting in a carwash so ruinously expensive that it could have kept the economy of Bo, in Sierra Leone, going for a couple of days.

Bikes

39 The Vespa story

After the Second World War, an Italian aeroplane-maker called Enrico Piaggio decided to stop making planes and make a new kind of motor scooter for the knackered Italian roads. The American Cushman scooters he had seen during the war, buzzing military personnel around the bomb-cratered streets were the source of his idea.

Helicopter designer General Corradino D'Ascanio had already designed such a scooter for rival Ferdinando Innocenti, who had asked for a cheap, simple and strong passenger vehicle, which men and women could both use on the blasted Italian thoroughfares without dirtying their clothes. D'Ascanio designed him a motor scooter with its engine mounted on the back wheel. Gears were changed on the handlebar and a shield at the front protected the rider from wind and weather. Like a lady's bicycle, the leg area could be stepped through so that men as well as women in skirts or dresses could ride the thing without snarls. Rigid rear suspension and 8 in. (200 mm) wheels added further nippiness and gave ample room even for fat legs. Importantly, D'Ascanio also got rid of the filthy motorcycle chain, introducing instead internal mesh transmission. Gone were the oil and muck.

But, of course, D'Ascanio and Innocenti fell out (they were Italian, don't forget). So D'Ascanio went round to Enrico Piaggio's with his elegant designs and knocked on the door. He was asked inside and given (I imagine) some spaghetti, as well as the job of producing his new scooter. Innocenti, meanwhile, rolled up his sleeves and began designing a competing bike that he named the Lambretta.

The Vespa, as D'Ascanio's scooter came to be called, was ready in

1946. It had a distinctive aerodynamic pressed steel body that combined a grease-and-muck-isolating engine-cowling, a flat foot-protecting floorboard and a characteristic, upright front fairing (windshield). The engine made a high buzzing sound and when Enrico Piaggio first heard it he reportedly said, *'Sembra una vespa!'* ('It's just like a wasp!') It looked a bit like one, too. And a name was born.

Rather as the Mini was to do in Britain, the Vespa became a huge hit in Italy, and, proving that product placement is a good idea, more than 100,000 flew out of the shops after Audrey Hepburn and Gregory Peck cuddled up on one as they went through the Roman streets in William Wyler's 1952 film, *Roman Holiday*. Marlon Brando and Dean Martin added their imprimatur by buying Vespas, and, before you could say crash helmet, the utilitarian scooter had become a fashionable thing to be seen putting your bottom on.

Over the next couple of years the Vespa's tentacles spread around Europe. Outside Europe the market varied. In the US a fanbase developed, particularly for the more modern designs, and Asia was a fruitful market. Germany and Spain took to the Vespa, too, but with nothing like the enthusiasm of the British.

In early 1960s Britain, the mods and rockers subculture was developing, and the mods quickly adopted the Vespa as their ideal form of transport: cleaner and dryer than the big bikes ridden by the rockers, who wore oily leather outfits and scorned the suit-wearing mods with opprobrious scoffs. Before long, huge scooter rallies began springing up and the UK was soon the biggest market for the Vespa outside its home country. For one brief period more Vespas were being sold in the UK than at home. Unimpressed, the rockers continued to regard the Vespa as a nancy-scooter ridden by weeds and woofters.

But as the petrol tank of time emptied, the Vespa's success started to wane. With the increase in people's disposable income over the next decade and the development of small cheap cars, the popularity of the Vespa withered. In common with the rest of the motor industry many ups and downs were visited upon the Vespa's manufacturers, including changes of ownership, foreign competition and modernization of the original design. In response to growing environmental rules a number of hybrid scooters had to be developed.

Nonetheless, by 1996, when the company celebrated its fiftieth anniversary, more than 15 million of its little wasps had been sold around the globe, making the Vespa the most successful motor scooter of all time.

Bzzzzzzzzzzzzzzzzzzzzzzzzzzzzzzzzzzzzzzzzzzzzzzzzzzzzzzzzzzzzzzzzzzzzzzzzzzz zzzzzzzzzzzzzzzzzzzzzzzzzzzzzzzzzzzzzzzzzzzzzzzzzzzzzzzzzzzzzzzzzzzzzzzzzzzzz.

40 From boneshaker to Stumpjumper: 200 years of the bicycle

'When did you first notice you had diarrhoea?' asked the doctor. 'When I took my bicycle clips off,' replied the vicar. That joke is as old as bicycle clips themselves, but not everything has changed in the cycling world. I went into a bicycle shop for advice the other day and came out with a Dutch bike that was designed in 1926 and hasn't changed a bit since then. This got me thinking about the history of the bike and it is quite fascinating.

Thomas Gray (1716–71) wrote his *Elegy Written in a Country Churchyard* among the graves of St Giles' church in Stoke Poges and this church has a seventeenth-century stained-glass window that includes the earliest known depiction of a true bicycle that might have actually worked. The window shows a trumpet-blowing naked figure on a wooden (presumably) two-wheeled thing without pedals.

The first practical bike is generally agreed, however, to be that of German Baron Karl von Drais, an officer to the Grand Duke of Baden. Drais patented his *Laufmaschine* (walking machine) in 1818. Its purpose was to help Drais get around the royal gardens more quickly. The bike was dubbed the Draisine by the English, but other names including 'hobby-horse' and 'dandy horse' also came to be used. The wooden walking machine had a steerable front wheel and was moved forward by the rider pushing his feet against the ground.

In 1839 a Scottish blacksmith, Kirkpatrick Macmillan, reportedly built

the first mechanically propelled bicycle and was said to have come up with a rear-wheel drive with mounted treadles connected to a rear crank, rather like a steam train. However, the first recorded commercially successful design was French.

Developed around 1863–4, it was simpler than the Macmillan bicycle, using rotary cranks, with pedals mounted on the steerable front wheel hub. Although the bicycle's wrought-iron frame allowed mass production, there was a limit to the driving wheel's rotational speed and it was hard to pedal. It was known formally as the velocipede (speed foot), but owing to the metal tyres and the cobblestones of the time, the contraption was better known as the boneshaker. Nonetheless, it became a hit.

The slow rotational speed of the front wheel was such a problem that it led in the 1870s to the development of the 'high-bicycle' or 'penny-farthing', so called because of the relative size of its huge front and tiny back wheels. Frenchman Eugene Meyer invented the wire-spoke tension wheel in 1869 and produced the classic penny-farthing design. It was stylish but dangerous, and riders were prone to break wrists and heads.

Englishman James Starley (1830–81) made significant developments to bicycle design over the next few years, reintroducing wheels of equal size, along with other improvements, and is generally accepted as the father of the British cycling industry.

The development of this so-called safety bicycle was a huge step – or pedal – forwards, turning what had been a dangerous novelty into a useful vehicle. John Kemp Starley, James' nephew, produced the first commercially successful version in 1885. It had wheels of equal size and a rear-wheel-drive chain. Ball bearings, solid rubber tyres and hollow steel frames now reduced weight and improved comfort. Queen Victoria owned one of Starley's bicycles.

An Irish vet called John Dunlop invented the pneumatic tyre in 1888, further improving comfort, and by 1890 safety bicycles had completely replaced the penny-farthing. Owing to its efficiency, the 'diamond' fame design was now the norm. Bicycles soon became popular with the bourgeoisie, and were enthusiastically taken up by women as well as men.

The derailleur gear (the one that lifts the chain on to a new sprocket) was developed in France in the first decade of the twentieth century. After a dip in production during the First World War, children's bicycles were introduced and remained a significant part of the market from then on.

By the 1950s there were two main bicycle styles: first, heavier hobby bikes, with balloon tyres, pedal-activated brakes (you back-pedal) and a single gear; second, lighter bicycles with hand brakes, narrow tyres, three-speed hub gears, dynamo headlamps, reflectors, kickstands and mounted bicycle pumps. These were the high-end machines.

In the early 1980s, Swedish company Itera invented a new type of bicycle, made entirely of plastic. This was a commercial failure. It sounded good, but just think of all the successful factories you'd have to refit. Innovation can be expensive.

Nowadays, there is a bicycle for everyone, from the granny-bicycle to high-end racing bikes with carbon or aluminium frames, and Olympic medallists' helium-filled things with wheels like flying saucers and a million gears. Racing bikes, mountain bikes, bikes with trailers (with children inside often) and recumbent bikes are, these days, all to be seen on British roads – and pavements. Commuters have increasingly taken to the bicycle and the fold-up hybrid or city bike is now common on trains. For teenage boys who enjoy racing through the mud and muck there's

always the BMX (bicycle motocross), and even the Mayor of London has been seen cycling to and from work in his special hat.

During the 1970s, off-road biking was becoming a big thing and in 1981 the first mass-produced mountain bike was launched. It was an immediate success. Mountain bikes have more robust frames than traditional bikes, wider, nobbly tyres for better traction, an upright sitting position, innovative front and rear suspension, and a drinks cabinet – oh no, *not* a drinks cabinet. Mountain bikes now reportedly sell better than all other bicycle types put together. The 'Stumpjumper' is typical of the latest in sophisticated trail bikes.

The bicycle may have come a long way, and the choice might be endless, but can you still buy vicar-style cycle clips anywhere? Answers on a postcard, please.

41 Puncture repair: coffee-spoon method

I was in the supermarket looking for shampoo the other day and I was annoyed by the enormous amount of choice – thousands of bottles. It's ridiculous; I'm sure they all do the same thing. And they all had instructions on the back, saying, 'Rinse and repeat', which looks to me like nothing more than trying to make you use twice as much shampoo as necessary.

All that choice isn't limited to shampoo, either. I couldn't help noticing that there are now more contraceptives on sale in supermarkets than you can shake a stick at. Buying these things was once a discreet arrangement whereby your barber would ask you quietly if you required something for the weekend. Now the multicoloured packets are spotlit and there's shelf after shelf of the things, all covered in boasts about what fantastic effects their contents will produce. It's quite shameless. Still, I suppose the Boy Scouts have it right: 'Be prepared.'

The diligent cyclist is always prepared. In his pannier will you find waterproof clothes, a spanner, maps, a packet of ginger nuts, and – most important – a puncture repair outfit and a pair of tyre levers. But what about the non-diligent cyclist who doesn't own tyre levers? What is he going to do when he gets a nail in his wheel, halfway up Ditchling Beacon? This is the answer.

Required

- Spanner
- Puncture repair outfit
- Two coffee spoons

Method

1 Get off the bike and stop swearing. Turn it upside-down and squat next to it. Loosen the axle bolts with your trusty spanner.
2 Push the chain and rotate the cranks with the other hand. Pop the chain off the sprocket and pull the wheel towards you.
3 Remove the chain from the cog. Boring, isn't it?
4 Insert the tips of your spoon handles under the bead of the tyre, at the 12 o'clock and 1 o'clock positions. (The bead is the part that anchors the tyre to the wheel rim.) Often you will find spoons nearby – kerbside cafés are great in this respect. Don't do what a friend of mine did and try it with wooden salad spoons. It won't work and you will look silly.
5 Pull the tyre's bead out. Move around the rim in a circle until the bead is out all the way round. Be very careful not to 'pinch' the inner tube during this whole process. You can cause another puncture rather easily that way.
6 Now press the valve stem into the tyre and pull the whole inner tube out. Check carefully inside the tyre for nails, glass, Japanese soldiers who believe the Second World War is still going on, etc.
7 Repair the puncture, following the instructions on the tin.
8 Allow the repair to 'cure'. Now is the time to uncork the cider, listen to the birds singing in the meadow and eat your packed lunch. If it's pissing with rain and you are surrounded by manure up a smelly lane in Croydon, you'll just have to make the best of it.
9 Replace the tube. It's important to align the valve stem and the hole

before you put the rest of the tube back inside the tyre. More swearing otherwise.

10 Putting the tyre back on is the fiddliest bit, where the serious cursing really starts. Go round the tyre in a circle, rotating your thumbs away from yourself, as you press the bead back inside the rim. If it's difficult – it always is – use your spoons for added leverage. That's the worst of it over.

11 Replace the chain on the cog and slide the wheel back into place.

12 Put the chain on the top of the sprocket and spin the cranks with your other hand. There's a knack to this. In fact, it helps to practise the whole thing in the warm and light before you have to do it one dark night in a blizzard.

13 Once the chain is on, pull the wheel back and tighten the bolts. There should be sufficient tension in the chain to prevent it pinging off as you climb the rest of the hill.

Or go by car.

ARTS AND LETTERS

English Literature

42 Samuel Pepys: the rude bits

Samuel Pepys wrote his famous diary, in a special shorthand, between 1660 and 1669. Being well connected and holding important public posts such as Surveyor-General to the Victualling Office, he was well placed to discuss such nationally important events as the King's dog crapping in the royal boat.

As well as describing momentous goings-on such as the Plague and the Great Fire of London, Pepys' diary reveals the footling trivialities of his home life and everyday concerns. These are often the best bits.

In spite of suffering from kidney stones, wind, a busy workload and being married, Pepys managed to have several affairs, recording these in his diary in an amalgam of English, French and Spanish, though they are not difficult to translate for anyone familiar with English swear words. The most entertaining entry for the modern reader is his description of being caught by his missus while diddling her companion Deborah Willet. Mrs Pepys' tongue-lashing put Mr Pepys to shame but caused no permanent alteration in his behaviour.

Pepys made his final entry on 31 May 1669, giving poor eyesight as his reason for stopping – and we all know what causes that. After his death, the boringly named John Smith spent three painful years decoding the huge volumes and transcribing them into English, unaware that the key to the shorthand lay in a book on a nearby shelf.

The human body and its multifarious functions were a rich source of material for Pepys. Here are a few illuminating extracts in chronological order:

7 February 1660

Mr Moore told me of a picture hung up at the Exchange of a great pair of buttocks shooting of a turd into Lawson's mouth, and over it was wrote 'The thanks of the house.' Boys do now cry 'Kiss my Parliament', instead of 'Kiss my [rump],' so great and general a contempt is the Rump come to among all the good and bad.

28 May 1660

At night I had a strange dream of bepissing myself, which I really did, and having kicked my clothes off, I got cold; and found myself all much wet in the morning, and had a great deal of pain . . . which made me very melancholy.

8 November 1660

From thence with him as far as Ratcliffe, where I left him going by the water to London; and I (unwilling to leave the rest of the officers) went back again to Deptford; and being very much troubled with a sudden looseness, I went into a little alehouse at the end of Ratcliffe and did give a groat for a pot of ale and there I did shit.

7 Septembeer 1662

Thence to my Lord's, where nobody at home but a woman that let me in, and Sarah above; whither I went up to her and played and talked with her and, God forgive me, did feel her, which I am much ashamed of, but I did no more, though I has so much a mind to it that I spent in my breeches.

25 May 1663

I up and there hear that my wife and her maid Ashwell had between them spilt the pot of piss and turd upon the floor and stool and God knows what, and were mighty merry washing of it clean.

6 October 1663

Thence home by water in great pain, and at my office a while, and thence a little to Sir W. Pen, and so home to bed, and finding myself beginning to be troubled with wind as I used to be, and in pain in making water, I took a couple of pills that I had by me of Mr Hollyard's.

7 October 1663

They wrought in the morning and I did keep my bed; and my pain continued on me mightily, that I keeped within all day in great pain, and could break no wind nor have any stool after my physic had done working. So in the evening I took coach and to Mr Hollyard's, but he was not at home; and so home again. And whether the coach did me good or no I know not, but having a good fire in my chamber, I begun to bread six or seven small and great farts; and so to bed . . .

23 October 1663

Thence to Mr Hollyard, who tells me that Mullins is dead of his leg cut off the other day, but most basely done. He tells me that there is no doubt but that all my slyme do come away in my water, and therefore no fear of the stone; but that my water being so slymy is a good sign. He would have now and then to take a clyster, the same I did the other day, though I feel no pain, only to keep me loose, and instead of butter, which he would have to be salt butter, he would have me sometimes use two or three ounces of honey, at other times two or three ounces of Linseed oil. Thence to Mr Rawlinson's and saw some of my new bottles made, with my crest upon them, filled with wine, about five or six dozen . . . That done, to bed.

28 September 1665

So I to bed, and in the night was mightily troubled with a looseness (I suppose from some fresh damp linen that I put on this night), and feeling for a chamber-pott, there was none, I having called the mayde up out of her bed, she had forgot I suppose to put one there; so I was forced in this strange house to rise and shit in the chimney twice; and so to bed and was very well again.

Lord's day. Up, and discoursing with my wife about our house and many new things we are doing of, and so to church I, and there find Jack Fen come, and his wife, a pretty black woman: I never saw her before, nor took notice of her now. So home and to dinner, and after dinner all the afternoon got my wife and boy to read to me, and at night W. Batelier comes and sups with us; and, after supper, to have my head combed by Deb, which occasioned the greatest sorrow to me that ever I knew in this world; for my wife, coming up suddenly, did find me imbracing the girl con my hand sub su coats; and endeed, I was with my main in her cunny. I was at a wonderful loss upon it, and the girl also, and I endeavoured to put it off, but my wife was struck mute and grew angry, and so her voice come to her, grew quite out of order, and I to say little… but she went on from one thing to another till at last it appeared plainly her trouble was at what she saw, but yet I did not know how much she saw, and therefore said nothing to her.

This final extract goes to show that three hundred years ago people were behaving exactly as they do today. Things haven't changed one jot or tittle. Especially not in the tittle department.

43 Lost and sometimes found again literary masterpieces

When I feel gloomy I cheer myself up by reading past winners of the Bulwer-Lytton Fiction Contest. This is a literary competition, in memory of the dire Victorian novelist Edward Bulwer-Lytton, in which entrants submit their own (deliberately terrible) opening sentence to a hypothetical novel. I especially liked the 2009 Special Award winner by Marguerite Ahl from Prescott Valley, Arizona. Here it is:

Fleur looked down her nose at Guilliame, something she was accomplished at, being six foot three in her stocking feet, and having one of those
long French noses, not pert like Bridget Bardot's, but more like the one
that Charles de Gaulle had when he was still alive and President of
France and he wore that cap that was shaped like a little hatbox with a
bill in the front to offset his nose, but it didn't work.

There are many rotten novels and plays that you wish had never been
published, but what about those good ones that weren't – or nearly
weren't? Here are three of those.

Seven Pillars of Wisdom: A Triumph

In 1919, T.E. Lawrence (Lawrence of Arabia) had completed a first draft
of his enormous autobiographical work, *Seven Pillars of Wisdom*. He
was carrying this with him in a briefcase when he had to change trains
at Reading railway station. Somehow he lost it there, except for the
introduction and the last two sections. Having spent months of toil on
this volume, he notified the press who alerted the public. But it never
turned up. Lawrence reckoned that the book would have amounted to
roughly 250,000 words, about twice the length of a heavy novel.

Not to be daunted, he quickly set about rewriting as much of it as he
could remember, having foolishly burnt all his notes after completing the
first draft. This second effort was nearly twice as long, and was described
by Lawrence as 'hopelessly bad'. The work was finally published in
different, frequently abridged, editions between 1922 and 1926 but made
Lawrence poorer rather than richer. Subsidizing a lavish 'Subscribers'
Edition' had left him almost bankrupt.

A Confederacy of Dunces

In 1969, following the suicide of her thirty-one-year-old son John Kennedy
Toole, after his inability to get a book published, Mrs Thelma Toole
stumbled upon a carbon copy of the manuscript in the house they had
shared. Toole, who considered his book a comic masterpiece, had sent a

copy to, among others, Simon & Schuster, who rejected it on the grounds that it 'isn't really about anything'. Mrs Toole became determined that her boy's work was going to see the light of day and, during her superhuman efforts, showed it to local author Walker Percy, who reluctantly read it. Despite his initial misgivings, Walker found it unputdownable, and finally managed to get it published as *A Confederacy of Dunces*, in 1980. The novel became a cult classic, won the Pulitzer Prize for Fiction the following year, and is still in print.

Under Milk Wood

Dylan Thomas' magisterial 'play for voices', *Under Milk Wood*, almost never happened, owing to the author being rat-arsed much of the time and consequently leaving the manuscript all over the place. He began the work in typically undisciplined fashion, mentioning in 1948 that he was writing a radio play set in Wales. The BBC expected daily to see a draft but nothing turned up and producers had to keep 'reminding' him to finish the piece, set in the fictional town of Llareggub, which, read backwards, is, 'bugger all'. Llareggyb as it finally became, at the BBC's insistence, has its roots in Laugharne and New Quay, Welsh towns Thomas knew well. According to Stuart Kelly in *The Book of Lost Books*, Thomas lost the manuscript several times, writing in 1953 to Charles Elliott of University College, Cardiff, 'Do you remember that I had with me a suitcase & a briefcase . . . ? Well, anyway, I left the briefcase somewhere . . . It's very urgent to me: the only copy in the world of that kind-of-a-play of mine, from which I read bits, is in that battered, strapless briefcase whose handle is tied together with string.' Despite its value to him, Thomas lost and found the manuscript twice more, on different continents. It was discovered, for the last time, in a pub – where else? – and against all the odds went on to become the drunken author's most popular work.

44 Best ever book titles

A book doesn't have to have a good title to be a big seller – take *The Highway Code* – but an eye-catching title does help. I remember one from that hypnotist fellow off the telly a couple of years back that was called, *I Can Make You Rich*. I bet that flew off the shelves. Indeed, it might better have been called, *You Can Make Me Rich*. Here are a few book titles that have an arresting quality to them. They are all real.

Knitting with Dog Hair

Proceedings of the Second International Workshop on Nude Mice

Play with Your Own Marbles

Crocheting Adventures with Hyperbolic Planes

Moles and Their Meaning

Collectible Spoons of the Third Reich

Invisible Dick

Reusing Old Graves

The Attractive Child

The Big Book of Lesbian Horse Stories

Cheese Problems Solved

Teabag Folding

Tattooed Mountain Women and Spoon Boxes of Daghestan

Scouts in Bondage

Lightweight Sandwich Construction

How to Live with a Bitch

Why Jesus Was a Man and Not a Woman

The Day Amanda Came

A Basic Guide to the Occult for Law Enforcement Agencies

Erections on Allotments

The History of Lesbian Hair

Proceedings of the Eighteenth International Seaweed Symposium

The Politics of Breast Feeding

What Kind of Bean is This Chihuahua?

How Nell Scored

Recollections of a Society Clairvoyant

Willie's Ordeal

Authentic Dreams of Peter Blobbs, MD

Afterthoughts of a Worm Hunter

Life Shortening Habits & Rejuvenation

Natural Bust Enlargement with Total Mind Power

Shag the Pony (for children)

45 The guaranteed failure that went wrong and succeeded by mistake

In 1969, *Newsday* columnist Mike McGrady found himself disenchanted with the 'Big Money' books that were dominating the bestseller lists. He decided to expose these vulgar paperbacks as the trash they were and shame lowbrow readers into buying better books.

To do this, McGrady hatched a sneaky plot. He asked 24 colleagues each to write one formulaic chapter of a Harold-Robbins-type novel. He had a few rules:

1 Everything they wrote should lack all literary merit but contain a lot of sex.
2 The book's overwrought prose must drip with cliché and the story must be chaotically disorganized.
3 Every character should be 'deeply shallow' and all the sex must be boring.

Concealing his writers' identities behind the sexy nom de plume, Penelope Ashe, McGrady gave his book the pretentious title, *Naked Came the Stranger*. The plot, such as it turned out to be, centres on a suburban housewife, Gillian Blake, who revenges herself against an unfaithful husband by fornicating a channel through the men of Long Island. Naturally enough, most of the book is taken up with descriptions of Mrs Blake's bed-hopping, including the unlikely 'curing' of a token gay man's homosexuality under the unstoppable influence of her stupendous breasts.

Some heavy editing was required on drafts of the book since the authors, unable to help themselves, had frequently strayed into good writing by mistake. But if McGrady was hoping that his novel's inconsistent, rubbishy, shallow, boring, inconsequential shapelessness would persuade book buyers to stop reading trash, he was wrong. Published under a lurid cover, the novel became an instant and enormous hit.

After years of producing a lot of good writing for unspectacular reward, his disillusioned authors found themselves earning handsome royalty incomes for badly written tripe. This began to cause them discomfort and they decided to act, leaking to the media the story of the book's true genesis. But instead of damping down demand the renewed publicity shot their crappy title into the *New York Times* bestseller list. Yet worse was to come. Cashing in on the success of *Naked Came the Stranger*, opportunistic publishers – an indirect target of McGrady's deception – immediately hijacked the formula, bringing out such successful heavyweight titles as *Naked Came the Manatee* and *Naked Came the Sasquatch*.

A highly successful, truly terrible film followed in 1975.

46 'Jabberwocky': *auf Deutsch*

Written in 1871, Lewis Carroll's *Through the Looking-Glass* contains the Western world's most famous nonsense poem, 'Jabberwocky'. Here it is, together with a translation into German done by philologist Robert Scott (1811–87).

Jabberwocky

'Twas brillig, and the slithy toves
Did gyre and gimble in the wabe:
All mimsy were the borogroves,
And the mome raths outgrabe.
'Beware the Jabberwock, my son!
The jaws that bite, the claws that catch!
Beware the Jubjub bird, and shun
The frumious Bandersnatch!'
He took his vorpal sword in hand:
Long time the manxsome foe he sought –
So rested he by the Tumtum tree
And stood awhile in thought.
And, as in uffish thought he stood,
The Jabberwock, with eyes of flame,
Came whiffling through the tulgey wood,

Der Jammerwoch

Es brillig war. Die schlichten Toven
Wirrten und wimmelten in Waben;
Und aller-mümsige Burggoven
Die mohmen Räth' ausgraben.
'Bewahre doch vor Jammerwoch!
Die Zähne knirschen, Krallen
kratzen!
Bewahr' vor Jubjub-Vogel, vor
Frumiösen Banderschnätzchen!'
Er griff sein vorpals Schwertchen zu,
Er suchte lang das manchsam' Ding;
Dann, stehend unterm Tumtum Baum,
Er an-zu-denken-fing.
Als stand er tief in Andacht auf,
Des Jammerwochen's Augen-feuer

And burbled as it came!	*Durch turgen Wald mit Wiffek kam*
One, two! One, two! And through and through	*Ein burbelnd Ungeheuer!*
	Eins, Zwei! Eins, Zwei! Und durch und durch
The vorpal blade went snicker-snack!	*Sein vorpals Schwert zerschnifer-schnück,*
He left it dead, and with its head	
He went gallumphing back.	*Da blieb es todt! Er, Kopf in Hand,*
'And hast thou slain the Jabberwock?	*Geläumfig zog zurück.*
Come to my arms, my beamish boy!	*'Und schlugst Du ja den Jammerwoch?*
Oh frabjous day! Callooh! Callay!'	*Umarme mich, mein Böhm'sches Kind!*
He chortled in his joy.	*O Freuden-Tag! O Halloo-Schlag!'*
'Twas brillig, and the slithy toves	*Er schortelt froh-gesinnt.*
Did gyre and gimble in the wabe:	*Es brillig war. Die schlichten Toven*
All mimsy were the borogroves,	*Wirrten und wimmelten in Waben;*
And the mome raths outgrabe.	*Und aller-mümsige Burggoven*

47 The best of *The Devil's Dictionary* by Ambrose Bierce

Ambrose Bierce (1842–*c*.1914) was an American satirical journalist and writer. He wrote *The Devil's Dictionary* over a period of several years in a series of newspaper columns. It was first published in book form in 1911.

Bierce's definitions are full of the flavour of his mordant wit, and they are still funny today because they are still true.

In 1913, at the age of seventy-plus, Bierce travelled to Mexico to observe the revolution alongside rebel troops. He disappeared, and was not heard of again. He left some great stuff behind him. Here are a few of the best definitions from his dictionary.

AMBITION   An overmastering desire to be vilified by enemies while living and made ridiculous by friends when dead.

AUCTIONEER   The man who proclaims with a hammer that he has picked a pocket with his tongue.

BAROMETER	An ingenious instrument which indicates what kind of weather we are having.
BIGAMY	A mistake in taste for which the wisdom of the future will adjudge a punishment called trigamy.
CLAIRVOYANT	A person, commonly a woman, who has the power of seeing that which is invisible to her patron, namely, that he is a blockhead.
CLARIONET	An instrument of torture operated by a person with cotton in his ears. There are two instruments that are worse than a clarionet – two clarionets.
CLERGYMAN	A man who undertakes the management of our spiritual affairs as a method of bettering his temporal ones.
DENTIST	A prestidigitator who, putting metal into your mouth, pulls coins out of your pocket.
EXILE	One who serves his country by residing abroad, yet is not an ambassador.
FEMALE	One of the opposing, or unfair, sex.
GHOST	The outward and visible sign of an inward fear.
HEARSE	Death's baby-carriage.
HUSBAND	One who, having dined, is charged with the care of the plate.
IMPUNITY	Wealth.
INDISCRETION	The guilt of woman.
JUSTICE	A commodity which is a more or less adulterated condition the State sells to the citizen as a reward for his allegiance, taxes and personal service.
KILT	A costume sometimes worn by Scotchmen in America and Americans in Scotland.
LABOR	One of the processes by which A acquires property for B.
LAWYER	One skilled in circumvention of the law.
LEARNING	The kind of ignorance distinguishing the studious.
MALE	A member of the unconsidered, or negligible sex. The male of the human race is commonly known (to the

female) as Mere Man. The genus has two varieties: good providers and bad providers.

NOVEMBER	The eleventh twelfth of a weariness.
OPTIMIST	A proponent of the doctrine that black is white.
POSITIVE, adj.	Mistaken at the top of one's voice.
QUILL	An implement of torture yielded by a goose and commonly wielded by an ass. This use of the quill is now obsolete, but its modern equivalent, the steel pen, is wielded by the same everlasting Presence.
RELIGION	A daughter of Hope and Fear, explaining to Ignorance the nature of the Unknowable.
SUCCESS	The one unpardonable sin against one's fellows.
TWICE, adv.	Once too often.
UGLINESS	A gift of the gods to certain women, entailing virtue without humility.
VOTE	The instrument and symbol of a freeman's power to make a fool of himself and a wreck of his country.
YEAR	A period of three hundred and sixty-five disappointments.
ZEAL	A certain nervous disorder afflicting the young and inexperienced.

48 Banned books

In 1999 an American newspaper reported that its local high school had told children that they must get special permission before they could read three very shocking plays by a long-haired English playwright. The school had already withdrawn these plays from the approved reading list because they contained what the governing body called 'adult language', as well as references to sex and violence. The corrupting titles of these works were *Hamlet*, *Macbeth* and *King Lear*, all by that disgusting pervert, William Shakespeare.

This was nothing new. Three years earlier, the filthy swine's *Twelfth*

Night had been pulled by a New Hampshire school owing to the school board's 'Prohibition of Alternative Lifestyle Instruction Act'. They were particularly upset by the bit where that tasty young woman, Viola, disguises herself as a boy and attracts a beautiful countess, Olivia. Quite right, too: who knows what kind of corrupt and depraved practices that would have led to behind the girls' bicycle sheds?

Psychologists often remark that those who cannot control their emotions instead try to control the behaviour of those who are upsetting them. But a censor is like is a man with a hammer looking for nails to hit. And when he has run out of nails he starts hammering flat surfaces. Here are a few titles that have been banned at one time or another.

- *Alice's Adventures in Wonderland* by Lewis Carroll: banned in China in 1931 for anthropomorphism.
- *Animal Farm* by George Orwell: it wasn't the anthropomorphism that upset people but Orwell's highly critical view of the USSR's undemocratic brand of 'Communism'. The USSR was an ally during the Second World War, so copies were suppressed in allied countries.
- *Brave New World* by Aldous Huxley: banned in Ireland in 1932 because of references to sexual promiscuity.
- *Candide* by Voltaire: seized by US Customs in 1930 for obscenity.
- *The Da Vinci Code* by Dan Brown: not much liked in the Vatican and banned in Lebanon as offensive to Christianity.
- *The Diary of Anne Frank* by Anne Frank: banned from schools in Culpeper County, Virginia, after complaints about 'sexual themes'. In 1983 the Alabama State textbook committee called the book 'a real downer' and demanded its rejection.
- *Doctor Zhivago* by Boris Pasternak: banned in the USSR for criticism of the Bolshevik Party.
- *Frankenstein* by Mary Shelley: South Africa's apartheid regime banned this in 1955, calling parts 'indecent' and 'obscene'.
- *The Grapes of Wrath* by John Steinbeck: banned in California for its unflattering portrayal of the region. Seems a bit harsh.

- *Gone with the Wind* by Margaret Mitchell: in 1978 the Anaheim Union High School District in California banned this book because they were upset by Scarlett O'Hara's behaviour, and took exception to the depiction of slaves. Remember, this is 1978.
- *Lady Chatterley's Lover* by D.H. Lawrence: banned in Australia, the US and the UK for violating obscenity laws. At the British trial in 1960 prosecutor Mervyn Griffith-Jones asked whether the book was one 'you would wish your wife or servants to read?', revealing himself to be a bit out of touch with ordinary mortals.
- *Lolita* by Vladimir Nabokov: banned in France, the UK, Argentina, New Zealand and South Africa on grounds of obscenity. A famous edition later appeared showing a girl on the cover, sucking a lollypop.
- *Madame Bovary* by Gustave Flaubert: generally agreed to be a classic work of literature. Flaubert was prosecuted for offences against public morals.
- *Rights of Man* by Thomas Paine: this was banned in the UK and Paine was charged with treason because he supported the French Revolution.
- *The Satanic Verses* by Salman Rushdie: this was banned all over the place for alleged blasphemy against Islam, thus selling many more copies. The fatwa urging the murder of the author and his publishers made Rushdie's life very difficult.
- *Spycatcher* by Peter Wright: this 1985 autobiographical book by an ex-MI5 man was banned – in England anyway – by the government of Margaret Thatcher. It was something to do with official secrets and, apparently, its publication was going to lead to the collapse of the Realm. In reality, the book was an embarrassment to the government. If they were going to ban it, they should have banned it for being so dull. In any case, you could still buy it quite legally in Scotland and bring it back to Primrose Hill on the train. Complete waste of everyone's blimmin' time.
- *The Story of Little Black Sambo* by Helen Bannerman: banned from Toronto public schools in 1956 for its perceived racially stereotyped illustrations. I read it as a boy and was only interested in the tigers.

- *Tropic of Cancer* by Henry Miller: seized by US customs for sexually explicit content. Miller's work was generally unpopular with moral guardians in the United States, but when the ban was lifted, and people read the rude bits, nothing awful happened.
- *Ulysses* by James Joyce: banned in the UK during the 1930s and in the US for its sexual content. I got to page 6. Twice. Shan't bother again.
- *Uncle Tom's Cabin* by Harriet Beecher Stowe: banned in the southern US because of its anti-slavery message.
- *United States-Vietnam Relations, 1945-1967: A Study Prepared by the Department of Defense* commissioned by US Secretary of Defense, Robert Strange McNamara: better known as *The Pentagon Papers*. President Nixon tried to squash publication allegedly because the study contained classified information. The real reason was, as usual, that the unvarnished report of US doings in the Vietnam War was embarrassing to Nixon personally and highly damaging to a succession of administrations.
- *The Well of Loneliness* by Radclyffe Hall: Radclyffe Hall is not an Oxford college but the name of a lesbian author, whose book was banned in the UK in 1928 because it had a homosexual theme.

There's nothing like banning a book to increase its circulation and, in fact, none of these bans did any good. Most lasted only a short time.

English Language

49 Mark Twain's plan for the improvement of English spelling

At one time, spelling reform was all the rage. George Bernard Shaw wrote about it, pointing out that a perfectly defensible spelling of 'fish' would be 'ghoti': 'gh' is 'f', as in 'tough', 'o' is 'i', as in 'women', and 'ti' is 'sh', as in 'station'. Some obsessive exponents of the spelling reform movement developed mad staring eyes and became very boring. The following joke at their expense is probably the work of numerous authors, possibly none of whom is Mark Twain.

A Plan for the Improvement of English Spelling

In Year 1 that useless letter 'c' would be dropped to be replased either by 'k' or 's,' and likewise 'x' would no longer be part of the alphabet. The only kase in whlch 'c' would be retained would be the 'ch' formation, which will be dealt with later. Year 2 might reform 'w' spelling, so that 'which' and 'one' would take the same konsonant, wile Year 3 might well abolish 'y' replasing it with 'i' and Iear 4 might fiks the 'g/j' anomali wonse and for all.

Jenerally, then, the improvement would kontinue iear bai iear with Iear 5 doing awai with useless double konsonants, and Iears 6–12 or so modifaiing vowlz and the rimeining voist and unvoist konsonants. Bai Iear 15 or sou, it wud fainali bi posibl tu meik ius ov thi ridandant letez 'c,' 'y,' and 'x' – bai now jast a memori in the maindz ov ould doderez – tu riplais 'ch,' 'sh,' and 'th' rispektivli.

Fainali, xen, aafte sam 20 iers ov orxogrefkl riform, wi wud hev a lojikl, kohirnt speling in ius xrewawt xe Ingliy-spiking werld.

50 Medical mnemonics you will remember

I was once having a pint in a pub called The Jeremy Bentham, just off Gower Street, in London. University College Hospital was next door and the pub was frequented by tasty trainee nurses and hard-drinking medical students. On this occasion a number of the boys came in after class and began a display of the filthiest swearing I have ever heard. It made even me blanche and one old lady near the fruit machine started to cry. The students were letting off steam because they were under enormous pressure. Their studies required them to commit to memory a huge amount of information, including long lists of ridiculous Latinate terms for parts of the body. To help themselves out, they often relied on mnemonics, which tended to be obscene. One student I knew left medicine because he said, although he could remember the mnemonics, he couldn't remember what they stood for.

Rude mnemonics are easier to recall than clean, but occasional liberties are sometimes taken with spelling. In the 1960s Alan Bennett performed a monologue about a man dictating a telegram to his girlfriend, which he'd signed, 'NORWICH', standing for Nickers Off Ready When I Come Home. When the lady on the phone told him he'd misspelled 'knickers', he pointed out that he knew this, having been to Oxford, where it was one of the first things they taught him. Here are a few mnemonics of the medical variety for you to try.

- For the branches of the facial nerve – Temporal, Zygomatic, Buccal, Mandibular and Cervical: *Two Zulus Buggered My Cat.*
- For the shoulder muscles of the rotator cuff – Teres minor, Infraspinatus, Supraspinatus, Subscapular: *Tarts In Silk Stockings.* (Though the Latin terms themselves could do with mnemonics.)
- For the sperm pathway through the male reproductive tract – Seminiferous tubules, Epididymis, Vas deferens, Ejaculatory duct, Nothing, Urethra, Penis: *SEVEN UP.*
- For the order of the branches of the external carotid artery – Superior thyroid, Ascending pharyngeal, Lingual, Facial, Occipital, Posterior

auricular, Maxillary, Superficial Temporal: *Suzy Always Lays Flat On Pillows Making Sex Terrific.*

- For the symptoms of renal failure – Malaise, Breathlessness, Nausea, Vomiting, GI motility, Headache, Pruritus, Pigmentation: *My Big Nob Vibrates Gently In Her Pulsating Pelvis.* (You have to forgive the uncommon spelling of 'nob', which is comparable with the 'NORWICH' example above.)
- For the following nerves – Olfactory, Optic, Oculomotor, Trochlear, Trigeminal, Abducens, Facial, Vestibular, Glossopharyngeal, Vagus, Accessory and Hypoglossal: *Oh, Oh, Oh! To Touch and Feel Very Good Virgins And Homosexuals.*

With such a crazy spelling, the word 'mnemonic' needs a mnemonic itself; and the following has been recommended: *My Nob Ejaculates Mercilessly On Nuns In Classy Stockings.*

51 Man bites dog: funny real newspaper headlines

Good newspaper headlines must sum up the story in a few words. The best are clever, apt and often humorous. Here are a few corkers, both intentionally and accidentally amusing.

- In the late 1930s, when the British were being encouraged to economize, the news that students at Oxford University had decided to cancel their summer dances was announced with the classic: 'Undergraduates scratch balls'.
- DeForest Kelley, who played Dr Leonard 'Bones' McCoy in the TV series *Star Trek*, died in 1999 and a great headline playing on his famous catchphrase appeared in a newspaper: 'It's worse than that, I'm dead Jim!'
- Then there's the 'held-over' problem: 'Teenager held over penguin' and 'Police hold man over prostitutes' are fine examples.
- Accidental humour resulted also from 'Woman kicked by her husband

said to be greatly improved', which is either good news or a sexist slur, depending on the way you read it, and your attitude to women, of course.

- A clever, or bored, subeditor came up with the lovely 'Book lack in Ongar' to describe a funding problem in the Essex library system, while a prize was awarded to one newspaper for its coverage of a story featuring the deeply disappointed manager of an Indian curry restaurant that had come second in a national competition. The headline: 'Tears on my pilau'.

- In 2005, when Sir Elton John and David Furnish's civil partnership ceremony took place to great fanfare it was described in one paper like this: 'Elton takes David up the aisle'. And if you find that amusing, you shouldn't.

- Sometimes it seems that a story must have been fitted to an existing headline. One about the death of Ken Dodd's father's pet was headed: 'Ken Dodd's dad's dog's dead'.

- But genuine Oscar winners crop up occasionally, too. When the then Labour leader Michael Foot chaired a European group formulating plans to ban nuclear weapons the headline ran: 'Foot heads arms body'.

- Three wartime classics that should be mentioned in dispatches are, first, the one concerning a French military push that had contained and held back an important flank of Hitler's armed forces, which was headed: 'French push bottles up German rear'. Eye-watering, but surely a prize-winner. Second was the simpler, if dizzying, 'Macarthur flies back to front'. The third, from the same war, was reported by Alistair Cooke. It was caused when a compositor carelessly muddled his type, switching an *O* for an *A*, and inadvertently created the deathless 'Churchill puts anus on cabinet'.

- In the 1960s, premier Harold Wilson, who was savagely reshuffling his cabinet, suffered the indignity of 'Out comes the Wilson chopper'. It must have been at about this time also that newspaper readers learnt that round-the-world-yachtsman Sir Francis Chichester had successfully navigated the stormy Cape: 'Chichester conquers the Horn', it said.

■ Finally it's time for the number-one world-beater. When the English explorer Sir Vivian Fuchs announced that he was setting off for the South Pole, there appeared the now legendary headline 'Dr Fuchs off to south ice'. This was capped months later when a further visit was announced with 'Dr Fuchs off again'. Subeditors, and readers it seems, were more innocent in those days.

52 Twenty-five rules for improving your English

Have you ever yearned to write a novel? Many people have, and there's certainly nothing wrong with literary ambition. The problem is that, unlike wannabe violinists, many wannabe novelists begin without having acquired the rudiments of their craft. Furthermore, in contrast to, say, cross-Channel swimmers who haven't bothered to learn to swim, they are not penalized by death; indeed, a number of them go on to make good money from the book racket. Here's an example of the sort of thing I mean, cobbled together from several real efforts.

Her Desert Heart

Hank and Tracy had never met. They were like two birds of Paradise who had also never met, exact opposites: she a ballerina who could rise gracefully *en Pointe*, one slender leg extended behind her like a dog at a lamppost, he as lame as a duck. Not the metaphorical lame duck, either, but a real duck that was actually lame, probably from having a leg disease when he was a boy or something. He was as tall as a six-foot-three-inch tree with a hungry look – the kind you get from not eating for a while, she was short, her eyes two round circles with completely black dots in the centre. They had first met by the duck pond in their suburban neighbourhood near Croydon that had those little white fences a bit like Esther Rantzen's teeth going round the gardens. A storm had been brewing as they watched a little boat drifting across the water exactly the way a cannon ball wouldn't. Then the thunder began, at first ominous sounding, much like the sound of a thin sheet of metal being shaken backstage during the storm scene in a play. The whole atmosphere was like a high-pitched atmosphere of surrealism, just like when something really surreal happens. Suddenly a loud handful of shots rang out, as shots are wont to do ...

Now, there are several problems with this piece, including contradiction, tortured syntax, clichés, mixed metaphors, 'gorged-snake' sentences, bathos and an unequal struggle with similes. So for beginners at the novelist's trade and freshman wordsmiths of every stripe, here are my twenty-five rules for improving your English and avoiding a few of the beginner's mistakes.

Twenty-five rules for improving your English

1 Use words correctly, irregardless of the way others use them.
2 Be careful not to carelessly split infinitives.
3 Avoid clichés like the plague.
4 Use the apostrophe in it's proper place and not when its not needed.
5 Only allow a low level of alliteration.
6 Be more or less specific.
7 And don't start sentences with conjunctions.
8 Check for inadvertant spelling errors.
9 Parenthetical remarks (however relevant) are unnecessary (usually).
10 Verbing nouns weirds language.
11 No sentence fragments.
12 Contractions aren't necessary so don't use them.
13 Never generalize about anything.
14 Prepositions are not the best words to end sentences with.
15 Verbs has to agree with their subjects.
16 Never use no double negatives.
17 Ampersands & abbreviations etc. are N.G.

18 Puns are for children, not groan readers.

19 Don't use a sesquipedalian word if a short one will do.

20 Check you're work for embarrassing homophones.

21 <u>Avoid exclamation marks.</u>

22 No underlining!

23 Capitals should NOT be used for emphasis.

24 Your work will be more powerful if written in the active voice.

25 Eliminate all, unnecessary, commas.

26 Proofread carefully to see if you any words out.

Painting

53 Brushes with death: famous painters and what they died of

Artists can be a bit odd. Not content with dying of old age or slipping away quietly in a retirement home, many go out in style. Here are the things that killed a few of them.

- Henri de Toulouse-Lautrec (1864–1901): this fellow was an inbred midget whose grandmothers were sisters. As a result he had unusually weak bones and several other congenital health conditions. He died at the age of 36 from causes unrelated to these problems: syphilis and chronic alcoholism – Veni, Vici, VD.
- Dante Gabriel Rossetti (1828–82): a sybarite of the old school, Rossetti died of a galloping addiction to chloral.
- Édouard Manet (1832–83): the painter of the famous *A Bar at the Folies-Bergère*, Manet wasn't a well man. He had syphilis, rheumatism and locomotor ataxia (possibly from the syphilis). He had his left leg amputated as a result of gangrene from an ergot overdose and died 11 days later.
- Vincent Van Gogh (1853–90): a wonderful painter, famous for being bonkers, Van Gogh shot himself in a corn field when he was feeling a bit down in the mouth.
- Giotto (*c*.1267–1337): the Black Death (probably bubonic plague) got him.
- Morris Louis (1912–62): an American painter of colourful drippy abstract paintings, he died after years of inhaling the fumes from

paint and powerful paint remover in his poorly ventilated studio.

- Barbara Hepworth (1903–75): this English Modernist sculptor died in a studio fire.
- Titian: (1473/1490–1576): aged nearly a hundred (possibly), Titian just missed out on a telegram from the Queen. He was struck down by the Venice plague and was the only one of its victims to get a church funeral.
- Salvador Dalí (1904–89): heart failure and wilful self-neglect.
- Peter Lanyon (1918–64): Peter Lanyon was a Cornish artist of the St Ives School, painting busy, colourful abstracts with a strong landscape feel. He loved the outdoors, not wisely but too well, dying after a glider he was in crashed into his beloved countryside.
- Paul Klee (1879–1940): the abstract painter who 'took a line for a walk' died of the wasting disease, scleroderma.
- Paul Cézanne (1839–1906): this Post Impressionist pre-Cubist French painter was a diabetic, and died from pneumonia after going out in a thunderstorm, which he shouldn't have done. He left his wife out of his will.
- Paul Gauguin (1848–1903): another Post-Impressionist, his live-now-pay-later life caught up with him in the end. He suffered from multiple venereal diseases caught, perhaps, from those sultry babes on Tahiti, where he went in 1891. Dissipated and alcohol-softened, he was done for by syphilis in the end.
- Mark Rothko (1903–70): after years of smoking, drinking, painting gigantic abstracts and sitting still, Mark Rothko developed an aortic aneurysm that left him impotent. One day he'd had enough of everything and slit his wrists at the kitchen sink. Sad really.

54 How to draw a cat

Winston Churchill and Adolf Hitler were both amateur painters. If one had declared art-war on the other it would have ended, probably, with Churchill winning by a nose. Their technical level was what you might call almost-Rolf-Harris-but-not-quite; 'facile' is probably the word. Nonetheless, there are many less accomplished artists around, of whom you may be one. If you are the kind of chap whose drawings of his family resemble sausages dancing with footballs, or something by L.S. Lowry after he got back from the pub, then you'll appreciate this simple lesson in cat drawing. You'll need a pencil, a rubber, and a sheet of paper – or two.

1   Begin by drawing a circle. It needn't be perfect.
2   Next, draw two triangles in the position shown in picture 1. These will be the cat's ears, so make them the right size or you'll end up with either a grotesque rabbit sort of thing, or a cat with nipples where its ears ought to be.
3   Now, draw two almond-shapes. These are to be the eyes. Their lower points should be on the circle's equator, their upper points about two-thirds of the way up. Don't make them too small or your cat will look like a gormless runt. The pupils are best drawn as almost vertical straight lines in the centre of the almond. Just make them a bit fatter in the middle (picture 2). If it's all going a bit wrong, use your rubber and try again. Rome wasn't built in a day.
4   Think of the nose as a heart (picture 3). Draw it in and colour it in. Then, make a small vertical line, shorter than the pupils, but not much, descend from the heart's point. Now draw a flaccid 'W' – a sort of upside-down bird – with its middle attached to the vertical. That's the mouth done.

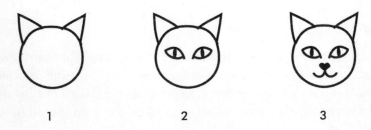

1   2   3

5 The cat's shoulders and legs (picture 4) are the next bit, and it's often here that everything goes all wrong. When I was practising earlier I made the mistake of starting the shoulders too low and drawing the legs too small. By the time I'd finished, my cat looked like a deformed House-of-Wax or Dr Mengele type of experiment, with a huge head, rescued from the Cats Protection League. I don't mean the head was rescued from the Cats Protection League, I mean the whole cat was rescued and that it had a big head. *Do try to keep up.* The two sides of the cat mirror each other, so get one right and you'll be OK with the other. Watch out for the feet, because those toes can be tricky. And keep the body slim – just a bit wider than the head.

6 The back legs (picture 5) are hidden by the front of the cat, so they are just simple curves. Remember to finish them high enough or the back feet will look abnormal. They are further away than the front feet so they look higher. This is called perspective. Am I blinding you with science?

4

5

6   7

7   The tail is up to you. You can put it on the floor, like drawing number
    6, or go mad and make a big 'question mark' of it.
8   Finally (picture 7), add some long whiskers and erase the head-circle
    where it intersects the ears. Draw some ear holes. You don't want
    your cat to be deaf, do you?

If you are wishing I had shown you how to draw a fire engine or the
Japanese flag, using a ruler and compasses, remember that this cat
drawing will impress a girl much more than something mechanical. Once
you've practised a bit, you'll be able to whip out a napkin in the pub, do
your drawing on it, and autograph your artwork along with your phone
number and the dedication, 'Here's to pussy!' Or something like that.

55 The incredible story of Salvador Dalí

That Salvador Dalí was a funny fellow. He had a crazy curly moustache, which looked as if it was made of wire, and did those wacky paintings of melting clocks and landscapes full of stretched-out bodies. One of his most famous paintings is called *The Great Masturbator* (1929) – I bet that competition was oversubscribed by teenage boys. When I put the title into a search engine I got all kinds of pictures I wasn't expecting. I had to sit down quietly and have a large scotch. I will never learn.

Salvador Felipe Jacinto Dalí I Domenech was born in 1904, in Spain, in a town called Figueres, at the foot of the Pyrenees. I suppose if he'd been born a little further south he would have been in the 'Pyrenankles'. Sorry.

Dalí's talent as a draughtsman was recognized early, when he held his first one-man show in Barcelona in 1925. Just three years later his paintings were on show in the US, receiving international acclaim. Along with a born gift for self-publicity, his success in America was fundamental to Dalí's lifelong worldwide popularity – and his healthy bank balance.

Salvador Dalí spent several years in Madrid and Paris, growing his flamboyant moustache in honour of the one worn by seventeenth-century Spanish painter Diego Velázquez. In 1929 he joined the Surrealist group, led by the 'Dadda' of the Daduists, André Breton. He also made, with Luis Buñuel, a very famous Surrealist film, *Un chien andalou* (*An Andalusian Dog*). I saw this when I was a student and thought it was a load of rubbish. At about this time (not when I was a student – *in 1929*), Dalí met Gala Éluard, wife of the poet Paul Éluard, and they began an affair. She became his closest companion and remained so for the rest of his life. The pair married and set up home together in Port Lligat, a picturesque village on the Costa Brava, where Gala acted as Dalí's manager. The house is today a museum.

Dalí was now a well-known Surrealist 'eccentric', and his painting, *The Persistence of Memory* (1931) – that's the famous one with the melting clocks you see everywhere – soon became the public's idea of what a proper Surrealist painting should be. But the Surrealists didn't think so and Dalí was booted out of the movement in 1934, after a sort of 'trial'. Breton began referring to Dalí as 'Avida Dollars', an anagram of his name. In French *avide à dollars* means 'mad-keen on dollars'.

During the Second World War, Mr and Mrs Dalí went to America, where there was less chance of a Nazi sticking his bayonet in your bum. They stayed for eight years. Dalí went all religious (Catholic, naturally) and started churning out religious subjects.

In 1941, the Museum of Modern Art in New York organized his first major retrospective. It was all happening. The following year he published his 'autobiography', *The Secret Life of Salvador Dalí*. In his review of the book George Orwell described Dalí as a fine – if old-fashioned – draughtsman and, at the same time, a 'disgusting' sexual pervert. He had 'arrived'.

Alfred Hitchcock hired Salvador Dalí to conceive the look for some dreamy scenes of mental delusion, featuring Ingrid Bergman, in his 1945 film *Spellbound*. The Dalí-look is noticeable but reactions were mixed. The director described his film as 'just another manhunt story wrapped in pseudo-psychology'.

In 1955, Dalí's religious painting, *The Sacrament of the Last Supper*, went on show in Washington, DC, rapidly elbowing out Renoir's *Girl with a Watering Can* as number one for popularity. On the Last Supper table is the meal. It consists of a torn loaf of bread and one tumbler of red wine – or possibly Ribena. Not much to go round, you might think.

Interestingly enough, it was discovered in 2010 that the food portions depicted in paintings of the Last Supper have been supersized over time. Cornell University studied fifty-two paintings done over more than a thousand years, by El Greco, Leonardo, Rubens and others, and discovered that the main courses, the bread and the plates had all grown in size by up to two-thirds. The meals grew by 69 per cent and the plates by 66 per cent. What's more, the bread was some 23 per cent bigger in the eighteenth-century paintings than in the oldest, a first-century painting. All I can say is that if they had included Dalí's *Last Supper* it would have brought that average right down.

In the 1970s, Dalí and his paintings were still a huge commercial success, with major retrospective exhibitions in Paris and London as well as Dalí's native Spain. But after the death of his wife in 1982 he started to neglect himself and was becoming a Howard Hughes-like recluse. His heart was giving up and he was forgetting to eat. In 1984 Dalí was burned in a fire at his home – a huge and stark castle in Púbol. He died in January 1989 from heart failure and breathing problems.

You can take Dalí's work or you can leave it. For me, the most interesting thing about his paintings is that they always remind me of that football score: Real Madrid – 4; Surreal Madrid – Fish.

Music Strangeness and the Problem of Noise

56 The story behind the Rolling Stones

You don't really think of Mick Jagger as a student at the London School of Economics, do you? But that is where he was off to one day in 1960 when Keith Richards, who was going to Sidcup Art College, got into his train carriage. Richards was an old friend of Jagger's from their days singing 'All Things Bright and Beautiful', and eating school-dinners shepherd's pie at Wentworth Primary School in Dartford in Kent. Richards noticed that Jagger had a Muddy Waters record under his arm.

The two renewed their friendship and, along with another Sidcup Art College friend, Dick Taylor, they began working together in an amateur band called Little Boy Blue and the Blue Boys. Whether this was meant to refer to the Little Boy Blue in the nursery-rhyme, who had the horn, is not recorded. Before long the Blue Boys met a chap called Brian Jones, who was playing slide guitar with Alexis Korner's rhythm-and-blues band, Blues Incorporated. This band contained a couple of other interesting looking musicians: Ian Stewart and Charlie Watts.

Stewart and Jones decided to start their own R&B band, and were joined by Mick Jagger and Dick Taylor. Jagger suggested asking Keith Richards to join, too. So in June 1962, together with drummer Tony Chapman, Jagger, Richards, Stewart, Jones, and Taylor became the members of a new, still nameless, band. Keith Richards remembers Brian Jones ringing *Jazz News* to place an ad for the group. When he was asked for the band's name he found himself at a loss and his attention was caught by a Muddy Waters LP on the floor. On it was the track 'Rollin'

Stone', and Jones borrowed the name. The new band was now, suddenly and accidentally, the Rollin' Stones.

In July 1962, with Mick Jagger fronting, the Rollin' Stones played their first gig, at the famous Marquee Club in central London. Their repertoire was Chicago blues, with some Chuck Berry and Bo Diddley numbers mixed in. Bill Wyman joined them as bass player and, when drummer Tony Chapman left the group, Charlie Watts replaced him.

The Stones were soon booked into the Crawdaddy Club in Richmond, where they attracted large crowds every Sunday. The Beatles' sometime publicist, nineteen-year-old Andrew Loog Oldham, was told to look out for them by a journalist-friend. He turned up to see them and became their manager. He was so young that his mum had to sign the papers.

Under Oldham's wily management, the Rollin' Stones signed with Decca and were given an unusual three-year contract with a royalty rate three times the usual, as well as artistic control of their recordings and ownership of the master tapes, which they then leased back to Decca. This was a technique that had been used successfully by Phil Spector, before he began wearing enormous wigs and being sent to prison.

Oldham cashed in on the perceived contrast between the 'nasty' Stones and the boy-next-door Beatles. He also changed the spelling of the band's name to the Rolling Stones, dropped the 's' from Keith Richards' surname – because he thought 'Richard' looked 'more pop', and made Ian Stewart the band's road manager and occasional studio pianist since, in his opinion, he was less gorgeous-looking on stage than the others. 'Keith Richard' used his stage name until the late 1970s, which is why it varies throughout this tale. Despite being a novice in the recording studio, Oldham also became the Stones' producer. In due course, he acquired a 'bodyguard' called 'Reg', who kept rivals at arm's length.

The Rolling Stones' first single, a version of Chuck Berry's 'Come On', was released in June 1963 but the Stones hated it and refused to play it live, though they did perform it on ITV's *Thank Your Lucky Stars,* where Oldham was advised to fire 'that vile-looking singer with the tyre-tread lips'. With little publicity for the single from Decca, Oldham sent Stones fans out to buy copies at record shops that he knew were polled by the charts people. The effect was that the single shot into the charts, missing out on a top 20 position by just one place.

On the back of this success, Oldham and his partner Eric Easton booked the band on their first UK tour, supporting Little Richard and the Everly Brothers. Oldham's connection with Brian Epstein and the Beatles allowed him to introduce the Fab Four to the Rolling Stones, and during the tour they recorded 'I Wanna Be Your Man', a Lennon and McCartney number that the Stones released before the Beatles' own version. It got to number 12 in the charts. Their third single was Buddy Holly's 'Not Fade Away' in 1964. That reached number 3.

Wanting to focus the band's music on their largely teenage audience, and avoid royalty payments to other writers, Oldham next told Jagger and Richard to co-write some original songs. The first to be recorded was 'Tell Me (You're Coming Back)'. Two new songs also appeared, credited to the mysterious 'Nanker Phelge'. This was a pseudonym invented for songs written by the whole band – an unforgettable name.

Over the years, the Rolling Stones have had enormous success in the US, where it matters, being described as 'The greatest rock band of all time'. But Bill Wyman describes their first tour, in 1964, as a disaster. 'When we arrived, we didn't have a hit record or anything going for us,' he says. The band appeared on *The Ed Sullivan Show* and Sullivan took exception to them, saying he would never book them again, though once they were successful, he mysteriously had them back repeatedly.

During the US tour, the Stones stayed one night in a motel in Clearwater, Florida. In the middle of the night Keith Richard woke up with a tune running through his head and recorded it on to his tape recorder. In the morning he played it to Jagger and told him that the words were 'I can't get no satisfaction'. Richard explained that this was the working title only, remembering later, 'It could've been, "Aunt Millie's Caught Her Left Tit in the Mangle",' although this doesn't have quite the same ring to it. Jagger wrote some lyrics beside the motel pool but Richard didn't like them and the song was recorded in the teeth of his objections. 'I never thought it was commercial enough to be a single,' he said, which just goes to show that artists are often the last people to ask about their own work. 'Satisfaction' became the Stones' first international number 1 hit in June 1965. It also became, over time, their most famous song and their unofficial anthem. It remained at the top of the US charts for four weeks, setting the seal on the Rolling Stones' reputation as a top class international act.

Professional things continued big for the band for a very long time after this, though, unsurprisingly, it wasn't all that long before 'substances' reared their head. Dick Taylor remembered that even at art college in Sidcup, 'Keith and I were on a pretty steady diet of pep pills, which not only kept us awake but gave us a lift. We took all kinds of things – pills that girls took for menstruation, inhalers like Nostrilene, and other stuff.' In May 1967, Jagger and Richard found themselves before the courts on drugs charges. Brian Jones was also separately arrested and charged. Jagger and Richard were sentenced to long prison terms that shocked many people, including the un-groovy William Rees-Mogg, who defended them in *The Times*. He compared the doling out of such harsh sentences, which were later reduced, to putting a butterfly on the rack. At about the same time, Andrew Oldham and the Stones parted company.

In 1968 Brian Jones, who was in a wobbly state of repair owing partly to his experiences with 'substances', agreed that he was unable to go on the road again and was immediately replaced by guitarist Mick Taylor. He received a pay-off containing many noughts. But on 3 July 1969 Jones was discovered dead, face down in the swimming pool of his home, Cotchford Farm, in Sussex. This house had been the country retreat of A.A. Milne, author of the Winnie the Pooh stories. Three decades later, Mr and Mrs Johns, the then residents, said that every year hundreds of people arrived on their doorstep looking for Pooh, or Brian Jones' pool. 'On the whole,' said Mr Johns, 'the Brian Jones lot are incredibly nice and polite. They apologise for the intrusion. The Winnie the Pooh bunch, on the other hand, think they own the place.'

In 1971, accountants advised the Rolling Stones to leave England for

France. They recorded successful albums in France and Germany over the next few years. At the end of 1974 Dick Taylor left the band to go back to art college. Ronnie Wood became Taylor's replacement in 1975. Unlike the rest of the band, Wood was an employee, and he stayed on salary for two decades.

During the 1980s the Jagger–Richards relationship was becoming strained and the band members were increasingly working solo. Then, in December 1985, the Stones' stalwart Ian Stewart died of a heart attack. In 1991 Bill Wyman left the group, his retirement being announced in 1992. Charlie Watts chose Darryl Jones as Wyman's replacement for their 1994 album, *Voodoo Lounge*, which won the 1995 Best Rock Album Grammy.

As the new century approached, the Stones were still wowing the crowds and selling bucketloads of music. Their European 'Bigger Bang' tour in 2007 made an incredible $437 million, landing the band in *The Guinness Book of World Records*.

Today the two Kentish cults, Mick Jagger and Keith Richards, are OAPs. In his stairlift years, Jagger is just a wrinkly version of his young self, but it must be said that Richards' face looks decidedly 'lived in'. Sometimes it looks as if it's been lived in by twenty reckless art students who have been partying non-stop behind the soiled curtains. Some party!

57 'Puff the Magic Dragon' and that rumour

When I was a schoolboy they made us do a play called *Custard the Dragon*, which was based on a poem by Ogden Nash. My friend Ken landed the part of Custard and I got some crappy man-with-spear type walk-on. It was the same when we did *Noah's Flood*: Ken was God while I got Mrs Noah. Humiliating! In later life the story was repeated: he became a much admired master at a famous school whilst simultaneously pursuing his vocation as an artist, with exhibitions in Cork Street and places, while I ended up on the 'deli island' in ASDA, slicing liver sausage all blimmin' day and coming home smelling of bacon.

Anyway, 'Custard the Dragon' was the inspiration for that famous song 'Puff the Magic Dragon', which was recorded in 1963 by the group Peter, Paul and Mary, becoming a ferociously popular and long-lived hit. The story behind the song is a fascinating one.

In 1959 Leonard Lipton, a nineteen-year-old Cornell University student who was missing his childhood, read Ogden Nash's poem 'Custard the Dragon' in the student union library. That evening Lipton was due to have dinner with a friend, but on arrival at his address, 343 State Street, nobody answered the door. Being a student, he went in anyway, headed straight for the typewriter, and in three minutes had typed out his own poem, inspired by Nash's 'Custard'. Having written it he promptly forgot it, leaving the paper in the typewriter, which happened to belong not to his friend but to his friend's housemate, fellow student Peter Yarrow.

Unbeknownst to Lipton, Peter Yarrow was already getting a name on the folk scene and would soon become the 'Peter' of the group Peter, Paul and Mary. On the night in question, says Lipton, Yarrow got home, found the poem in the typewriter, and wrote a tune for it.

Some years later a friend of Lipton's told him he had heard Peter, Paul and Mary singing a song called 'Puff the Magic Dragon'. He said that Yarrow was aware that Lipton was the author and was looking for him because the song was becoming a hit and seemed to be heading for royalty-heaven. Lipton, for the first time remembering his song, contacted Yarrow, who arranged for proper royalties to be paid to Lipton for his work, giving him a co-credit for the song, which not everyone would have done, especially since he had forgotten he'd written it.

But rumours of the song's psychedelic lyrics soon began to circulate and raise eyebrows. This was not an uncommon problem; the Beatles' 'Lucy in the Sky with Diamonds' would later be banned by the BBC for 'being about LSD', while actually having been inspired by a painting by John Lennon's young son Julian, which he said was a picture of his friend Lucy O'Donnell.

The word 'Puff' in the title was the first thing that got people going. Clearly this was a reference to marijuana ciggies. In case there was any doubt, there were also the shocking psychedelic lyrics about frolicking in the mist, and so forth. What's more, Puff's friend was called 'Jackie *Paper*' – how much more obvious could the roll-up references be, M'Lud?

But Lipton denies any such references. It's about 'loss of innocence and having to face an adult world,' he explains. 'I can tell you that at Cornell in 1959 *no one* smoked grass.' Yarrow also has no time for the druggy interpretations, claiming that similar interpretations are possible for 'The Star-Spangled Banner'. 'You can wreck anything with that kind of idiotic analysis,' he says.

In any case, the song has been a perennial hit and has been covered by everyone from Bing Crosby to Aled Jones to Alvin and the Chipmunks. It has been sung in French by Claude François as 'Poff, le dragon magique', in German by Marlene Dietrich as 'Paff, Der Zauberdrachen', and in Catalan by Joan Manuel Serrat as 'Puf, el Drac Màgic'. Not bad for a song written in three minutes by a student who forgot he'd written it.

58 Guitar heroes

Someone, I forget who it was, said that the best guitarists are never discovered – they just sit on their verandas picking away. So I don't know why I decided to do this list of heroes, which is just going to cause arguments anyway, because you'll never get everybody's favourite on there and preferences tend to change. If you don't see your current favourite below please don't write me letters.

- Hannes Coetzee (1944–): Mr Coetzee is from the Karoo region of South Africa. He is best known for playing slide guitar by holding a spoon in his mouth and sliding it up and down the strings. This technique is called '*optel en knyp*' in Afrikaans, which means something like 'pick and pinch'. An inveterate wearer of small-brim hats.
- Andrés Segovia (1893–1987): Segovia did more than anyone to popularize the classical guitar and drag it out of its well of neglect

and into the twentieth century. Over the course of his long life Segovia taught many students, but John Williams – the guitarist, not the film composer – found him a poor teacher: 'The general mood in all of his classes was one of great fear,' he said. Sounds horrible. Segovia fathered a son at the age of seventy-seven but was too fat and old to pick him up.

- Steve 'The Colonel' Cropper (1941–): an American soul guitarist, songwriter, and producer best known as a member of the Blues Brothers band and as the guitarist of Booker T. & the MG's, whose 1962 hit tune 'Green Onions' became very popular in the UK after being featured in the 1979 film *Quadrophenia*.
- Derek Bailey (1930–2005): Derek Bailey studied classical guitar as a young man and went on to become a session musician, playing for such seminal names as Gracie Fields and Bob Monkhouse and working on such high-brow television shows such as *Opportunity Knocks*. In time Bailey turned, perhaps understandably, to the squeaky gate and broken glass-sound of 'free music'. Many listeners, including this author, find the unpredictable chaos of these noises hard to listen to for more than a few minutes at a time. But, since this music would be the first thing a fascist government would abolish, I've put Derek Bailey on the list.
- Jimi Hendrix (1942–70): many people put Hendrix at number one in their list of great rock guitarists. You know all about him; what else can I tell you? Perhaps only that he lived at No. 23 Brook Street, right next door to George Frideric Handel, who lived at No. 25 – years earlier, of course. Hendrix died in unexplained circumstances, having asphyxiated on his vomit, which mainly consisted of red wine. I would have put him down as more of a beer man, myself. It just goes to show, you never can tell. His hats tended to be of the wide-brim variety.
- Baden Powell (1937–2000): widely regarded as the greatest Brazilian guitarist of all time – and that's saying something. Yes, his dad was a fan of the Scouting movement. Drank too much, smoked too much, and it did for him in the end.

- John Fahey (1939–2001): an American finger-style guitarist and composer, his minimalist style was much imitated by the 'American Primitivist' school. A skinny pioneer of the steel-string guitar as a solo instrument, he began in the folk and blues traditions but later absorbed flavours of South American and Indian music, moving finally into the world of improvisational and 'experimental' music. A rough-hewn crusty man, who went through wives and bottles at a steady rate, he managed his life badly and ended up fat, ill and poor. He wrote a book called, wonderfully, *How Bluegrass Music Destroyed My Life*.

- Eric Clapton (1945–): English blues-rock guitarist and musician, member famously of the Yardbirds and Cream, who always scores very high on great guitarist lists. After an unusual childhood, during which he believed his mother to be his sister (!), Clapton took up the guitar. His enormous professional success has been mirrored by great personal turbulence, including the usual trouble with 'substances', alcoholism, family unhappiness, including the death of his young son, and, less usually, accusations of racism. Better just listen to the music.

- Egberto Gismonti (1947–): another Brazilian guitarist, composer and pianist, Gismonti plays a ten-string classical guitar and his influences range from Django Reinhardt (see below) to serialism. Wears a crocheted tea-cosy thing on his head.

- Les Paul (1915–2009): what can you say about Les Paul? As a youth he believed that nothing was playable above the third fret but went on to disprove his theory – in spades. After a car crash he had his arm set in a bent plaster cast so that if the elbow joint remained immobile he would still be able to play. Paul invented multi-tracking and, as if this weren't enough, the solid-body electric guitar. He teamed up with Gibson to produce his signature instrument, the Gibson Les Paul, available in all good guitar shops. Dedicated hard work was the countersign he shared with other great guitarists.

- Julian Bream (1933–): his mum once introduced herself to a friend of mine in Russell Square. After starting as a jazz guitarist, Bream did much to rekindle interest in the Baroque lute and turn the guitar into an instrument considered worthy of study by musical academies. A big fan of Django Reinhardt (see below), he also persuaded Benjamin Britten, William Walton and others to compose works for him. Like Les Paul, he once damaged his arm in a car crash, and like Jan Akkerman (see below) he has a penchant for wearing hats indoors. Bald, but not as bald as Joe Pass (see below). More power to his plectrum.

- Chester 'Chet' Atkins (1924–2001): Segovia much admired this hugely influential, technically brilliant finger-picker and wily country-music producer. Atkins recorded that tune they used to use on *The Benny Hill Show* when those speeded-up semi-naked women chased him round trees: 'Yakety Axe' it's called.

- Joe Pass (1929–94): a very bald Jazz guitarist with an unmistakable, profoundly influential, solo style. An expert in chord substitution, and if you don't know what that means you can either look it up or do what I do and forget it. Life's too short.

- Elizabeth Cotten (1895–1987): left-handed and self-taught, Cotten played the guitar upside-down and back to front. A performer of great charm, who wrote the much-recorded 'Freight Train' when she was a girl. The royalties poured in when she became famous.

- Django Reinhardt (1910–53): enormously influential gypsy jazz guitarist, Django co-founded and played with the Quintet of the Hot Club of France. He had only two working fingers on his left hand after a fire incinerated his caravan and left him severely burnt. Despite this, his left-hand technique was scintillating. I've never seen a picture of him wearing a hat.

- Reverend Gary Davis (1896–1972): blind, black, religious and from the Southern United States, Gary Davis was almost bound to become a blues guitarist. Playing guitars big enough to sail in, the Baptist preacher used them to get his message across, with a percussive, rough-around-the-edges but virtuosic technique. He strongly influ -

enced the playing of such musicians as Bob Dylan, Stefan Grossman and the Grateful Dead. Comprehensively bald, he usually had a hat on.

- Pierre Bensusan (1957–): a French-Algerian guitarist, Bensusan is a fine innovator, and interpreter of Celtic music. His guitar influences include Big Bill Broonzy, Reverend Gary Davis, Mississippi John Hurt, Django Reinhardt, Doc Watson, Wes Montgomery, Jimi Hendrix, Ralph Towner, Ry Cooder, Pat Metheny, Martin Carthy, Bert Jansch, John Renbourn, Nic Jones, Paco de Lucía and John McLaughlin, which covers almost everything. He is an exponent of 'DADGAD' guitar tuning but, having had an enormous amount of hair when young, has considerably less today.

- Jan Akkerman (1946–): with a name like that, you've got to be Dutch, and he is. The son of a scrap-metal dealer, Akkerman is another hat-wearing innovator whose interest in Renaissance and Medieval music intriguingly led him to introduce the lute into a rock band. Like Les Paul and Julian Bream, he suffered a nasty car crash, but is still strumming away like a goodun.

59 'Silent Night': how it happened

It is Christmas Eve, 1818, and Franz Gruber, the teacher, organist and choirmaster of the snowbound Nikolaus-Kirche (Church of St Nicholas) in the picture-postcard village of Oberndorf, near Salzburg in Austria, is desperately trying to solve a problem. The sad and urgent fact is that the church organ has broken down and unless something can be done the Christmas Eve service – at a church dedicated to Santa Claus – is going to be without music for the first time in living memory. Something must be done.

But Gruber's guardian angel is looking down on him. Suddenly, miraculously even, he is touched by a creative inspiration that will be remembered for generations to come. Gruber decides to write down the haunting melody that has just come into his head: a slow lullaby on the theme of the Christ-child, to be sung in a reflective 3/4 time. Picking up a quill, he writes down the music and words, in German, and, in a stroke of brilliance, arranges the tune for guitar in place of the organ, something unheard of in Austria at the time. Gruber calls his carol 'Stille Nacht', in English, 'Silent Night'.

As he is putting the finishing touches to his work the choir arrives, and, after what little rehearsal they have time for, they stand in suspense as the members of the congregation, stamping the snow from their boots, file into the church. It is now time to sing the new carol and, as the light from a thousand candles dances among the pine trees, the choir of the little church of St Nicholas in Oberndorf begin the soft, unforgettable melody, accompanied by the exquisite playing of their brilliant choirmaster, Franz Gruber.

The surprise of the congregation at hearing a guitar in the Nikolaus-Kirche turns at once to joy as the beautiful music fills the building to its rafters. Not the stoniest heart is untouched by the melody; not an eye remains dry at the simple message. Franz Gruber has done the impossible, he has snatched victory from the jaws of defeat, and solved the problem of a silent Christmas Service with a song *about* silence. He has also composed, without labour, a timeless Christmas carol, the most beautiful ever, some will say, and a song that will outlive its author for hundreds of years. Before long, 'Stille Nacht' will be the most asked-for carol, one sung in a thousand tongues by choirs and congregations around the world.

Except that this is all balls.

As with many wonderful stories, the embroidery of this oft-told tale has obscured the plain fabric of the truth. For a start, Franz Gruber was not the author of the words to this carol, which was written in German by Austrian priest, Father Joseph Mohr, and the idea that they were written, in an emergency, on Christmas Eve 1818 is wrong. In fact, Mohr wrote the words as a six-stanza poem in the nearby Alpine village of Mariapfarr in 1816, some two years earlier. He moved to Oberndorf the following year and struck up a relationship with Gruber. Then, on Christmas Eve 1818, he took along his song, asking Gruber to set the words to music in an arrangement for two solo voices and choir, with guitar accompaniment. The earliest known manuscript in Mohr's handwriting is thought to date from around 1820 but it confirms these facts.

Contrary to the story about Gruber's organ being out of order – which has been turned into a rude joke by modern organists – there is no reference in the Austrian records to any kind of problem. Gruber left no reference to it himself, and according to the resonantly named Renate Ebeling-Winkler Berenguer, an expert on the subject, the first mention of the knackered organ appeared in an American book.

Another misconception is that the use of a guitar in church was previously unknown. In fact, it was common practice for guitars to be used in churches at this time, so Mohr's request for a guitar arrangement was unremarkable. Indeed, he might have played the guitar accompaniment himself.

Gruber published various arrangements of 'Stille Nacht' during his life, realizing its popularity. The international spread of the carol was aided by Christian missionaries who took it around the world at the beginning of the twentieth century. Today, according to experts at the Silent Night Chapel in Oberndorf, there are more than 300 known translations. And since there are estimated to be between 5,000 and 10,000 languages in the world (big difference there), this seems not unlikely.

John Freeman Young published the English translation that is best known today in 1819. The melody of the modern carol differs slightly from Gruber's original. Moreover, Gruber's tune was not a slow lullaby in 3/4 time, but a syncopated 6/8 dance, reminiscent of native Austrian folk tunes of the period.

With the realization that the story of 'Silent Night' is largely a myth, it is nice to recognize the authenticity of an associated tale. This is the touching *true* story of the simultaneous singing of the carol by British and German troops within earshot of each other during the Christmas truce of 1914. It wasn't, though, sentiment over the ditty that prompted this bilateral sing-song so much as its being known in their own language by British and German soldiers both.

60 The Monkees: a potted history

A friend of mine, who is a newspaper journalist, once told me that when computers were first introduced into her office many elderly hacks took some time to get used to the technology. She remembered one old fellow who persisted in obliterating his typos by painting correction fluid on to his screen. As soon as he scrolled the page, of course, he was left with a white splurge in the wrong place. I understand he retired early owing either to congenital Luddism or an overexposure to the overpowering smell of Tipp-Ex, Liquid Paper, or whatever it was.

Liquid Paper was invented by a secretary called Bette Nesmith Graham, in 1951. She supplied other secretaries with bottles of the product, which she called 'Mistake Out', changing its name five years later to 'Liquid Paper', and ultimately making herself a fortune. Half of this money she left to philanthropic organizations; the other half went to her son, Robert Michael Nesmith.

Robert Michael Nesmith might be better known to you as Mike Nesmith, a businessman, producer (executive producer, *Repo Man*), writer, actor and philanthropist. Mike Nesmith was also, most famously, one of the Monkees, a pop-rock quartet that starred in the television series of the same name. This is how it happened.

In 1966, inspired by The Beatles film *A Hard Day's Night*, producers Bob Rafelson and Bert Schneider set out to fabricate a Beatles-like group especially for TV. In September 1965 they advertised in newspapers for musicians to act as 'four insane boys' in their new series. From some 400 aspirants, they hand-picked just one, songwriter and guitarist Michael Nesmith, who was the only Monkee to have seen the original press ads. The other three musicians had been recommended by industry professionals and consisted of two likely American youngsters: sometime child-actor Micky Dolenz and Greenwich Village folk musician Peter

Tork, as well as an English musician, Davy Jones, around whom the show was initially intended to revolve. The boys were to be supervised by a music publisher and producer called Don Kirshner, who had been taken on to provide catchy songs for the show. The deal was that each Monkee received a royalty of 1.5 per cent on the songs, while Kirshner got 15 per cent. The Monkees sang the songs but were forbidden by Kirshner to play them. Mike Nesmith, who remembers watching as musicians such as Glen Campbell played songs Nesmith himself had written, told Kirshner, 'Hey, the music isn't a hit because somebody wonderful is making it, the music is a hit because of the television show.'

But the arrangement seemed to work, producing two hit singles, 'Last Train to Clarksville' (1966) and 'I'm a Believer' (1966), the latter written by Neil Diamond, with Dolenz providing the lead vocals on both tracks. There were also two successful albums. But when the public learned that the Monkees were using session musicians (a common practice little understood by the screaming fans), they rudely dubbed them the prefab four, and threw eggs at them. After a year, the boys were itching to choose their own material, perform it themselves, have a say in what was released and stop the flying eggs.

Things were going badly with Don Kirshner and it all came to a head in January 1967, when Nesmith tackled him in his suite at the Beverly Hills Hotel, demanding that the band be given musical control. When Kirshner demurred, Nesmith punched a hole in the wall, saying, 'That could have been your face . . . !', followed by what the British Board of Film Classification used to call 'the Oedipal noun'.

Without telling the Monkees, Kirshner then released another Neil Diamond song, 'A Little Bit Me, A Little Bit You', with Davy Jones alone. The show's producers had had enough and Kirshner was dismissed. The song was pulled from record shops and re-released with Nesmith's own song, 'The Girl I Knew Somewhere', on the B-side. The Monkees were now allowed to perform on their recordings.

On their third album, *Headquarters*, issued in May 1967, the music was played mainly by the Monkees themselves and the album reached number 1, being overtaken only by the the Beatles' *Sgt. Pepper's Lonely Hearts Club Band*.

The Monkees TV show was cancelled in 1968, but Bob Rafelson directed them in a feature film mysteriously entitled, *Head*. The name was allegedly chosen so that in the promotion for the supposed sequel, posters could read: 'From the producers who gave you *Head*'.

61 The mysteries of Dad Rock

What is the worst punishment a father can inflict on his son? That's right – to go to his school and do a dance in the classroom in front of all his friends. And what would be dad's music of preference? Why, 'Dad Rock', of course.

There are arguments about exactly what counts as Dad Rock, with everyone from Tom Jones to Oasis on the list. If you are yourself a baby boomer, say between the ages of thirty-eight and fifty, wearing a cardigan and stuck in the past, then turn up your gramophone player – or cassette player, if you have one of those newfangled things – plug in your deaf-aid, and spray some Brut on your comb-over because it's time to boogie on down to the ultimate 2CD Dad Rock track listing below. (Note: a CD is a modern device for playing music, which is unlikely ever to be superseded.) If your favourite track isn't here, I'm sorry, but you cannot please all of the people all of the time, as Abraham Lincoln didn't say. Pass the Werther's Originals and let's shake a wicked hip.

CD 1

1 'Born in the USA': Bruce Springsteen
2 'Sailing': Rod Stewart
3 'It's Not Unusual': Tom Jones
4 'Addicted to Love': Robert Palmer
5 'Down Down': Status Quo

CD 2

1 'I Am the Resurrection': Stone Roses
2 'Rebel Yell': Billy Idol
3 'Smoke on the Water': Deep Purple
4 'Reward': Teardrop Explodes
5 'Maneater': Hall & Oates

CD 1

6 'We Will Rock You': Queen
7 'Bat Out of Hell': Meat Loaf
8 'Cold as Ice': Foreigner
9 'The Eton Rifles': Jam
10 'All Right Now': Free
11 'Hit Me With Your Rhythm Stick': Ian Dury and the Blockheads
12 'The Joker': Steve Miller Band
13 'Boys Are Back in Town': Thin Lizzy
14 'Eye of the Tiger': Survivor
15 'Here I Go Again': Whitesnake
16 'Live Forever': Oasis
17 'Free Bird': Lynyrd Skynyrd
18 'House of the Rising Sun': Animals
19 'Gimme All Your Lovin'': ZZ Top
20 'Highway Star': Deep Purple
21 'Wild Thing': Troggs
22 'The Road to Hell': Chris Rea
23 'Come On Eileen': Dexys Midnight Runners

CD 2

6 'Silver Machine': Hawkwind
7 'Steppin' Out': Joe Jackson
8 'Bitter Sweet Symphony': Verve
9 'Jungle Boogie': Kool & the Gang
10 'Park Life': Blur
11 'Message in a Bottle': Police
12 'Saturday Night's Alright For Fighting': Elton John
13 'Lola': The Kinks
14 'Layla': Derek and the Dominos
15 'Ace of Spaces': Motörhead
16 'Can't Get Enough': Bad Company
17 'Run to the Hills': Iron Maiden
18 'Purple Haze': Jimi Hendrix
19 'I Love Rock 'n' Roll': Joan Jett
20 'Iron Man': Black Sabbath
21 'Hotel California': Eagles
22 'Another Brick in the Wall': Pink Floyd
23 'Stairway to Heaven': Led Zeppelin

HOBBIES

Old-fashioned Activities
in the Shed

62 The ship in the bottle

I saw a magician in a pub once doing a few bar tricks. I remember he borrowed a large coin and pushed it slowly into the neck of a small beer bottle, where it rattled around. Then he shook it out again. I had a good look at that bottle afterwards but there was nothing wrong with it. The trick was more of a puzzle than a piece of great magic but it put me in mind of the ship in the bottle, which you see sometimes in museums and old hotels.

If you've ever seen a ship in a bottle, you'll agree that it is an intriguing effect. How the devil did they get that enormous great thing in there? If you think about it for a moment, though, you will realize that unless the bottle was blown around the ship it must have gone in through the neck.

The upright masts are what really makes this a puzzling puzzle, and one way to accomplish it is to build the ship's pieces each with a diameter small enough to fit through the neck, then push them into the bottle one at a time, starting with the hull. Once you have made the hull secure, attach the masts, sails and rigging using your special long-handled tools. Easy, isn't it!

Ok, a simpler method is to assemble the ship with special turned-back masts attached to long threads, which run out of the neck. The masts have a 90-degree hinge at the point where they meet the deck and are attached to the hull, folded flat. Don't forget to apply glue at the hinged points just before you push the ship inside.

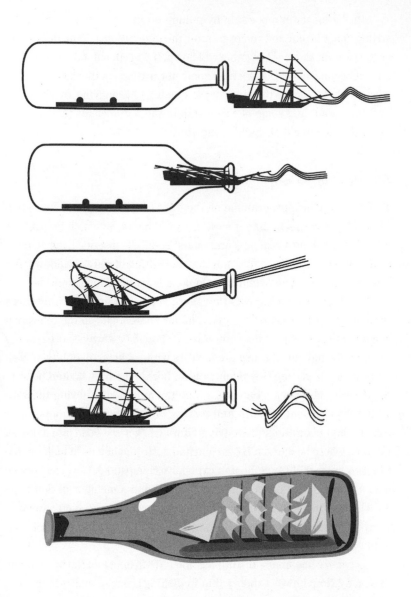

Lift the masts into position by pulling on the strings. Naturally, the strings must be cut and removed after the glue has dried and before the bottle goes on show, or the game will be up. If you consult the illustration, all will become clear. Bottles with some aberrations in the glass are best because they disguise the hinge-trickery a bit. Like juggling, there is a lot to think about, and some of these ship-in-the-bottle chaps must have a hard time keeping their balls in the air.

63 How to tie a fly

There used to be a programme on the telly, presented by a fellow called Jack Hargreaves, who had a scratchy grey beard, in which he sat in a fake shed smoking a real pipe and talked about the disappearing country crafts, such as willow-basket making, the cutting of water meadows, fly-tying and artificial insemination. Oh no, not artificial insemination.

The interesting thing was that there was more to Jack Hargreaves than met the eye. He was, in fact, a major shareholder in the television company that produced the show. Also, although he always wore a funny hat on telly and one of those green vests with pockets full of bits of cork and things for getting Boy Scouts out of horses' hooves, he had been to Sandhurst and was a clean-shaven lieutenant-colonel during the war, with a superbly cut uniform and a mirror-like shine to his boots. After this, he had been the suit-wearing editor of *Picture Post* magazine in London, where he dated a *Vogue* journalist. He had homes in fashionable Chelsea, cosmopolitan Soho and expensive Hampstead. Hargreaves was also a major figure in the setting up of ITV and a member of Southern TV's board of directors. So it wasn't exactly a case of what-you-saw-was-what-you-got; it was more a case of what-you-got-was-not-what-you-didn't-see.

I seem to remember Jack talking about fly-fishing and the proper way to tie a fly. Now, I have a theory that fly-fishing is one of those things that lowers the blood pressure, like porridge. If that's true, then tying a fly probably puts you into a coma. Talk about small and fiddly. I was going to describe in easy steps the process of tying a fly, but when I mentioned this to my friend Ralph, who is an expert in fly-tying, he looked at me as if I had suggested describing on an envelope the best way to do a bilateral cingulotomy.

In fact, fly-tying is a skilled art that requires a load of practice. But – hooray! – you can buy a kit which comes with all the bits and pieces you need and a book of words. The equipment you'll typically get in a kit includes such items as a fly-tying vice, scissors, a whip finisher, hackle pliers, a dubbing needle, a bobbin threader and a hair stacker. Then you'll need hooks and things like dubbings, threads, dumbbell eyes, hare's mask and head cement (*don't even ask*). Among the flies you will then be able to tie is one called the wooly bugger streamer.

If all this takes your fancy, you should really talk to an expert to see if you can get some apprenticeship in. That's the proper way to learn.

64 How to dissolve your wife

In 1949, forty-year-old John George Haigh died when he fell down a hole and broke his neck. It wasn't an accident; he was being hanged for murdering six people and dissolving their bodies in concentrated sulphuric acid.

If you're fed up with your wife you might decide that this is a good way to dispose of her. But there's an even better way, which is already used to dispose of large animal carcasses and which some cheerful people would like to see introduced as a sort of liquid cremation for humans. It's called alkaline hydrolysis, from 'hydro-', having to do with water, and '-lysis', which is the chemical disintegration of a cell by the rupture of its wall or membrane.

The stuff you need to do this is sodium hydroxide (NaOH), also known as lye, caustic soda or, more commonly, drain cleaner. So getting hold of it is not going to be hard. Caustic soda is an alkali not an acid. If you drank some you wouldn't digest it: it would digest you. You can see the effect if you look at some chap making lutefisk, that weird but traditional

Scandinavian dish. What they do is soak dried ling or cod in a solution of lye over several days. The fish swells and becomes jellified, its protein content decreasing by more than half. It is important that your Nordic man does not leave it in the sodium hydroxide for too long because the fats in the fish might then turn to soap (saponification). In Finnish this spoiled fish is called is *saippuakala* (soap fish).

Anyway, to get back to things. There is some special equipment you will need to dissolve your wife, apart from the sodium hydroxide. The first thing is a large, specially designed, pressure-cooker-style tank. No, I don't know where you can get one: try a DIY store as I don't think Tesco is going to have one. If you draw a blank there, you could try doing it in the bath but it's going to take longer. Once you have all your equipment to hand, put your wife into the tank and fill it with a solution of caustic soda and water. (Ideally, she will be dead first.)

You must now heat up the liquid to several hundred degrees, and apply 60 lb of pressure per square inch, which is about the same as that in your bicycle tyre. Just think pressure cooker. Now leave it to cook. Why not go and see a film?

After a few hours, when you open the pressure cooker you will find the remains of your unloved one in the form of a shallow layer of crumbly, sterile, bone solids and a coffee-coloured liquid residue with the consistency of motor oil and a strong ammonia smell. Luckily this is inert, so you can safely pour it down the drain.

You might complain that this whole process is undignified. All I can say is that so are those trousers that teenage boys wear round their knees with their pants showing. This is no time for niceties.

Of course, you could just try being nice to your wife. Who knows, maybe she's already thinking about dissolving *you*.

House and Garden DIY

65 How to make a smokehouse out of an old fridge

My grandma, putting down her knitting, once told me that she had just two remaining ambitions. One was to punch someone in the face and the other was to be shut inside an old fridge. I remember thinking that this must be the first sign of her going bananas. She was at that time being kept alive on a heroic regimen of coloured pills for everything from bad feet to itchy teeth and I thought they might be interacting poorly. But apparently she wasn't off her head; these were long-held desires. Of course, her fridge suggestion was a dangerous one so my brother-in-law Pete instead made her a smokehouse out of an old refrigerator, later cold-smoking some of the most succulent trout I've ever eaten. Here's how to make the patent 'smokerator' electric smoker.

Your smokerator consists of a smoke/heat source in the bottom and somewhere to put the meat. It's that simple. Vents at the top and bottom control the airflow, regulating the temperature and smoke-flow.

Required

- An old fridge (metal shelves, not plastic)
- A small cast-iron frying pan
- A can of your favourite beer
- A single-burner electric hotplate
- A hammer and chisel or old screwdriver
- Tin snips
- Self-tapping screws
- Proprietary smoking-wood sawdust: chunks or pellets

Method

1   Remove all the innards from your fridge. Don't leave *any* plastic in there. There should already be a couple of holes in the back and bottom, where the wires and pipes used to emerge but you need one more. Using a chisel or an old screwdriver or something else, whack a hole in the top about 1.5 in. (4 cm) in diameter. *Mind your fingers.*

2   Drink the beer.

3   Cut the beer can into smallish pieces with your snips (*not your sister's nail scissors*). These will act as movable flaps to let you control the flow of air through your smokerator. Screw one into place over each hole with some self-tapping screws.

4   Mount the hotplate in the bottom of the fridge and position the frying pan on top (on top of the hotplate, obviously, not on top of the fridge).

5   Run the cord out of one of the holes in the back and plug it in. Turn it on medium-low and fill the pan with the sawdust, following the instructions on the packet.

6   Place your properly prepared meat on the shelves and close the door. (Get out first.)

7   Refill the pan every 3–4 hours until the meat is well smoked. It takes between 12 and 24 hours, depending on what you're smoking.

8   'Cold smoking' is smoking at a temperature lower than 100°F (37°C). For cold smoke you need a smoke source outside the unit, so cut a 4 in. (10 cm) hole in the side of the fridge, towards the bottom and use an old wood stove connected to the smokerator via a 4 in. (10 cm) metal pipe. The length of the pipe will determine the temperature of the smoke.

9   Get smoking.

66 Build your own log cabin

Abraham Lincoln was born in a one-room log cabin in 1809 and if it was good enough for him it ought to be good enough for anybody. Of course, building your own log cabin is not exactly quick or easy, but it is rewarding. Just imagine how proud you'll feel as you finally step back to admire your completed work. In three years' time. Just remember, though, this is a two-person business; indeed, the more people you can rope in to help, the merrier.

Required

- A broadaxe for tree felling and chopping
- An adze (an axe with its blade on sideways) for shaping and working

Your pioneer's log cabin will be based on the traditional kind, which was generally just one story high and the length of one log. Depending on log size, each long wall was made typically of, say, five thick logs up to where the roof started, and on the short ends, five more logs forming the tapering top half of the gable up to the roof apex. The inside of your cabin will consist of just one room, which will be big enough to accommodate a small family.

Method

1. Dress in something robust. A dinner jacket is not right.
2. Select your site: you are looking for a sunny spot that requires little clearing and offers good drainage. If you can rest your cabin corners on rock, so much the better. An earth floor requires no foundations, but foundations keep the damp out.
3. Cut down about twenty-five trees with your broadaxe. There's not much to say about this except get someone to help you. The best trees for the purpose are old and very straight, with few branches (fewer knots).
4. Lay the logs at right angles, one on top of the other. If you've picked the best trees, very little hewing should be required. You will be building with round logs with the bark still on. Join the corners with notches in the form of half-moon grooves hacked with your adze into the sides of the lower of the interlocking logs. Keep going until you have the basic hut shape, about five logs high.
5. Fill any gaps with 'chinking': woodchips and 'daub', which is a mixture of moss, grass and mud-and-sand. Careful notching in the previous step will minimize the chinks between the logs. Cracks in

the logs are common as the wood dries but you can ignore them as they only add to the charm.

6   Hack your doorway in one of the gable ends. Make it a sensible size. A clapboard door secured by battens and hung from wooden hinges is a must.

7   Cut your window. Do this by cutting horizontally into the lower (top of the window) and upper (bottom of the window) halves of two logs in one of the long sides of your cabin, then join the horizontal cuts with two vertical cuts to make a rectangular hole. Cover this with greased paper. Paper windows used to be all the rage.

8   Make the shutters using long clapboards fastened to frames of split-wood. Fashion hinges from the same material; a wooden latch may be made for the inside. In the old days, a leather latch-string hanging from the outside was a signal of a warm welcome on the inside.

9   Put the roof on. The easiest roof to make is one of stout but slimmer horizontal logs notched at each end into the uppermost logs of the gable walls. Each of these logs is a little shorter than the one below it, thus forming the characteristic pointy tip, and it is this that determines the pitch of your roof. The purlins run from one gable end right across to the opposite. Once you've got them all on, make your roof. You do this by splitting enough 4 ft (1.2 m) long oak clapboards to cover the area, keeping them in place under weighty timber poles.

10 Furnish your log cabin with a wood stove, two or three beds, a table and chairs, your exercise bike, TV, washing machine, microwave, computer and so forth: all the essentials of the simple life.

11 Go upmarket: if you want to impress the neighbours when you've finished, you can lay a plank floor using split ash or poplar, smoothed with your broadaxe on one side. Or you could just have a rest.

67 'Uncle Podger hangs a picture' by Jerome K. Jerome

Three Men in a Boat by Jerome K. Jerome is the tale of a holiday on the Thames, published in 1889 It is the antidote to such novels as Thomas

Hardy's *Jude the Obscure*, a flipping miserable book written at about the same time. Unlike the work of Dickens, Hardy and the rest, Jerome's style has barely dated; his characters and their troubles seem just like us and ours; what's more, *Three Men in a Boat* is eye-wateringly funny. Here's the bit about Uncle Podger doing a bit of DIY.

Uncle Podger Hangs a Picture

You never saw such a commotion up and down a house, in all your life, as when my Uncle Podger undertook to do a job. A picture would have come home from the frame-maker's, and be standing in the dining-room, waiting to be put up; and Aunt Podger would ask what was to be done with it, and Uncle Podger would say: 'Oh, you leave that to me. Don't you, any of you, worry yourselves about that. I'll do all that.'

And then he would take off his coat, and begin. He would send the girl out for sixpen'orth of nails, and then one of the boys after her to tell her what size to get; and, from that, he would gradually work down, and start the whole house.

'Now you go and get me my hammer, Will,' he would shout; 'and you bring me the rule, Tom; and I shall want the step-ladder, and I had better have a kitchen-chair, too; and, Jim! you run round to Mr. Goggles, and tell him, "Pa's kind regards, and hopes his leg's better; and will he lend him his spirit-level?" And don't you go, Maria, because I shall want somebody to hold me the light; and when the girl comes back, she must go out again for a bit of picture-cord; and Tom! – where's Tom? – Tom, you come here; I shall want you to hand me up the picture.'

And then he would lift up the picture, and drop it, and it would come out of the frame, and he would try to save the glass, and cut himself; and then he would spring round the room, looking for his handkerchief. He could not find his handkerchief, because it was in the pocket of the coat he had taken off, and he did not know where he had put the coat, and all the house had to leave off looking for his tools, and start looking for his coat; while he would dance round and hinder them.

'Doesn't anybody in the whole house know where my coat is? I never came across such a set in all my life – upon my word I didn't. Six of you! – and you can't find a coat that I put down not five minutes ago! Well, of all the—'

Then he'd get up, and find that he had been sitting on it, and would call out: 'Oh, you can give it up! I've found it myself now. Might just as well ask the cat to find anything as expect you people to find it.'

And, when half an hour had been spent in tying up his finger, and a new glass had been got, and the tools, and the ladder, and the chair, and the candle had been brought, he would have another go, the whole family, including the girl and the charwoman, standing round in a semi-circle, ready to help. Two people would have to hold the chair, and a third would help him up on it, and hold him there, and a fourth would hand him a nail, and a fifth would pass him up the hammer, and he would take hold of the nail, and drop it.

'There!' he would say, in an injured tone, 'now the nail's gone.'

And we would all have to go down on our knees and grovel for it, while he would stand on the chair, and grunt, and want to know if he was to be kept there all the evening.

The nail would be found at last, but by that time he would have lost the hammer.

'Where's the hammer? What did I do with the hammer? Great heavens! Seven of you, gaping round there, and you don't know what I did with the hammer!'

We would find the hammer for him, and then he would have lost sight of the mark he had made on the wall, where the nail was to go in, and each of us had to get up on the chair, beside him, and see if we could find it; and we would each discover it in a different place, and he would call us all fools, one after another, and tell us to get down. And he would take the rule, and re-measure, and find that he wanted half thirty-one and three-eighths inches from the corner, and would try to do it in his head, and go mad.

And we would all try to do it in our heads, and all arrive at different results, and sneer at one another. And in the general row, the original number would be forgotten, and Uncle Podger would have to measure it again.

He would use a bit of string this time, and at the critical moment, when the old fool was leaning over the chair at an angle of forty-five, and trying to reach a point three inches beyond what was possible for him to reach, the string would slip, and down he would slide on to the piano, a really fine musical effect being produced by the suddenness with which his head and body struck all the notes at the same time.

And Aunt Maria would say that she would not allow the children to stand round and hear such language.

At last, Uncle Podger would get the spot fixed again, and put the point of the nail on it with his left hand, and take the hammer in his right hand. And, with the first blow, he would smash his thumb, and drop the hammer, with a yell, on somebody's toes.

Aunt Maria would mildly observe that, next time Uncle Podger was going to hammer a nail into the wall, she hoped he'd let her know in time, so that she could make arrangements to go and spend a week with her mother while it was being done.

'Oh! you women, you make such a fuss over everything,' Uncle Podger would reply, picking himself up. 'Why, I like doing a little job of this sort.'

And then he would have another try, and, at the second blow, the nail would go clean through the plaster, and half the hammer after it, and Uncle Podger be precipitated against the wall with force nearly sufficient to flatten his nose.

Then we had to find the rule and the string again, and a new hole was made; and, about midnight, the picture would be up – very crooked and insecure, the wall for yards round looking as if it had been smoothed down with a rake, and everybody dead beat and wretched – except Uncle Podger.

'There you are,' he would say, stepping heavily off the chair on to the charwoman's corns, and surveying the mess he had made with evident pride. 'Why, some people would have had a man in to do a little thing like that!'

68 Health and safety madness

Last winter it snowed where I live. A neighbour knocked on my door to say that the dustmen wanted her to let us know that they were not allowed to collect our rubbish in case they slipped over, hurt themselves and decided to sue. They weren't even allowed to come and tell us this, which is why she had volunteered to knock on doors. In the next few minutes a procession of pregnant ladies, bleary gentlemen in cravats and cardigans, frail old dowagers and this author dragged their wheelie bins on to the main road in the driving snow. It was a case of health and safety madness, yet again. Here are some other recent examples. The identities of these people have been concealed to prevent them being lynched, but they are all true.

- In 2007, a firefighter was investigated by his brigade for breaching safety rules when he rescued a drowning woman from the River Tay. He was told that by risking his life he had broken the brigade's standing safety instructions.
- In 2009, children who wanted to play conkers in the playground at a primary school in Macclesfield, Cheshire, were ordered to wear safety goggles by their head teacher. She said, 'Conkers are generally frowned on now because a child somewhere in the country, at some point, has been hurt playing a game. So we decided it was a case of better safe than sorry.'
- In 2009, St George's Day flags on Liverpool lampposts were torn down by council workmen. Officials said they posed a danger to pedestrians and motorists.
- In 2007, council officers told Bramcote Crematorium in Nottinghamshire to replace 40 memorial benches that an inspector had found to be three inches lower than the 'allowed minimum' height. Under health and safety laws park benches must be more than 17.75 in. (45 cm) high so that the old and infirm can get off them easily. The crematorium was also instructed to pay a crippling £200,000 for lighting because the new benches must be lit at night, under the same rules.

- In 2007, a Scottish local council decided to leave the lights on in derelict buildings so that vandals and burglars did not hurt themselves.
- In 2007, the only place residents of East Prawle in Devon were able to get a mobile-phone signal was the village bench. When the parish council applied to build a £100 replacement concrete plinth, dubbed 'phonehenge', they were told that health and safety laws required the provision of wheelchair access, safety railings and a security night-light.
- In 2007 the word 'accident' was banned from the new edition of *The Highway Code*.
- In 2008, several London councils deliberately knocked over or 'removed' some 10,000 graveyard headstones for fear that they might fall on passers-by and injure them. Many mourners who turned up to lay flowers on family graves found that their gravestones had been kicked over by municipal vandals so as to make them safe. This official desecration was ordered by robotic functionaries, in the face of statistics showing that you are 4,000 times more likely to be injured by a bus than by a gravestone.

THE MEDIA

Famous Radio and Television Performances

69 The first ever pissed commentator

In 1937 the BBC were to cover the Illumination of the Royal Navy Fleet at Spithead with live radio commentary given by Lieutenant-Commander Thomas (Tommy) Woodrooffe, author of *Best Stories of the Navy* (1941).

Pre-transmission naval hospitality had been lavish and the convivial Woodrooffe was already listing heavily to port on a tide of pink gins. The transcript of the subsequent radio masterpiece cannot convey the full eloquence of his commentary, filled as it is with prolonged gaps, repetition, vagueness, sudden changes of tone from obsequious to aggressive, and the intermittent whistling and crackling of the vintage equipment.

In addition to being three sheets to the wind, Woodrooffe speaks with the 'posh' accent so characteristic of the Establishment-class of yesteryear. All his 'offs' are 'awfs' and his 'lamps' are 'lairmps', which only adds to the fun.

Here then is Tommy Woodroofe's magisterial effort that night, from his vantage point on the fleet flagship.

ANNOUNCER: Once again we're taking you on board HMS *Nelson* for a description of the scene at Spithead tonight, by Lieutenant-Commander Thomas Woodrooffe. [*Muffled bumbling noises.*]

WOODROOFFE: At the present moment, the whole fleet is lit up! When I say 'lit up', I mean lit up by fairy lamps. We've forgotten the whole Royal Review [*whistling noises*] . . . we've forgotten the Royal Review

. . . the whole thing is lit up by fairy lamps. It's a fantastic . . . it isn't the fleet at all. It's just . . . er, it's fairyland, the whole fleet is in fairyland . . . In the next few moments . . . you'll, you'll find the fleet doing odd things . . . and when I say the fleet is lit up . . . in lamps, I mean she's outlined. The whole ship's outlined. In little lamps. [*Long gap.*] I'm sorry, I was telling some people to shut up talking. Umm . . . what I mean is this. The whole fleet is lit up. In fairy lamps. And each ship is outlined . . . the ships are all lit up. They're outlined. The whole lot. Even destroyers are outlined. In the old days, you know, destroyers used to be outlined by a little kind of pyramid of lights. And nowadays . . . destroyers are lit up by . . . the outline themselves. In a second or two, we're going to fire rockets, and erm, we're going to fire all sorts of things. And . . . you can't possibly see them but you'll hear them going off, and you may hear my reaction when I see them go off. Because erm . . . I'm going to try and tell you what they look like as they *go off*. But at the moment there's a whole huge fleet here. The thing we saw this afternoon, [*whistling sounds*] this colossal fleet, lit up . . . by lights . . . and the whole thing is in fairyland! [*Suddenly aggressive*] It isn't true! It isn't here! And as I say it . . . It's gone! It's gone! There's no fleet! It's, it's disappeared! No magician whoever could have waved his wand could've waved it w . . . with more acumen than he has now at the present moment. The fleet's gone. It's disappeared. Er, I'm trying to give you, ladies and gentlemen, [*loud crackling*] . . . I was talking to you in the middle of this damn, *ahem*, in the middle of this fleet . . . At a signal by the Morse code . . . at a signal by the fleet flagship, which I'm in now, they've gone, they've disappeared. There's nothing between us and heaven. There's nothing at all . . .

At this point Woodrooffe was faded out and replaced by music. Suspended briefly by the BBC, he later denied being 'lit up' himself, claiming to have been affected by the emotion of the occasion – possibly the first recorded example of this now exhausted broadcasters' euphemism.

70 The most disastrous chat-show guest ever

After Dark was a late-night series broadcast live on Channel 4 between 1987 and 1991, featuring discussions between 'experts' on sofas in a pitch-black studio. Droll commentators were already calling the show 'After Last Orders', owing to the perceived wobbliness of some participants, but they hadn't seen anything yet.

Disaster finally struck one momentous night in 1991, when lawyer Helena Kennedy was moderating a discussion about masculine violence. Male contributors included a psychoanalyst, the author of a book on serial killers, a military historian with a moustache and a sourpuss journalist. Seated alongside were various female opinion-holders, including the noted feminist author Kate Millett.

Unfortunately, inexplicably and, as it turned out, very unwisely, someone had also invited along Oliver Reed, an actor well known for his 'robust stance' on women's issues. Reed was also a notorious enthusiast for the 'falling-down liquid', evidenced by a history of bleary appearances on chat shows, where he could be seen clutching jugs of a mysterious orange substance from which he took copious swigs.

On the night in question Reed had arrived in a frightening state of gobby inebriation, and, sweating for England, with a wine-glass gripped unpredictably in his paw, he lost no time in helping himself to gallons of a colourless fluid from a green bottle. He was soon in what one medically minded observer referred to as 'a seriously pissed condition', belligerently interjecting incomprehensible remarks into the conversation and apparently farting into the sofa he was sharing with Kate Millett.

In the middle of an earnest exchange between the psychoanalyst and an American lady, Reed suddenly adopted a loud Yorkshire accent and barked irrelevantly, 'I've put my plonker on the table; I won't take it off unless you give me my mushy peas.' Helena Kennedy looked as if she was unused to this kind of thing in her day job.

To add to the accelerating confusion, a hoax caller now rang the show, claiming to represent Channel 4's Chief Executive Michael Grade, saying that Grade wanted the programme 'off the air now!' In a flash the picture disappeared from viewers' screens to be replaced by a soothing film about coal.

But the hoax was soon realized and *After Dark* was back on, with an apologetic though nonetheless grinning Reed promising to behave. It didn't last. In response to the question, 'Why do people commit serial murders?' Reed astonished the panel with a rhetorical teaser of his own: 'Why did Ratty and Mole in *The Wind in the Willows* have a love affair?', a question so original it brought conversation to a juddering halt.

To general relief, Reed then left the set for what he referred to as 'a slash'. On his return, two pointed shirt collars sprouting maniacally from either side of his shiny face, he rolled extravagantly over the back of his sofa, frightening the wits out of Kate Millett and nearly kicking her in the head. 'I want a smoke!' he yelled. The expert on serial killers lit him a cigarette.

Reed now began an exhibition of five-star swearing. He started, as Millett tried to make a point, by yelling 'Shout away, big tits!' before treating everyone to an eye-wateringly coarse reference to the female pudendum.

Things were now getting alarmingly out of hand with moderator Kennedy looking like someone trying to put kangaroos into a box. Then, just as people were beginning to fear for their safety, Reed grabbed hold of Kate Millet's head and kissed her forcibly on the face. Having taken about as much of this sort of thing as anyone could reasonably be expected to take, she quietly asked to have Reed ejected, backed up without demur by the others.

Reed made his exit in crestfallen and contrite manner, though he was still to be heard for some time bumbling around in his rustling seersucker jacket, giggling into the darkness behind the cameras.

The series was cancelled.

Oliver Reed died in 1999 after reportedly drinking three bottles of Captain Morgan's rum, eight bottles of lager and several double scotches, and beating five young sailors at arm wrestling in a pub called The Pub.

71 Archie Andrews and other things not to do on the radio

There used to be a programme on the telly called *Muffin the Mule*, which I think is an activity now banned under the Sexual Offences Act 2003. Whatever the case, I feel sure that mule-muffin' would have sounded even more disgusting on the wireless than it looked on the TV. There are several other things that are not best suited to doing on the radio. Here are a few of them, starting with one that they actually tried, and which became popular despite the insanity of the basic proposition.

- *Ventriloquism: Educating Archie* was a BBC radio show broadcast in the 1950s. It starred Archie Andrews, a ventriloquist's dummy in the shape of a cheeky child, with a man called Peter Brough's hand up his shirt. It wasn't such an odd idea; American ventriloquist Edgar Bergen and his dummy Charlie McCarthy had been doing a similar thing since the 1930s. Although the illusion was completely lost on the wireless, one big advantage was that you couldn't see Brough's lips moving, which was just as well since they were moving a lot. At its height, *Educating Archie* drew an audience of 15 million people; future stars such as Benny Hill, Bruce Forsyth and Julie Andrews got their start on the programme. Peter and Archie made the move to BBC television in 1956, but to general dismay Brough's lips were seen to move even when Archie was saying things like 'Eh?', and the show didn't survive.

- *Magic tricks:* actually this is another one that has worked. In 1949 Australian magician Sydney Piddington and his wife Lesley, known – somewhat unsurprisingly – as the Piddingtons, performed startling mindreading and telepathy effects on BBC radio. Twenty million listeners tuned in to hear as Lesley, locked in the Tower of London, correctly received the randomly chosen sentence fragment, 'abandoned as the electricians said that they would have no current,' which her husband had sent telepathically all the way from Piccadilly. I met Lesley Piddington once; she was clever and charming – but not telepathic.

- Gurning: the annual Egremont Crab Fair is home to the World Gurning Championship, in which contestants pull grotesque faces through a horse collar, or 'braffin'. Would this be any good on the radio? No.
- The Miss World Contest: even intelligent answers to such questions as 'what is your assessment of occidental bicameralism?' are going to pall if you are unable to eye the babes' lineages.
- Belly dancing: same. And that music is going to get on your nerves after a bit, too.
- Origami: this is tedious enough on television.
- Programmes for the deaf: it's time for one of my pills.

Behind the TV Classics

72 Doctor Who

Doctor Who hardly needs introducing. The programme was conceived by the BBC as a family science fiction drama about the adventures of a mysterious, two-hearted alien 'time lord' known as 'the Doctor', who zooms about time and space in his TARDIS (Time And Relative Dimensions In Space). This is a 1950s police box, which, unlike John Prescott, is bigger on the inside than it is on the outside. The Doctor is accompanied on his travels by various companions – often fruity young women in ridiculously short skirts – and, on one occasion, by a kilted Peter Purves, off *Blue Peter*. The Doctor encounters lots of delinquent monsters in his travels, but always sorts everything out by the end of the series, leaving everyone but the baddies happy. This proves he is not human.

Doctor Who first appeared on television in 1963. Initiated by Canadian Sydney Newman (also responsible for *The Avengers*), the show was produced by Verity Lambert and starred as its first Doctor an elderly William Hartnell. The famous, and superb, theme tune was composed by Australian composer Ron Grainer, who had written the *Steptoe and Son* theme and would later write the ones for *The Prisoner* and *Tales of the Unexpected*. Grainer's tune was 'realized' by Delia Derbyshire of the BBC Radiophonic Workshop. It so impressed Grainer when he heard it that he tried to get Derbyshire a co-credit. This was resisted by the BBC's men in suits. The Radiophonic Workshop was responsible also for the famous creepy sound of the TARDIS dematerializing, which was made by recording a man on his knees dragging his house keys down the strings of a piano and playing the tape backwards with distortion. The main swirly title sequence was equally innovative, using video feedback, a usually unwanted effect caused by pointing a TV camera at a monitor displaying the camera's own output.

Over the decades the monsters came thick and fast, with such blood-chilling examples as the Cybermen, the Ice Warriors, Ronald McDonald, Davros and, most famously, the Daleks. The Daleks were created by writer Terry Nation and designed by BBC designer Raymond Cusick, who was asked to create the look of a woman in a ballgown sweeping along without any sign of motive power. Sydney Newman had been keen to avoid the traditional man-in-a-crappy-monster-suit look. It is a false rumour that the name was chosen when Nation looked at his encyclopaedias and noticed on the spine of one volume, 'DAL–EK'.

The Dalek voices were created by two genius performers, Peter Hawkins, who was also the voice of Captain Pugwash, and David Graham, who was the voices of Parker, Brains and Gordon Tracy in *Thunderbirds*. The delivery was a sort of aggressive and staccato imperative, created by feeding the actors' wonderfully urgent performances through something that I seem to recall was called a 'wobulator', surely the most descriptive word in the world.

Doctor Who remains the longest-running science-fiction television show in the world, and the most successful science-fiction series of all time. After a production hiatus between 1989 and 2003, the programme was relaunch - ed in 2005, with the help of co-production money from the Canadian Broadcasting Corporation (CBC). The show now has a more sophisticated look and a younger doctor. A fifth series of the relaunched programme was broadcast in 2010, with the Doctor in his eleventh incarnation.

73 M*A*S*H

In 1979 the Meibion Glyndwr (the Sons of Glyndwr) began an English-cottage-burning campaign in protest at the influx of English second-homers into the Welsh countryside. During their twelve-year campaign some 200 English holiday homes went up in smoke. It was shortly after this that an English friend of mine moved to Wales with his Welsh wife. His cottage was called 'Hafod y Wennol', which means 'Swallows' Summer Dwelling'. He was advised to change it, which he thought preferable to asking his missus to burn the house down. An apparently friendly man in the village sold him a new sign which read, 'Cala Goeg', and said it meant 'Welcome Stranger', but when my friend got back to the house his wife explained that he'd bought a sign that translated as 'Dildo'.

This is just the kind of prank that Hawkeye Pierce from *M*A*S*H* would have played on that pompous character Charles Emerson Winchester III. What do you mean, you've never seen *M*A*S*H*? It is a classic of TV comedy. Here's a quick fly-by history.

The *M*A*S*H* TV series had its origins in a 1968 novel by Richard Hooker about three army doctors at the fictitious 4077th Mobile Army Surgical Hospital in Uijeongbu, South Korea. The book was based on Hooker's own experiences in the Korean War. A film followed in 1970 and Larry Gelbart was asked to adapt it for television.

The black comedy ran from 1972 until 1983, the final programme emptying streets across the US as 106 million people (almost 5 times the entire population of Australia) stayed in to watch. For a quarter of a century this remained the most-watched television episode ever.

Here are some interesting facts about *M*A*S*H*.

- Author Richard Hooker's home state was Maine, just like Hawkeye Pierce. His real name was H. Richard Hornberger and he remained a surgeon his whole working life.
- *M*A*S*H* lasted almost three times longer than the Korean War itself, which ran from 1950–53.
- Many early stories were based on the real memories of Mobile Army Surgical Hospital surgeons.
- The Vietnam War was still going on when the show began and many people saw the show's anti-war slant as a clear reference to that conflict.

- The *M*A*S*H* 4077th was based on the real 8055th.
- Creators Larry Gelbart and Gene Reynolds wanted *M*A*S*H* transmitted without a laughter track, 'Just like the actual Korean War,' said Gelbart. But CBS rejected the notion. Nonetheless, some episodes did omit the laughter track, and laughs were left off scenes in the operating theatre. The laughter track was omitted in Britain.

74 Mission: Impossible

In football a 'hat-trick' is the scoring of three goals by the same player in any one game. The term comes from cricket, a game for gentlemen with very hard balls, in which, at one time, a bowler who dismissed three batsmen with three successive deliveries was awarded a prize in the form of a hat. I'd rather have had large numbers of high denomination notes stuffed through my front door. A cricketing hat-trick is a hard thing to accomplish but they do happen – roughly once every 50 test matches – so they could best be described as improbable rather than impossible. Do you see where we're going with this?

Mission: Impossible was an American television series created, written and produced by Bruce Geller, a Yale graduate who had worked on the TV cowboy shows *Rawhide* and *Have Gun – Will Travel*. The series was first broadcast on CBS between 1966 and 1973.

The weekly programme featured the adventures of a team of secret agents, the Impossible Missions Force or IMF (not to be confused with the International Monetary Fund), and followed a trusted formula. It would begin with the well-dressed team leader Jim Phelps picking up a packet hidden somewhere public. This always contained photographs of the frequently international criminals the team were supposed to deal with, often by unmasking them or rescuing their hostages. The instructions were read to Phelps by an authoritative voice on a tape recorder which began by announcing, 'Good morning Mr Phelps,' and which always used the words, 'Your mission – should you decide to accept it . . .', as Phelps flipped through the pictures, often with his raincoat over his arm. Finally, he was warned that if his team failed in its mission, 'the Secretary will disavow any knowledge of your actions,' which reminds me of a boss I once had. The tape would then famously self-destruct, with plenty of smoke. Why someone couldn't just telephone him was never made clear.

Phelps was played after the first season by an impossibly good-looking Peter Graves (real name Peter Aurness), who was brought in to replace religiously observant actor Steven Hill, who found it impossible to combine *Mission: Impossible*'s impossible shooting schedule with the impossibly strict rules for the Jewish Sabbath. Graves had previously appeared – brilliantly – in Charles Laughton's chilling and wonderful *The Night of the Hunter* (1955).

Graves' character would pick a different team each week; they were played by a small and polished repertory company. Among the characters were Cinnamon Carter, a fashion model and actress played by Barbara Bain (real name, Millicent Fogel), who was then married to Martin Landau (see below); 'Barney' Collier, an electronics expert played by Greg Morris; Willy Armitage, a strongman played by bodybuilder Peter Lupus; Rollin Hand, a master of makeup and disguise played by Martin Landau, who had featured as a superb creepy slimeball in Hitchcock's *North By Northwest*. Landau was later replaced by 'Leonard 'Spock' Nimoy as 'The Great Paris'.

The intricately plotted shows always featured elaborate deceptions involving if not actually impossible, then highly *improbable*, imperson ations, sophisticated makeup and high-tech equipment. The whole thing was hooey of a high order and it was not uncommon to see characters who had just leapt from second-storey windows or fallen down flights of stairs stand up with never a hair out of place. Baddies would be instantly knocked out by being lightly tapped on the back of the neck, and masks made of boiled-up rubber with eyeholes cut out would instantaneously turn the wearer into an identical version of the target. Suspension of disbelief was vital for the viewer.

Mission: Impossible's hugely exciting theme was composed by

Argentinean composer Lalo Schifrin, who had also created *The Man from U.N.C.L.E.* theme as well as many films scores. It is one of a handful of TV theme tunes that has continued to live on long after the programme for which it was composed.

Mission: Impossible was an international hit and led, three decades later, to a series of blockbusting action thrillers starring Tom Cruise. When asked for his opinion of the films, Peter Graves seemed unimpressed, remarking that the original show had been a 'head game' and that the movies were a 'stunt game' – this from the man who had gone on to star in knockabout comedy *Airplane* (1980) as an incontinent, dribbling paedophile.

This page will self-destruct in five seconds.

75 'Energize!' The story of *Star Trek*

In 1964 Gene Roddenberry, who had been writing for the successful western series *Have Gun – Will Travel*, pitched an idea for a space fantasy that would parallel the adventures of the early western pioneers. He saw the show as a 'wagon train to the stars'. NBC picked up the idea and shot a pilot episode, called 'The Cage'. Of the cast of this first stab at *Star Trek*, only two would make it to the series – Leonard Nimoy and Majel Barrett, who played unnamed first officer, Number One, and happened to be the girlfriend of Gene Roddenberry. NBC executives were apparently incensed by Roddenberry's doling out a leading part to an unknown woman, whose chief qualification seemed to be that she was his girlfriend.

The pilot was rejected and a second commissioned with a new cast. This was called 'Where No Man Has Gone Before' and was the first of the famous 'voyages of the *Starship Enterprise*'. It featured William Shatner in the lead role of Captain James Kirk. Leonard Nimoy was Science Officer Spock, Canadian James Doohan played Chief Engineer Montgomery 'Scotty' Scott and George Takei was Helmsman Hikaru Sulu. NBC accepted the pilot in 1966.

Fascinating facts

- Actress Majel Barrett (Mrs Roddenberry) is the only actor to have been involved in every version of *Star Trek*, including the animated series and films.
- The show was first broadcast, in the US, on 8 September 1966. It finished its first run on 2 September 1969.
- The show's opening announcement contains the most famous split infinitive ever: 'to boldly go where no man has gone before'.
- The imaginary *Starship Enterprise* is 953.7 ft (290.7 m) long, the length of 34 London buses.
- James Doohan ('Scotty') lacked a middle finger on his right hand.
- The *Enterprise*'s 'transporter' was an economy measure that made it unnecessary for the 'ship' to 'land' on the various planets (expensive).
- Roddenberry admitted that *Star Trek* was influenced by the film *Forbidden Planet* (check it out).
- Leonard Nimoy created Spock's Vulcan neck-pinch during the episode 'The Enemy Within', when his character was supposed to hit a baddie over the head. Nimoy felt that this was out of character and substituted the less oafish pinch.
- NBC disliked the look of Spock and asked Gene Roddenberry to get rid of the 'guy with the pointy ears'. Roddenberry refused.
- The line 'Beam me up, Scotty!' was never uttered in *Star Trek*. The correct instruction was, 'Energize'.
- Roddenberry reportedly created the character of Pavel Andreievich Chekov as a Russian version of the Monkees' lead singer, Davy Jones.
- DeForest Kelley (Dr 'Bones' McCoy) was originally offered the role of Spock.
- Lieutenant Uhura's name means 'freedom' in Swahili.
- Martin Luther King Jr talked Nichelle Nichols (Uhura) out of leaving the show.
- Nimoy and Shatner were the only two actors to appear in every episode of the original series.

Batman was a 1960s American TV series based on the DC comic book character of that name. The show starred Adam West and Burt Ward as 'Dynamic Duo' Batman and Robin, two costumed heroes who fought a series of exotic baddies in a version of New York City named 'Gotham City'. The show was broadcast by ABC from 1966 to 1968 in half-hour episodes, twice a week, with a cliffhanger ending at the end of the week's first episode.

The idea for a TV *Batman* surfaced after the popular re-release in the early 1960s of two black-and-white movie serials, *Batman* (1943) and *Batman and Robin* (1949). ABC executive and *Batman* fan, Yale Udoff, suggested a series of prime-time *Batman* shows, which he foresaw as being somewhat in the style of NBC's hip, light, but dramatic *The Man from U.N.C.L.E.* ABC picked up the idea, transferring the rights ultimately to William Dozier and his Greenway Productions.

But Dozier hated comic books and decided to make the show as a comedy, full of Swinging Sixties hipness. A team of writers were instructed to inject high doses of campery, slapstick and political satire into the show's scripts, which they did. Lorenzo Semple Jr wrote a pilot and four actors were tested for the roles of Bruce 'Batman' Wayne and Boy Wonder Dick 'Robin' Grayson. Adam West and Burt Ward landed the parts. West had previously starred as Captain Q in an advert for Nesquik and Burt Ward, who had been labouring under the name Sparky Gervis, had been an estate agent.

The set-up was that clean-cut playboy Bruce Wayne lived in a gigantic mansion along with his young and equally clean-cut 'ward' Dick Grayson. This scenario immediately terrified executives who insisted on the introduction of Aunt Harriet, a character whose chief purpose was to defuse suspicions of pederasty, which might have been inferred from the prodigiously athletic older Batman's close relationship with, and physical proximity to, his handsome and somewhat naive young ward. The boys' frequent sliding down poles and wearing of silk French knickers outside ridiculously figure-hugging tights did nothing to help lessen the homosexual flavour. And just what was it that Batman carried in that 'utility belt'? The final character in this unusual ménage was an English butler, Alfred, whose place on the sexual spectrum was hard to guess.

The scripts coruscated with hilarious dialogue such as:

ROBIN: Batman, maybe I should stay home tonight. Homework, you know.

BATMAN: I think you should acquire a taste for opera, Robin, as one does for poetry and olives.

DICK: Bruce, let me ride Waynebow. I'm light enough.

BRUCE: No, Dick, I couldn't allow my own ward to ride my thoroughbred. People might think it was funny.

BATMAN: Drop that golden pussy Robin – it may be radioactive.

One of the most enjoyable aspects of the show's witty scripts was the recruitment of 'serious' performers to play the villains. Broadway Shakespearean actor Burgess Meredith played the Penguin; movie 'Latin Lover' Cesar Romero played the Joker; and three actors played Mr Freeze: George Sanders (sometime husband of Zsa Zsa Gabor and voice of Shere Khan in Disney's *The Jungle Book*), bad-tempered film director Otto Preminger and *The Good, the Bad and the Ugly* actor Eli Wallach.

Another sought-after part was the 'Batclimb Cameo' in which the 'Caped Crusaders' were filmed sideways climbing what, even on transmission, were obviously horizontal 'buildings'. Halfway up, a 'window' would open and a head emerge for a brief chat. Some of the performers who landed these enviable roles were Edward G. Robinson, Sammy Davis Jr, Jerry Lewis and Bruce Lee.

The programme's fantastically famous theme tune was written by jazz trumpeter and composer Neal Hefti, who also wrote the theme for *The Odd Couple*. The tune is an apparently simple but subtly orchestrated three-chord twelve-bar blues, with flatulent horns and an eight-voice chorus doing the 'Batmans'. The words are easy to learn as they consist entirely of the word 'Batman!' chanted ten times, together with a final 'Da da na na na na na na na na naaaaa: Batman!' Try it.

Cinema

77 Great war films

General Patton once said, 'The object of war is not to die for your country but to make the other bastard die for his.' You can see his point. While people always die in wars, nobody real ever died in a war film, which is partly why they are such great fun. Here are a few really good ones plucked randomly from the kitbag.

- *The Great Escape*: this 1963 American film is about a mass escape by Allied prisoners of war from tunnels dug below a German POW camp. It is based on the novel by Paul Brickhill about an actual escape from Stalag Luft III during the Second World War. The film, directed by John Sturges, stars Richard Attenborough, Steve McQueen, James Garner, Donald Pleasance and many other well-known actors. The famous motorcycle stunts were done by Steve McQueen himself, who also doubled some of the German parts in the bike chase. He was protected from being scratched to bits in the final crash into a barbed wire border fence by the simple expedient of having the barbs made of snipped-off rubber bands tied around ordinary wire. Elmer Bernstein's highly whistleable theme tune is as famous as the film itself. No man's Christmas is complete without a showing of this movie, which has conflict, drama and thrills from the outset.
- *The Caine Mutiny*: this lesser-known 1954 American film is based on a novel by Herman Wouk and was directed by blacklist victim Edward Dmytryk. The plot concerns the mutiny on board a US Navy minesweeper, the USS *Caine*, during the Second World War and the

consequent court-martial of two of its officers. It stars an ageing Humphrey Bogart giving the performance of a lifetime as Lieutenant Commander Captain Philip Francis Queeg, an inflexible, tough and haunted man who, it turns out, is suffering from a serious mental illness. The taut courtroom scenes in which Bogart changes from confident authority figure to frank nutcase are made all the more chilling by his obsessive jiggling of two large ball bearings whenever he is under stress. A young unknown actor called Maurice Micklewhite was one day in Leicester Square trying to come up with a stage name in a hurry. Looking around he saw signs for *The Caine Mutiny* at the Odeon Cinema and chose the name Michael Caine there and then. He chose wisely – he could so easily have ended up as 'Michael Mutiny' or, if he had looked over at the Empire cinema, 'Michael One Hundred and One Dalmatians'.

- *The Bridge on the River Kwai*: this is a 1957 film by David Lean, based on a novel by French writer Pierre Boulle. The film concerns the building by Allied POWs of the Burma-Rangoon 'Death' Railway in 1942–3. It stars Alec Guinness, Jack Hawkins, William Holden and Sessue Hayakawa, as the Japanese camp commandant. The film is fictitious in nearly all its details. In fact, the art director was so unhappy with the look of the real bridge that he designed a new, more dramatic one for the movie. David Lean, who was notoriously unpleasant to work for, finished one scene with British cast members and announced, 'Now you can all fuck off and go home, you English actors. Thank God I'm starting work tomorrow with an American actor.' This is known as motivational speaking. During the war, British soldiers had given the film's famous 'Colonel Bogey March' rude words that referred to Hitler's alleged monorchism (look it up, it's a good word). Lean used the tune knowing that the audience would recognize it as a symbol of defiant British contumacy (that's a good one, too).

- *The Dam Busters*: this marvellous 1955 British war film directed by Michael Anderson is based on the true story of the RAF's 617

Squadron and the dropping of the 'bouncing bomb' on the Ruhr dams in Germany. It stars Michael Redgrave as inventor Barnes Wallis and Richard Todd as Wing Commander Guy Gibson. Eric Coates' 'The Dam Busters March' has become one of Britain's unofficial national anthems. In 2008 Peter Jackson began work on a remake and much tooth-sucking was being done over the problem of the unfortunate name of Gibson's dog – 'Nigger'.

- *Where Eagles Dare*: this 1968 action-adventure spy film stars Richard Burton, Clint Eastwood and Mary Ure, and was directed by Brian G. Hutton. It was based on the book by Alistair MacLean who wrote the screenplay at the same time. Yakima Canutt, the legendary Hollywood stuntman, worked on the action scenes alongside British stuntman Alf Joint, best known for a high dive from a cliff in a famous TV commercial for chocolates. Ron Goodwin, who, four years later, would write the score for Hitchcock's *Frenzy* (1972), wrote the music. The plot is set during the Second World War, when US Army Brigadier General George Carnaby, who is planning the Normandy invasion, is shot down and taken to Schloss Adler (Castle of the Eagles) for interrogation. A team of commandos must now parachute into the castle and rescue General Carnaby before the Germans can get the information they need.

- *A Bridge Too Far*: a 1977 American film based on the book by Cornelius Ryan and directed by Richard Attenborough, it concerns the failed Operation Market Garden during the Second World War, when the Allies tried to seize a number of bridges from behind the German lines. The fantastic cast included Dirk Bogarde, James Caan, Michael Caine, Sean Connery, Denholm Elliott, Elliott Gould, Edward Fox, Gene Hackman, Anthony Hopkins, Laurence Olivier and several other A-list actors. The music was by John Addison, who had written the music for Hitchcock's *Torn Curtain* (1966). Alf Joint was again performing the stunts. Busy fellow.

- *The Way to the Stars*: the screenplay to this 1945 film was written by Terence Rattigan, and stars Michael Redgrave and John Mills. I mention it only because it was directed by Anthony Asquith, son of British Prime Minister H.H. Asquith. Unlike David Lean, Asquith was an extremely charming and gentle man, famous for his good manners. One evening, as he was walking across a dark and empty sound stage, an electrician who was coiling a cable in the shadows saw him trip over a stage weight and say, 'Oh, I *do* beg your pardon.' They don't make 'em like that anymore.

78 The best and worst movie dialogue

There used to be a sign on a platform at Penrith railway station in Cumbria that read, 'Keep back from the platform edge or you may get sucked off.' You knew what they meant but they didn't quite have what it took in the words department. It's the same with film dialogue: there's an art to it. Here's a collection of the good, the bad and the ugly.

Bad

- *Plan 9 from Outer Space* (1959): 'And remember my friends, future events such as these will affect you, in the future'; 'One thing's sure: Inspector Clay's dead – murdered. And somebody's responsible'; 'This is the most fantastic story I've ever heard.' 'And every word of it's true too.' 'That's the fantastic part of it'; 'Modern women!' 'Yeah, they've been that way all down through the ages.'
- *The Postman* (1997): 'You're a godsend – a saviour.' 'No, I'm a postman.'
- *Mad Max* (1979): 'When I was a kid, me and my pop used to go for long walks; I remember staring down at his shoes. They were special shoes. Brown. And he always kept 'em real shiny.'
- *Goldfinger* (1964): 'At least they won't be using heroin-flavoured bananas to finance revolutions.'
- *Flash Gordon* (1986): 'I love you, Flash, but we only have fourteen hours to save the Earth.'
- *X-Men* (2000): 'You know what happens when a toad gets struck by

lightning? The same thing that happens to everything else.'

- *Troll 2* (1990): 'They're eating her . . . and then they're going to eat me. Oh my Gooooooooooooooooooooooooooooooooooooood!'

Good

- *Duck Soup* (1933): 'Go, and never darken my towels again.'
- *Casablanca* (1942): 'Round up the usual suspects.'
- *Dr. Strangelove* (1964): 'Gentlemen, you can't fight in here. This is the War Room.'
- *Gone with the Wind* (1939): 'Frankly, my dear, I don't give a damn.'
- *Carry On Cleo* (1964): 'Infamy, infamy, they've all got it in for me.'
- *Jaws* (1975): 'You're gonna need a bigger boat.'
- *Citizen Kane* (1941): 'Rosebud.'
- *The Graduate* (1967): 'I just wanna say one word to you – just one word.' 'Yes Sir.' 'Are you listening?' 'Yes I am.' 'Plastics.'
- *Airplane* (1980): 'Surely you can't be serious.' 'I am serious. And don't call me Shirley.'
- *When Harry Met Sally* (1989): 'I'll have what she's having.'

79 Coming in Hindi: Bollywood explained

Bollywood is the name of the Mumbai-based, Hindi-language part of the Indian film industry, the largest producer of films in India and one of the largest film production centres in the world. The word is a conflation of Bombay (now Mumbai) and Hollywood, and resembles the 1932 portmanteau word 'Tollywood', itself a fusion of Tollygunge – a town in West Bengal, the centre of Indian cinema at the time – and Hollywood.

Your typical Bollywood film today is a brightly coloured escapist musical with a large helping of shamelessly commercial cheese. Many Bollywood films are released in the UK, catering to the vibrant British 'bolly' fan base, which is the largest outside India. Plots tend to be formulaic melodramas featuring archetypal characters from central casting. These include separated twins, tarts with hearts, ill-fated gorgeous young lovers, corrupt politicians, Indian Mafia types and wily good-for-nothings, who experience classical Greek-style come-uppances, dramatic hamartia, romance, family turmoil, violence, thrills and spills, and unfeasible coincidences in a three-hour-long extravagantly spicy 'masala' – with intermission.

Bollywood music is what might be called 'bouncy Indian-global' with a noticeable Western influence. The same influence is apparent also in costume, sets, makeup and lighting. Songs are generally pre-recorded by professional singers and mimed by the actors. Dialogue and effects are usually post-recorded entirely in the studio, with the actors, many of whom become huge international stars, dubbing their lines – not always in perfect synchronicity – while watching their performance on screen.

Few Bollywood films fail to include at least one big song-and-dance or so-called 'item' number, in which a fruity babe or 'item girl' sings a real foot-tapper while displaying her corporeal attractions. The item girl commonly used to be depicted as a high-class tart, dancing in cabaret or for her wealthy 'client'. God knows what sort of feminist analysis might be done of all this at one of those concrete universities. More usually these days, the item number is shoehorned in as a disco scene or celebration dance, and is often entirely uncontaminated by relevance or connection to the film's characters or plot.

So influential has Bollywood now become that in 2010, just before MGM went tits up and the movie was shelved, the producers of the 23rd James Bond film were scouting locations in India and lining up various gorgeous Bollywood actresses for the role of the latest Bond babe.

Will it be popcorn or naan bread with that?

80 Attack of the 50-foot B-movie

B-movies are low budget films, often of such dire quality that they drop out of the B-movie section altogether, sometimes right into the Z-movie category. Some are so bad they are good and become cults, while others are good films but without a proper budget. This type is the rarest but includes such titles as *Kiss Me Deadly* (1955) and the classic *Cat People* (1942). *Creature from the Black Lagoon* (1954), which features the 'man-beast from the dawn of time' (man in suit) who snatches the gorgeous Julia Adams and swims away with her – lucky swine – looks like a B-movie but was actually a 3D film with a proper budget. So you have to be careful with your classifications. Here are a few more, starting with the low-budget but not bad *Attack of the 50 ft Woman* and moving rapidly downwards.

- *Attack of the 50 ft Woman* (1958): Nancy Archer, 'once a normal voluptuously beautiful woman', is propelled into a 'nightmare of horror' when she meets an enormous alien with a giant, human-looking hand with fur on its fingers. This makes her grow into an 'incredibly huge' and frankly sultry babe, whose 'incredible desires for love and vengeance' cause her to become a big problem for her unfaithful husband and his bit on the side. The trailer warns the viewer to expect 'shock'. Yes, shocking model-making.
- *Glen or Glenda* (1953): this was the first of a number of seriously bad B-movies made by Ed Wood, who was posthumously given a Golden Turkey Award for Worst Director of All Time. His films were bad in every way, with out-of-place stock footage forced into incomprehensible plots with crazy casting and weird dialogue. *Glen or Glenda* is a sort of transvestite documentary, starring Wood himself in the titular role. Wood, a heterosexual transvestite himself, remarked, 'If you want to know me, see *Glen or Glenda*. That's me, that's my story, no question.'
- *Reefer Madness* (1936): originally financed by a church group and called *Tell Your Children*, the film began as a finger-wagging – literally at one point – warning against the 'monstrous extravagances' that occur when a few high-school students try some marijuana. These include suicide, rape and 'incurable insanity'. It starts very uncinematically with a two-minute hand-lettered rolling caption, which consists of a laughable diatribe on 'the frightful toll of the new drug menace which is

destroying the youth of America in alarmingly-increasing numbers'. That 'alarmingly-increasing' gives you an idea of the quality of the script. This morality tale was sold on and re-cut as an exploitation film. It's dire in both forms. I hope you get the chance to see it.

- *Plan 9 from Outer Space* (1959): Ed Wood described his *Plan 9 from Outer Space* as 'my pride and joy' but it's bad. Terrible cheap sets, mind-blowingly awful scripts and wooden acting, which is either mahogany or ebony judging by its density, mark this out as a contender for worst-ever. At one point a man in a shirt with a space-type logo – he may be an alien, it's hard to tell – says, 'The rays of sunlight are minute particles.' Nope, they are not particles, mate, they are rays. The film features the final appearance of Béla Lugosi in the form of test footage shot before his death in 1956. Owing to the absence of Lugosi at the time he was making the film, Wood asked his wife's bald chiropractor to double for him. Lugosi had always had plenty of hair and the two men were of noticeably different heights and builds. Wood's answer: 'Hold the cape in front of your face.' It doesn't work.

- *They Saved Hitler's Brain* (1966): directed by David Bradley and written by Steve Bennett and Peter Miles, this film was lengthened with extra footage shot by UCLA students. The problem was that the first half was filmed in 1968 and the characters look of their time. They wear no ties, have big moustaches, wide lapels and long hair, and talk in a much less formal way than in the second half, which was filmed first, in 1961. This section looks like a 1950s film noir, with different haircuts, different lighting, pre-war suits and uptight forelock-tugging actors. The quality of the film stock is also quite different, and new unannounced characters suddenly appear. Some intercutting of scenes that had been filmed seven years apart was tried. Unconvincingly. The acting is shocking in both halves. Forget the plot, that's the least of your worries.

- *The Beast of Yucca Flats* (1961): directed without sound by Coleman Francis, a narration was added later. The half-nude necrophilic prologue is unrelated in every way to the remainder of the film.

- *The Creeping Terror* (1964): directed by Arthur J. Nelson. The special effects in this film leave much to be desired, even if you squint through your lashes. Library shots of a rocket launch are played backwards in a penny-pinching attempt to depict the landing of an alien spacecraft. The Creeping Terror of the title is played by several characters shuffling around together, wearing carpets. The occasional glimpse of their trainers spoils the effect somewhat. Unhappily, dialogue reels were lost and although there is some half-hearted dubbing of speech here and there, most of the time a narrator is forced to explain what the actors are silently mouthing. You can't sink much lower than that.

- *Santa Claus Conquers the Martians* (1964): because Martian children have never met Santa and only see him on television, their parents decide to kidnap him. The film stars an unlucky John Call as Santa Claus and characters include Kimar (King Martian), Momar (Mom Martian) and their children Girmar (Girl Martian) and Bomar (Boy Martian). Your niece could come up with better names for her school play. They wear grey Martian suits with helmets and wield a 'tickle ray' to make each other laugh. The plot is ridiculous, but the sets and lighting aren't too bad. And it is in colour. I'm trying to be nice.

- *Monster A Go-Go* (1965): recently described as a 'surreal anti-masterpiece', *Monster A Go-Go* often wins first place for worst ever film. It was a resuscitation of the unfinished *Terror at Halfday* by Bill Rebane, filled out with some extra material by Herschell Gordon Lewis several years later. He was unable to use all of the original cast owing to the passage of time so almost half the characters disappear without explanation halfway through the film. One of the original actors who was able to appear had changed so dramatically that he was forced to play his own brother. Publicity featured the line, 'A genuine ten-foot tall monster to give you the whim-whams . . . When you walk out you'll wonder what you've seen.' In reality, the disjointed plot finishes with the narrator revealing the anticlimactic news that 'there was no monster'. Can I have my money back please?

81 The Oscars that went wrong

As the 46th Academy Awards ceremony was drawing to its close on 2 April 1974, a moustachioed streaker – thirty-three-year-old Robert Opel – suddenly ran on to the stage behind the poised and urbane David Niven, who was about to introduce Elizabeth Taylor. A huge laugh alerted Niven that something was up and, consummate professional and man of the world that he was, he didn't miss a beat. Dipping into his deep well of apposite witticisms he pulled out the following: 'Well, ladies and gentlemen, that was almost bound to happen. But isn't it fascinating to think that probably the only laugh that man will ever get in his life is by stripping off and showing his shortcomings.' Usually when things go wrong at the Oscars, it isn't this interesting. Generally, it's to do with the wrong films or actors winning the prizes, so here's a list of some 'Best Picture' Oscars that went a bit wrong.

1930–31	Not nominated: *City Lights*, *Frankenstein* Best Picture winner: *Cimarron*
1932–3	Not nominated: *King Kong* Best Picture winner: *Cavalcade*
1936	Not nominated: *Modern Times* Best Picture winner: *The Great Ziegfeld*
1937	Not nominated: *Snow White and the Seven Dwarfs* Best Picture winner: *The Life of Emile Zola*
1941 (a notorious year)	Best Picture nominees included: *Citizen Kane*, *The Maltese Falcon*, *Suspicion* Best Picture winner: *How Green Was My Valley*
1944	Not nominated: *Laura*, *Meet Me in St Louis* Best Picture winner: *Going My Way*

1955	Not nominated: *The Night of the Hunter*, *The*
(another notorious year)	*Blackboard Jungle*, *East of Eden*, *Kiss Me Deadly*, *Rebel Without a Cause*, *Bad Day at Black Rock*, *Oklahoma!*, *To Catch a Thief* (all good films, some extremely good, and one, *The Night of the Hunter*, a masterpiece)
	Best Picture winner: *Marty* (good, but not the best by any means)
1958	Not nominated: *Vertigo*, *Touch of Evil*, *South Pacific*
	Best Picture winner: *Gigi* (charming musical, but *Vertigo* and *Touch of Evil* were both much better)
1968	Not nominated: *2001: A Space Odyssey*, *Rosemary's Baby*
	Best Picture winner: *Oliver!*

We'll stop there because the Golden Age was over. I mean, look at 1941 and 1955. You wouldn't get as many great films in one year nowadays. It isn't just the Best Picture award that goes to the wrong film, either. Alfred Hitchcock never won a Best Director Oscar, which is insane. But there again, look at who wins the Turner Prize.

RELIGION
FOR THE
PRACTICAL MAN

Christianity Explored

82 Bananas as proof of God's existence

Those who try to debunk intelligent design need only look at what experts are calling the 'atheists' nightmare': the humble banana. I met a man at a party who explained it to me. He said that, just as drinks companies have designed their cans to be perfect for humans to drink from, so God has designed the banana as the perfect human food. Here is the evidence, in ten crystal-clear points, which are all pretty obvious.

1 The ridges down a banana perfectly correspond to the grooves in the human hand, with three ridges on the far side and three grooves on the fingers. There are two ridges on the nearside, too, with two corresponding grooves on the thumb side of the hand. It's a perfect fit.

2 God has made the banana with a non-slip surface.

3 The banana's skin has been designed to tell you whether it's ready to eat: green means too early, yellow is just right and black too late. Natural traffic lights.

4 At the top of a banana the maker has attached a convenient tab for opening it, just like a drinks can. But it's better than a drinks can because it won't spray in your face when you open it.

5 The banana's container, the skin, is biodegradable.

6 It is designed ready to tear conveniently along its ridges, with no hassle.

7 When peeled, its skin is designed to hang naturally over the fist, out of the way.

8 The banana has a mouth-size rounded point at the top, for ease of entry. The perfect shape.

9　As a bonus, the designer has made the fruit curve towards the face to make the process of eating it as easy as possible.

10　The banana is soft and sweet, with no nasty seeds – ideal for eating, even if you are a baby or a toothless old man.

As a rebuttal of atheistic scepticism the banana argument looks perfect. But, hang on, there are a few problems. Let's take the points one at a time.

1　The banana's ridges only fit the hand because we *say* they fit the hand. It makes no sense to talk about the 'far side' and a 'nearside' of a banana, nor a 'top' and 'bottom'. In any case, the banana fits a chimpanzee's hand – or foot – as well as that of a human.

2　The banana's skin does have a sort-of non-slip quality but so does a stick and you can't eat that. Furthermore, eels don't and you can eat them.

3　While it's true that you know a banana will be sweet and soft when it's yellow there's no guarantee that a ripe-looking melon or strawberry will be ready to eat. Half the melons and strawberries I try aren't, and I'm assuming God was responsible for them, too.

4　That tab at the top is not at the top because the banana doesn't have a top. And it's not a tab.

5　The banana skin is certainly biodegradable, but so are brown paper bags from the greengrocer.

6　OK, it tears conveniently along its ridges, but if this is supposed to show intelligent design all I can say is coconuts! Try getting one of those open. They must be an example of *unintelligent* design, along with pineapples.

7　Yes, the skin hangs down nicely but not if you eat it in bed. And what about potato peel? That's not very user-friendly.

8　Undoubtedly a banana is the ideal shape and size for the human mouth but so is the deathcap mushroom. Moreover, the banana will also fit up your bum (I'm guessing).

9   Curved towards the face? Only if you hold it that way. Turn it round
    and it curves away from the face.

10 Soft and sweet, with no nasty seeds? I'm afraid this is where the whole
    argument unravels. Wild, natural, 'real' bananas are nothing like the
    slim, cultivated, yellow things you are used to. They have tough, leathery,
    nobbly blue-green skins and are more squat in shape: you can't hold or
    peel them like a 'dessert' banana. Inside is an unappetizing, inedible
    flesh packed full of hard tooth-like seeds. The nice easy-peel soft, sweet,
    yellow banana is a human-made thing, the result of people's horticulture
    and deliberate hybridization over thousands of years. It's intelligent
    design all right – intelligent *human* design.

When I raised these points with the man at the party, he said, 'Ah yes, but
God gave us the knowledge and ability to change the banana, to turn it
into the perfect food.' I mean, *honestly*. There's one born every minute.

83 Great bits from *The Bible*

In 1611 *The Bible* was translated into English in an edition which became
known as the 'Authorised' or 'King James Version'. The translators were
a team of Jacobean scholars who wrote their translation in a language
'understanded of the people' that remains crystal clear today. This book
has some superb stuff in it, though there are many strange passages and
a good deal of sex and violence, mostly, but not all, in the Old Testament.
Here are a few of the weirder and ruder bits.

Testicles

In the following excerpt 'Put your hand under my thigh' means 'Put your
hand under my testicles', which is the way solemn oaths were once taken.
When your lawyer next uses the words 'testament' and 'testify' remember
that he or she is using words with the same root as 'testicle'. Just so long
as you are not asked to put your hand there . . .

Genesis 47:29: 'And the time drew nigh that Israel must die: and he called his son Joseph, and said unto him, If now I have found grace in thy sight, put, I pray thee, thy hand under my thigh, and deal kindly and truly with me; bury me not, I pray thee, in Egypt'.

Excommunication of the emasculated

Deuteronomy 23:1: 'He that is wounded in the stones [testicles], or hath his privy member cut off, shall not enter into the congregation of the LORD'.

Circumcision and foreskins

The authors of *The Bible* seem to have had an unhealthy preoccupation with circumcision and foreskins. According to infidels.org, the words 'circumcise', 'circumcised', 'circumcising', 'circumcision', 'uncircumcised', 'uncircumcision', 'foreskin' and 'foreskins' appear 157 times in the *King James Bible*, which ought to be enough for anyone. Here are a random couple.

Romans 2:25–7: 'For circumcision verily profiteth, if thou keep the law: but if thou be a breaker of the law, thy circumcision is made uncircumcision. Therefore if the uncircumcision keep the righteousness of the law, shall not his uncircumcision be counted for circumcision? And shall not uncircumcision which is by nature, if it fulfil the law, judge thee, who by the letter and circumcision dost transgress the law?'

1 Samuel 18:25–7: 'And Saul said, Thus shall ye say to David, The king desireth not any dowry, but an hundred foreskins of the Philistines, to be avenged of the king's enemies. But Saul thought to make David fall by the hand of the Philistines. And when his servants told David these words, it pleased David well to be the king's son in law: and the days were not expired. Wherefore David arose and went, he and his men, and slew of the Philistines two hundred men; and David brought their foreskins, and they gave them in full tale to the king, that he might be the king's son in law. And Saul gave him Michal his daughter to wife.'

Coitus interruptus

After God kills Onan's brother Er, Onan is told to impregnate Er's widow, so that his offspring will become Er's heirs (try saying that after a bottle of White Lightning). Onan 'spills his seed' on the ground and God punishes him, rather unforgivingly, you might think.

Genesis 38:8–10: 'And Judah said unto Onan, Go in unto thy brother's wife, and marry her, and raise up seed to thy brother. And Onan knew that the seed should not be his; and it came to pass, when he went in unto his brother's wife, that he spilled it on the ground, lest that he should give seed to his brother. And the thing which he did displeased the LORD: wherefore he slew him also.'

Sewing plants and clothes

Leviticus, written by Moses, is the third book of the Old Testament and it is full of 'abominations', mainly sexual and dietary prohibitions, some of which seem a bit odd today. I'm not sure I can wear my new suit, or grow my peas next to my beans, based on this bit.

Leviticus 19:19: 'Ye shall keep my statutes. Thou shalt not let thy cattle gender with a diverse kind: thou shalt not sow thy field with mingled seed: neither shall a garment mingled of linen and woollen come upon thee.'

Death as punishment for Sunday working

Leviticus 35:2: 'Six days shall work be done, but on the seventh day there shall be to you an holy day, a sabbath of rest to the LORD: whosoever doeth work therein shall be put to death.'

Enforced nudity as punishment

Nahum 3:5–6: 'Behold, I am against thee, saith the LORD of hosts; and I will discover thy skirts upon thy face, and I will shew the nations thy nakedness, and the kingdoms thy shame. And I will cast abominable filth upon thee, and make thee vile, and will set thee as a gazingstock.'

Infanticide as punishment for bad manners

Exodus 21:17: 'And he that curseth his father, or his mother, shall surely be put to death': few boys would reach manhood these days.

Cannibalism

2 Kings 6:29: 'So we boiled my son, and did eat him: and I said unto her on the next day, Give thy son, that we may eat him: and she hath hid her son.'

Coprophagia and urophagia

2 Kings 18:27: 'But Rabshakeh said unto them, Hath my master sent me to thy master, and to thee, to speak these words? hath he not sent me to the men which sit on the wall, that they may eat their own dung, and drink their own piss with you?'

'Pissing'

The phrase 'him that pisseth against the wall', appears repeatedly in *The Bible* and means something like 'any mother's son'. Still, I bet the vicar wouldn't like it.

1 Samuel 25:22: 'So and more also do God unto the enemies of David, if I leave of all that pertain to him by the morning light any that pisseth against the wall.'

Contamination of food with human excreta

Ezekiel 4:10–13: 'And thy meat which thou shalt eat shall be by weight, twenty shekels a day: from time to time shalt thou eat it. Thou shalt drink also water by measure, the sixth part of an hin: from time to time shalt thou drink. And thou shalt eat it as barley cakes, and thou shalt bake it with dung that cometh out of man, in their sight. And the LORD said, Even thus shall the children of Israel eat their defiled bread among the Gentiles, whither I will drive them.'

Titillation

Proverbs 5:19: 'Let her be as the loving hind and pleasant roe; let her breasts satisfy thee at all times; and be thou ravished always with her love.'

Whores

Ezekiel 23:8–11: 'Neither left she her whoredoms brought from Egypt: for in her youth they lay with her, and they bruised the breasts of her virginity, and poured their whoredom upon her. Wherefore I have delivered her into the hand of her lovers, into the hand of the Assyrians, upon whom she doted. These discovered her nakedness: they took her sons and her daughters, and slew her with the sword: and she became famous among women; for they had executed judgment upon her. And when her sister Aholibah saw this, she was more corrupt in her inordinate love than she, and in her whoredoms more than her sister in her whoredoms.'

Whores and sodomites

Deuteronomy 23:16–17: 'There shall be no whore of the daughters of Israel, nor a sodomite of the sons of Israel.'

This book should be kept on the top shelf.

84 Those you may not marry, from the *Book of Common Prayer*

I remember a friend telling me that when she was a court reporter one exchange stuck in her mind. It went like this:

> **PROSECUTION:** 'What is your sister-in-law's name?'
> **WITNESS:** 'Jeffers.'
> **PROSECUTION:** 'What is her *first* name?'
> **WITNESS:** 'I can't remember.'
> **PROSECUTION:** 'She's been your sister-in-law for seven years, and you can't remember her first name?'

WITNESS: 'No. I'm too nervous. They're all looking at me. [*Rising and pointing to her sister-in-law*] Jean, for God's sake, tell them your name.'

You feel for that witness because it can be hard these days to keep track of exactly who is and who isn't a consanguineous (blood) relation, especially in large families or where parents with children have divorced, remarried and had more children by another spouse. It's a good job, in this maelstrom of interrelationships, that the Church of England keeps a list of exactly who you may and may not marry. It's reproduced for your entertainment and approval and comes from the 1662 *Book of Common Prayer*.

A table of kindred and affinity wherein whosoever are related are forbidden by the Church of England to marry together

A man may not marry his	*A woman may not marry with her*
mother	father
daughter	son
adopted daughter	adopted son
father's mother	father's father
mother's mother	mother's father
son's daughter	son's son
daughter's daughter	daughter's son
sister	brother
wife's mother	husband's father
wife's daughter	husband's son
father's wife	mother's husband
son's wife	daughter's husband
father's father's wife	father's mother's husband
mother's father's wife	mother's mother's husband
wife's father's mother	husband's father's father
wife's mother's mother	husband's mother's father

A man may not marry his	*A woman may not marry with her*
wife's daughter's daughter	husband's son's son
wife's son's daughter	husband's daughter's son
son's son's wife	son's daughter's husband
daughter's son's wife	daughter's daughter's husband
father's sister	father's brother
mother's sister	mother's brother
brother's daughter	brother's son
sister's daughter	sister's son

In this Table the term 'brother' includes a brother of the half-blood, and the term 'sister' includes a sister of the half-blood.

85 Guess the age of the church: English churches in a nutshell

When I visit an English town I don't know I like to get away from the screaming shoppers by going into an old church. I'm not sure about you, but I'm a bit of an ignoramus when it comes to working out when these churches were built so I thought I'd come up with a quick guide to guessing the age of a church. Of course, if you're not bothered you could just go into the local pub and guess the age of the beer.

In 1812, Thomas Rickman wrote a book called *Attempt to Discriminate the Style of Architecture in England* and, though styles tend to overlap a bit, his system is a better way of lumping churches together than 'Big Grey Ones With Funny Windows', 'Small Red Brick Ones', 'Ones With Spires', etc. Until well into the twentieth century most English churches were built in one of his styles, which are:

1 **Norman:** Norman Conquest to late twelfth century
2 **Early English Gothic:** Late twelfth century to late thirteenth century
3 **Decorated Gothic:** Late thirteenth century to late fourteenth century
4 **Perpendicular Gothic:** Late fourteenth century to Classical revival of English Renaissance

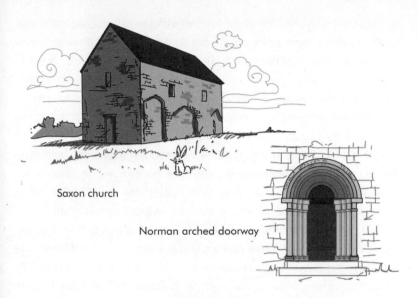

Saxon church

Norman arched doorway

Although he didn't put them on his list, a few Saxon churches also survive in England, built any time between about 410 and the Norman Conquest. St Peter-on-the-Wall in Bradwell-on-Sea is one of the best of these 'barns'. The village is better known nowadays for the Bradwell nuclear power station – a more hideous, unchurchlike building than which it would be hard to imagine.

After the Norman Conquest, Norman churches became the rule. These are massive stone structures with thick, weight-bearing walls and a sometimes rather rough-hewn look, but with spacious, light-filled interiors. Sometimes called Romanesque, these churches, with their characteristic semicircular Norman arches, have small openings for doors and windows to reduce the stress on the walls. Durham Cathedral is an example of a Norman church. By the way, a cathedral is a church – of any size – where a bishop has his seat, quite literally. '*Cathedra*' is the Latin word for 'chair'.

Where was I?

The Gothic style that followed on from Norman is, again, French, but is called Early English just to confuse you. Taller buildings with thinner walls were possible because of lighter ceilings. The walls of Early English churches are supported by buttresses, including so-called flying buttresses on the outside. Doors and windows are bigger than in Norman churches because the buildings can take it. Complex figurative carvings begin to appear alongside the weird mythological beasts and abstract architectural features of the Norman period. Noticeably, the round Norman arch is superseded by the pointed Gothic arch, an idea very likely nicked from the Holy Land by English masons. This Muslim arch is stronger and more flexible than its Christian cousin, allowing a wider span. Skinny, lance-like, 'lancet' windows (Muslim again) can now be grouped to provide big expanses of glass and, thus, more light. Indeed, the Early English style, spare and simple in character, is sometimes called 'Lancet Gothic'.

By the late thirteenth century, you get the Decorated Gothic style, so-called not because it looks fancier, but because of a development in window structure. Bigger windows with internal lancets divided by slender stone mullions and headed by geometrically curving tracery become the thing, and in-your-face circular rose windows begin to appear. Lighter and more complex ribbing for roof vaulting allows higher spaces than before, and walls are even thinner, and columns more

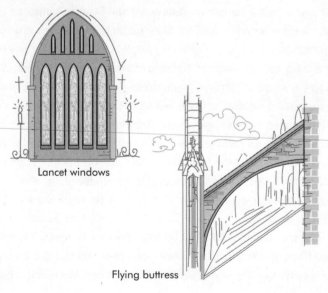

Lancet windows

Flying buttress

slender. Decorated Gothic is a sort of 'Weightwatchers Gothic'. Wells Cathedral is a superb example of the style.

Perpendicular Gothic style gets its name from the emphasis on vertical lines. This final development towards what would become the English Renaissance style is even more of the same, only higher, wider and lighter. Roofs, once steeply pitched for mechanical reasons, become flatter and are often decorated with carved wooden angels or Disney characters. *No, not Disney characters – what am I saying?* When new, the huge windows that increasingly occupied the wall space were full of stained glass. This was before the iconoclasts arrived with their hammers (see below). There is during this period an explosion of dramatic fan vaulting, where intricate ribbed fans spread the roof's load, making supporting pillars entirely redundant. In King's College Chapel, Cambridge, the fan vaulting is so magnificent it makes you laugh.

With the reign of Henry VIII this architectural feast came to an uncer - emonious stop, and with the accession of Edward VI (1547) destruction reigned down on the internal decoration of churches. Glass and font covers were broken, stone altars obliterated and wall paintings whitewashed. I was at school with some people who would have enjoyed doing that.

The Renaissance period, which followed the Gothic, coincided very roughly with the reign of Queen Elizabeth I (1558–1603), when much new building was secular rather than religious. It led to the English Classical style, from about 1660 up to the Industrial Revolution. St Martin-in-the-Fields, designed by James Gibbs in 1721, is a typically Classical church, with columns, a square footprint and the general feeling of being back in Ancient Greece. The London churches built after the Great Fire by such notables as Nicholas Hawksmoor and Christopher Wren are other fine examples. After Wren and Hawksmoor new Classical and, especially, Classical Baroque churches began to spring up across England.

Finally, before the advent of twentieth-century churches, many of which are less than lovely, though easy to identify, there was a burst of nineteenth-century architectural enthusiasm, with the building of many Victorian parish churches across England. A lot of these are so accurate

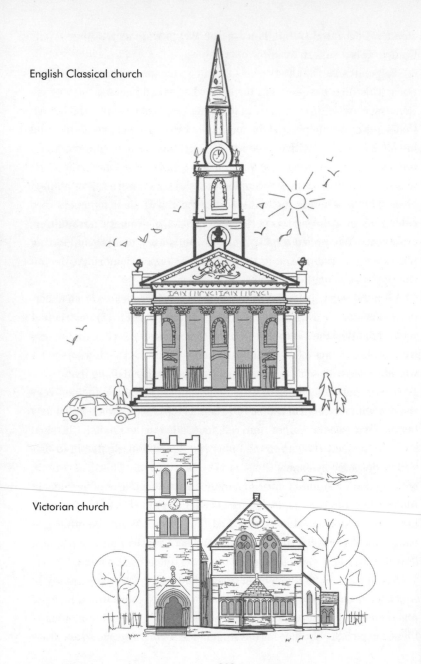

English Classical church

Victorian church

216

a recreation of the Gothic style that they are hard to spot as 'modern'. If in doubt ask the verger or something; I've got other things to think about.

86 The big monkey fight

On Saturday, 30 June 1860, seven months after the publication of Charles Darwin's *On the Origin of Species*, a group of prominent British scientists gathered at the Oxford University Museum of Natural History to join in what Alfred Newton, Professor of Comparative Anatomy at Cambridge University, called 'another hot Darwinian debate' on the subject of evolution. Speakers included Darwin's friend and champion of evolution, Thomas Henry Huxley, and the Bishop of Oxford, Samuel Wilberforce, a man Benjamin Disraeli described as 'unctuous, oleaginous, saponaceous'. 'Soapy Sam', as he came to be known, was nevertheless an outstanding, persuasive and practised public speaker who was expected to give one of his excoriating rebuttals of the contested theory of evolution, which had split the scientific community down the middle. Huxley, by contrast, was an inexperienced and unpersuasive speaker who had taken some arm-twisting to face Wilberforce in a public debate. More than a thousand people, fancying a good fight, were said to have stuffed the hall. Darwin, a famous hypochondriac, was too unwell to attend the meeting.

The main feature of the gathering was meant to be a presentation by John William Draper of New York University, entitled 'On the Intellectual Development of Europe, Considered with Reference to the Views of Mr Darwin and Others, that the Progression of Organisms is Determined by Law'. If you think that sounds the acme of dullness, just be glad you weren't there, because Draper's lecture was apparently ferociously long, boring and forgettable. Even when he had finished, there were other 'support bands' to sit through before it was time for the fancied act.

Known familiarly today as the Huxley–Wilberforce debate, the ensuing verbal punch-up is best remembered for a jab of Soapy Wilberforce's that hit Huxley bang on the nose. Wilberforce is said to have asked Huxley whether it was through his grandmother's side or his grandfather's that he was descended from a monkey. But the story has become embroidered over the decades and Wilberforce did not, in fact, make the crass error of confusing monkeys with apes. As Alfred Newton recorded in a letter at the time:

Referring to what Huxley had said two days before, about after all it's not signifying to him whether he was descended from a Gorilla or not, the Bp. [of Oxford] chafed him and asked whether he had a preference for the descent being on the father's side or the mother's side?'

But Huxley, adjusting his gumshield, returned a quick uppercut, as Newton recalled:

This gave Huxley the opportunity of saying that he would sooner claim kindred with an Ape than with a man like the Bp. who made so ill a use of his wonderful speaking powers to try and burke, by a display of authority, a free discussion on what was, or was not, a matter of truth, and reminded him that on questions of physical science 'authority' had always been bowled out by investigation, as witness astronomy and geology.

Huxley's response is said to have had a galvanizing effect on the audience, and Lady Brewster is reported to have fainted. However, the last speaker of the day, Joseph Dalton Hooker, mentioned in a letter to Darwin that Huxley had been mainly inaudible in the chamber and not much good against the persuasive, though 'silly', bishop.

Following the meeting everybody went off cheerfully to dinner in true gentlemanly style. Wilberforce and Darwin remained on good terms and, although the Huxley–Wilberforce debate is often portrayed as a fight between religion and science, many scientists of the time, including Darwin, were themselves religious men. Nonetheless, the growing polarity of thought and method between those who relied on religious 'authority' for access to the truth and those who favoured the investigation of evidence would, over the coming century, rend science from religion.

FOREIGN AFFAIRS

Geography

87 The continents: a reminder

When I was at school they told me to learn the periodic table of the elements, which I did. I've since forgotten it but occasionally I blurt out a right periodic table answer when *University Challenge* is on – usually it's 'plumbum'. While I was wasting my time learning this table they also told me that a continent was a continuous mass of land and that there were seven of them on the globe, which is true. There are also six, five or four, depending on what mood you are in, because the conventions for deciding which is which and what is what vary in different countries and for different purposes. This is the way they are generally divided at home.

- 7 continents: North America, South America, Antarctica, Africa, Europe, Asia, Australia (also known as Oceania and Australasia).
- 6 continents: North America, South America, Antarctica, Africa, Eurasia, Australia.
- 6 continents: America, Antarctica, Africa, Europe, Asia, Australia.
- 5 continents: America, Antarctica, Africa, Eurasia, Australia.
- 4 continents: America, Antarctica, Afro-Eurasia, Australia.

Some bits of these continents are called subcontinents, especially if they sit on a different tectonic plate to the rest of the continent. The Indian subcontinent and the Arabian Peninsula are possibly the best known of these. North and South America are subcontinents of the American continent, and the world's biggest island, Greenland, is also sometimes called a subcontinent.

So-called 'microcontinents' include Madagascar, the island off the right-hand side of Africa, about the size of the UK and Ireland joined together and sometimes called 'the eighth continent'. So-called 'supercontinents', which existed in geological times long gone, included Columbia, Gondwana, Kenorland, Laurasia, Rodinia, Pangaea and Vaalbara.

There are underwater continents, too, which include the almost totally submerged Kerguelen continent, in the southern Indian Ocean, and the partly submerged continent of Zealandia, also known as Tasmantis, of which New Zealand and New Caledonia are the bits that poke out of the water.

In order of geographical size, with land mass indicated as a percentage, the continents with which we are most familiar are:

- Asia: 29.5 per cent
- America: 28.5 per cent (North America: 16.5 per cent; South America: 12.0 per cent)
- Africa: 20.4 per cent
- Antarctica: 9.2 per cent
- Europe: 6.8 per cent
- Australia: 5.9 per cent

There are some fascinating figures here. Europe is hardly any bigger than Australia and is smaller than Antarctica, which you'd never guess from the news, and Africa is 4.1 per cent bigger than the whole North American continent, which is not the way it looks on the map. Ask yourself why.

88 The world's tiniest countries

Some of the world's countries are very small. They are known, by the people who make these things up, as microstates or ministates. Malta, Liechtenstein, Luxembourg, Monaco and Singapore are all microstates. The smallest recognized sovereign microstate is Vatican City, which despite having only 826 citizens (2009) and an area of less than a fifth of a square mile ($0.44\,km^2$), punches well above its diplomatic weight.

The Republic of Indian Stream is one of a few weirder microstates that resulted from mapping and treaty confusions. An anomaly in the Treaty of Paris, which ended the American War of Independence (1775–83), led to a claim over Indian Stream in Pittsburgh, New Hampshire, by both the US and Canada, to which it is adjacent. But residents refused to acknowledge either claimant and it became a republic for three years, until 1835, when Indian Stream was voluntarily annexed by New Hampshire.

Microstates should not be confused with self-proclaimed micronations, which are not recognized as sovereign countries. Although some micronations have their own flag, currency, stamps and passports, they are usually just ignored until the residents strike oil or something. The most interesting micronation is Redonda, which has a section all to itself later in this chapter. But here's a mention of a few of the others, in order of founding date.

- Llanrwst, founded 1276: this North Wales town was declared a 'free borough' by Llywelyn ap Gruffydd, Prince of Wales (Llywelyn the Last). The thirteenth-century Archbishop asked the Pope to overturn this, which he didn't. The town has its own coat of arms and flag, and in 1947 the town council applied, unsuccessfully, for a seat on the United Nations Security Council.
- Humanity, founded 1914: a micronation in the superbly named Spratly Islands, in the South China Sea, which in 1963 merged into the Republic of Morac-Songhrati-Meads (another micronation, founded by British naval captain James George Meads in 1878 or thereabouts).
- Frestonia, founded 1977: Freston Road in West London seceded from the United Kingdom in 1977 during a legal dispute over the unauthorized performance of *The Immortalist* by playwright- sculptor-poet-actor-painter-magician-graffitist, Heathcote Williams. He won a court ruling that Frestonia was *not*, for this purpose, part of the UK.
- Kingdom of Talossa, founded 1979: the bedroom kingdom of King Robert I (R. Ben Madison). It has its own language as well as an excellent 'heavy opera' company.
- Other World Kingdom, founded 1996: a Czech matriarchy in Prague

with a strict BDSM (bondage, discipline, sadism and masochism) ethos, in which women rule over men with a rod of iron. Sounds blimmin' awful.

- Copeman Empire, founded 2003: the Copeman Empire is run from a caravan park in Norfolk by its monarch, Nick Copeman, who changed his name to HM King Nicholas I by deed poll. And why not?
- BjornSocialist Republic, founded 2005: a self-proclaimed Marxist-religious-atheist state of some seven square yards (6 m²) on a stone that looks like a tractor, in front of the Bos Islands on the Sea of Immeln, Scania, Sweden.
- Austenasia, founded 2008: in September 2008, Jonathan Austen emailed the MP for Carshalton and Wallington, Tom Brake, to proclaim his house a separate state, his father, Terry, as Emperor, and himself as Prime Minister. In February 'Glencrannog', a nearby house, became part of Austenasia, and in March a Treaty of Annexation was also signed by Sir William Kingsnorth KOR, CAO, DSC, agreeing that his house would become the town of South Kilttown. The following month, 'God Save the Emperor' was adopted as the country's national anthem. Its tune is somewhat familiar, being identical to the British national anthem.

89 The thirty-eight countries of North America

At the time of writing, the number of countries and territories on the continent of North America is thirty-eight. Yes, that amazed me too. What's more, there are 514 million people living in these twenty-three sovereign states and fifteen dependent territories, except for Navassa Island, which is uninhabited, has no official language and produces nothing but bird crap.

Naturally enough, there's some debate about where, exactly, North America starts and stops. Central America, for example, is generally regarded as the southernmost part of the continent, even though some view it as a region in its own right. In fact, people argue about a lot of this stuff. Take Aruba, Netherlands Antilles, Trinidad and Tobago, and

Panama, which are all held to have territory in both North and South America. I've included Panama here as the bottom of North America. And before you write me a letter of complaint, I should stress that I don't mean that in a derogatory sense.

The countries and territories

- Anguilla (UK). Language: English. Main products: sugar, molasses and Sea Island cotton
- Antigua and Barbuda. Language: English, Main product: tourism
- Aruba (Netherlands). Languages: Dutch, English, Papiamento. Main product: tourism
- Bahamas. Language: English. Main products: tourism, rum, offshore finance
- Barbados. Language: English. Main products: rum, molasses, tourism (this tourism thing is *big*)
- Belize. Languages: English, Spanish. Main products: sugar, timber
- Bermuda (UK). Language: English. Main products: tourism, offshore finance
- British Virgin Islands (UK). Languages: English, Creole. Main products: tourism, offshore finance
- Canada. Languages: English, French. Main products: minerals, timber, cereals, manufactured goods
- Cayman Islands (UK). Language: English. Main products: tourism, offshore finance, turtle products(!)
- Costa Rica. Language: Spanish. Main product: coffee
- Cuba. Language: Spanish. Main products: beans, cassava, minerals, coffee, sugar
- Dominica. Language: English. Main products: bananas, fruit, tourism
- Dominican Republic (different place). Language: Spanish. Main products: sugar, minerals
- El Salvador. Language: Spanish. Main products: coffee, cotton
- Greenland (Denmark). Languages: Danish, Inuit. Main products: fish, further fish, more fish

- Grenada. Language: English. Main products: cocoa, nutmeg, bananas
- Guadeloupe (France). Languages: French, Creole. Main products: aubergines, bananas, pineapples, sugar cane
- Guatemala. Language: Spanish. Main products: coffee, minerals
- Haiti. Languages: French, Creole. Main products: coffee, sugar
- Honduras. Language: Spanish. Main products: bananas, coffee, timber
- Jamaica. Language: English, Creole. Main products: bauxite, bananas, sugar, tourism
- Martinique (France). Languages: French, Creole. Main products: bananas, flowers, pineapples, sugar cane
- Mexico. Language: Spanish, Main products: oil, minerals, textiles, steel
- Montserrat (UK). Languages: English, Creole. Main products: electronic components, vegetables, plastic bags (severe volcanic activity has decimated this country)
- Navassa Island (US/claimed also by Haiti). Language: None. Main product: guano (bird crap)
- Netherlands Antilles (Netherlands). Languages: Dutch, English, Creole. Main products: tourism, oil refinement, offshore finance
- Nicaragua. Languages: Spanish, English. Main products: coffee, cotton, meat
- Panama. Language: Spanish. Main products: canal traffic, banking, bananas
- Puerto Rico (US). Language: Spanish. Main products: minerals, cotton, fish, fruit, hydroelectricity
- Saint Kitts and Nevis (UK). Language: English. Main product: sugar
- Saint Lucia. Language: English. Main products: bananas, cocoa, textiles
- Saint Pierre and Miquelon (France). Languages: French, English. Main product: fish
- Saint Vincent and the Grenadines. Language: English. Main products: bananas, arrowroot, tourism

- Trinidad and Tobago. Language: English. Main products: oil, sugar, cocoa, coffee
- Turks and Caicos Islands (UK). Language: English. Main products: seafood, including lobster and conch
- United States (incl. continentally distant Hawaii). Language: English. Main products: foods, minerals, manufactured goods
- US Virgin Islands (US). Languages: English, Creole, Dutch. Main product: tourism

90 The incredible Kingdom of Redonda

The Kingdom of Redonda is a small, vaguely roundish but more slug-shaped Caribbean islet, 15 miles (24 km) to the northwest of Montserrat in the West Indies. It is about a mile (1.6 km) long and a third that width, with the stub of an extinct volcano on the top. Redonda was discovered by Christopher Columbus at 8 p.m. on 12 November 1493. Believing it to be round, he named it Santa Maria la Redonda, but didn't land. In more modern times, the island has been used for the harvesting of its rich seams of guano. The wandering goats would nibble the miners' shorts as they excavated mountains of reeking bird excrement in the blistering sun.

Redonda is regarded as the third island of the Nations of Antigua, Barbuda and Redonda, but the sovereignty has long been disputed. Nevertheless, Redonda has a king. Indeed, there are no fewer than four kings presently claiming to be Redonda's authentic monarch, despite its being a steep lump of unfriendly rock, uninhabited but for a few feral goats and the occasional wasp. There's no fresh water, only a bit of brown grass near the top, so no humans want to live there and, therefore, there is zero tax income.

The first chappie to mention Redonda as a kingdom was one M.P. Shiel (originally Shiell), a fantasy-author. In 1929 Shiel described how his dad, Matthew Dowdy Shiell, who was a Montserratish (Montserratoid? Montserratian?) banker, had claimed kingship over the island when his son was born. He reckoned this would be OK because he knew of no country having officially claimed the lump of rock as its territory. Shiel said that his father asked Queen Victoria for the monarchal title, which she granted on the condition that he agree not to revolt against her.

M.P. Shiel was crowned on the island by an Antiguan bishop at the age of just fifteen, but seems to have got a bit bored with being a king as he grew up, giving the title in due course to the writer Terence Ian Fytton Armstrong (also known as John Gawsworth – not to be confused with John Galsworthy). Gawsworth, who was also known as Orpheus Scrannel (look, I'm not making this up), was himself crowned King of Redonda in 1947, taking the title King Juan I.

Armstrong/Gawsworth/Scrannel/Juan I subsequently sold the title (several times) because he was in a permanent condition of pennilessness – he was a writer, don't forget – at one time bestowing the monarchy on somebody called Arthur John Roberts, who, it seems, abdicated in 1989, nominating William Leonard Gates (King Leo) as his successor. Confusingly, Jon Wynne-Tyson, a pacifist publisher who became Gawsworth's literary executor in 1970 and seems to have become King Juan II into the bargain, overlapped with Roberts. Wynne-Tyson abdicated in 1997, passing the title to the Spanish novelist and translator Javier Marías, who styled himself Xavier I, bestowing numerous titles during his reign, including that of Duke of Trémula upon the film director Pedro Almodóvar.

If you're still with me, you'll be fascinated to hear that a number of pretenders to the throne of Redonda are still knocking around in different countries. These include Americans W.I. Robert Williamson (King Robert the Bald), with his Queen Elizabeth, and Olen Atkins (King Alexander the Wise). There is also an Italian claimant, Giancarlo Ezio Noferi (King Giancarlo Ezio I of Montedoglio). In 2007, 'Sir' Robert Beech, landlord of the Wellington Arms in Southampton, unilaterally afforded himself 'diplomatic immunity' from the UK smoking ban by declaring his pub an 'embassy' of the country.

All stand for the national anthem.

Intercourse with Aliens

91 Best Portuguese chat-up lines

I once passed through Brazil on the way to somewhere else, and judging by the view out of the aeroplane window it is country worth visiting properly. One of the interesting things about it is that, just as Americans do not speak American because there's no such thing, neither is there such a language as Brazilian. Instead, the natives speak their own delightful version of Portuguese. I also noticed that they are not bashful when having a stab at English either, even when they are beginners. For instance, I saw a charming sign at the airport that said, 'If you are stolen, alarm a police', which I thought was nice.

Another place where Portuguese is commonly spoken is, of course, Portugal, now a favourite holiday destination and a grand place for chatting up bronzed girls. But you need the vocabulary, which they don't teach you at school, even though Portuguese is the official language of nine countries. Actually, they don't teach you this kind of Spanish or French vocabulary at school either, but it's a lot more useful than 'Monsieur Marsaud est dans le jardin' and 'Madame Marsaud est dans la cuisine', as they always seemed to be when I was at school.

Anyway, I thank Charles Neville-Smith for helping me assemble the stuff you need for your Portugal trip. Just put these essential phrases in your pocket next to the Diocalm and you'll be ready for anything. How will those Portuguese babes be able to resist flattery like this?

- Would you care to view my etchings? *Gostaria de ver as minhas gravuras?*

- Fascinate me some more with your knowledge of foot ulcers. *Fascina-me mais com o seu conhecimento das úlceras de pé.*
- Your stumbling attempts at English are charming me silly. *As suas tentativas tropeçados de falar inglês estão a encantar-me estupidamente.*
- The contours of that bum are geometrically perfect. *Os contornos daquele rabo são geograficamente perfeitos.*
- Your breasts are compelling. Are they real? Mind if I check? *As tuas mamas são cativantes! São naturais? Posso verificar?*
- Your place or mine? *Tua casa ou minha?*
- Take your clothes off. *Tire sua roupa.*
- What do you think of *this one*, lady? *O que você acha deste, senhora?*
- Shut up and bend over. *Cala-te e ajoelha-te.*
- Get your laughing gear round that. *Leva esta na boca.*

92 Filthy foreign food

Cheap air travel means that we now encounter foreign food products more than we used to. Unfortunately, the names of many of these items don't come over well to the English-speaking traveller.

Take Poland, where you can buy a soft drink called Fart. I suppose vigorous Poles must often be heard panting: 'God, I simply must have a Fart!' Things are no better in Ghana, where the sun beats down without mercy. Here they drink gallons of refreshing Pee cola. Fart or Pee? It's a tough decision.

If it's Spanish coffee you're after, the market leader is Bonka Natural, although telling the daughter of the hotel's proprietor that you 'want a Bonka' may not be the most felicitous way of putting it. For *café au lait*, you could do worse than go for Canada's interesting-sounding Homo Milk or try a mouthful of delicious German Sperm. How does it come? I'll tell you – in a white bottle, tasting like I don't know what.

American alcoholic refreshment can be a bit of gamble for the British visitor, though you can't go wrong with a Wanker – it's what your right arm's for. This delightful beer comes emblazoned with a girl in a swimsuit – to help things along, perhaps? The perfect whisky chaser is undoubtedly Knob Creek (mine's a large one). Back in the Old World, a can of Greek Vergina beer really hits the spot but requires nerve to ask for, as does a bag of Brazilian Prick crisps, French Cok' Bacon, or yummy Indonesian Super Titi 33.

When it comes to boring old bread rolls, how about a warm Jusipussi from Finland, filled perhaps with Peruvian Grated Fanny, a mouth-watering canned tuna that is surely a prize-winner in the world of unfortunate nomenclature. Now when Dad asks 'What's for tea dear?', Mum's answer will not be dreary old cucumber sandwiches but Grated Fanny, Fanny on toast or maybe even Fanny surprise. More Fanny, Vicar?

For dinner, how about sitting down to a bowl of Knorr's delicious Cock Soup, with Turkish Çemen sauce? Royco's New Improved Shito lends an air of haute cuisine to more formal occasions, as does a big wodge of Makrel Guf so long as somebody opens a window.

For dessert, you need look no further (indeed you *can* look no further) than Australia, for a Golden Gaytime, a sort of ice cream. And if that doesn't tickle your fancy, the Germans are right behind you, bringing up the rear with their tasty Bum Bum Banana – why not sit down to one of those? Alternatively, you could try Coming Lemon on the Japanese sweet trolley. If the very idea makes your eyes water, tuck in to a few Brazilian Muffs instead, with some Slagroom cream. Muffs are small cakes and for English-speaking amusement the drawing on the packet depicts a character diving into one.

If it's just a few sweets you want, I can heartily recommend Swiss Grany Maniac for sheer epithetic surrealism, while the Danish-English description on a packet of mouth-watering Spunk says all that anyone could wish to say on the subject of poor global-product-naming: 'Spunk is the "naughty" and tasty pastil for children. Two different kinds of Spunk is available; the popular salt pastil, and the funny, brilliantly coloured jelly gums.'

As you finish with a piece of Australian Coon cheese, don't forget the poor old dog. He'll be there, eagerly wagging his tail for a bowl of his favourite German doggy snack: Spurty Bones.

Bon appétit.

93 Latin and Greek for the practical ἄντρας

I'm thinking of getting a Latin motto engraved over my front door. My favourite so far is '*Quid quid latine dictum sit, altum videtur*', which I'm told means 'Anything said in Latin sounds profound', and how true that is. I couldn't help noticing that Sir George Martin, the Beatles' producer, has adopted the motto '*Amore solum opus est*' for his coat of arms. When I asked him what this meant, he told me, 'Love only is needed', or 'All you need is love'. Geddit? Sir Christopher Frayling is a Clint Eastwood fan and his motto is '*Perge scelus mihi diem perficias*', which may be translated as 'Go ahead punk, make my day', showing the truth of '*Quid quid latine dictum sit, altum videtur*'.

I think all this clowning started in 1978, when they translated Beatrix Potter's *The Tale of Mr Jeremy Fisher* as *Fabula de Domino Ieremia Piscatore*. Henry Beard took up the baton in 1990, producing *Latin for All Occasions* (*Lingua Latina Occasionibus Omnibus*), which contained entries that have become part of the common lexicon, such as 'Beam me up, Scotty!', '*Me transmitte sursum, Caledoni!*', and the useful 'The check is in the post', '*Perscriptio in manibus tabellariorum est*'.

Anyway, here are a few Latin and Greek mottoes along with some useful everyday phrases for the practical man.

Latin

- *SPQR*: an initialism from the Latin '*Senatus Populusque Romanus*', meaning 'The Senate and the People of Rome' and not, as I have heard it said, 'the Society for the Prevention of Quelty to Romans'. And before you write to tell me that *que* is not a separate word and doesn't deserve its own initial, you should know that *que is* a separate word, meaning 'and', but when used as a copulative particle it is affixed to the word it annexes. So there.
- *Per Ardua ad Astra*: 'Through Adversity to the Stars' is the motto of the Royal Air Force. It appears in adapted form on the gravestone of comedian and one time RAF pilot 'Professor' Jimmy Edwards in this form: '*Per risum ad honorem*', which I suppose means something

like, 'To honour through laughter'. An excellent motto.

- *Scientia est lux lucis*: 'knowledge is enlightenment', a favourite of Leonardo da Vinci, who can be accurately described either as 'the archetypal Renaissance man' or 'a left-handed homosexual bastard', depending on your level of mindless prejudice.
- *Castigat ridendo mores*: 'one corrects customs by laughing at them'. This is the equivalent of pulling down the mayor's trousers in front of the council. A good idea.
- *Mendacem memorem esse oportet*: 'Liars need good memories'. As true today as it was back then.

Greek

- Ἰησοῦς Χριστὸς Θεοῦ Υἱὸς Σωτήρ (*Iēsous Christos Theou Hyios Sōtēr*): 'Jesus Christ, Son of God, Saviour'. The initialism is: ΙΧΘΥΣ (*Icthys*), meaning 'fish', which led to the fish being adopted by some Christians as their symbol, mainly on the backs of Cortinas in South London.
- Θάλασσα καὶ πῦρ καὶ γυνή, κακὰ τρία (*Thalassa kai pŷr kai gynē, kaka tria*): 'Sea, and fire, and woman: three evils'. Can't argue with it, really.
- Μὴ χεῖρον βέλτιστον (*Mē cheíron béltiston*): 'The least worst is the best' is exactly the kind of thing you think before deciding whether to be burnt at the stake or hung, drawn and quartered – or which way to vote in an election. Often a tough one.
- Διαίρει καὶ βασίλευε (*Diairei kai basileue*): 'Divide and rule'. This is not a geometry problem but what our governments do to us.
- Ἐν οἶδα ὅτι οὐδὲν οἶδα (*Hen oida hoti ouden oida*): 'The only real wisdom is knowing you know nothing' or 'I know, through not knowing' is a saying attributed to Socrates. It didn't do him much good in the end because they made him drink hemlock and he died. It could have been worse: they could have made him drink Toilet Duck or Kaliber alcohol-free lager.
- Τὸ δὶς ἐξαμαρτεῖν οὐκ ἀνδρὸς σοφοῦ (*To dis examartein ouk*

andros sophou): 'To commit the same sin twice is not a sign of a wise man'. A bit like drinking Toilet Duck two days running.

All this reminds me of that limerick:

There was a young curate from Kew,
Who kept a pet cat in a pew.
He taught it to speak
Alphabetical Greek,
But never got further than $M\mu$.

94 The twenty-two official languages of India

There are hundreds upon hundreds of 'mother-tongue' languages spoken across the Indian subcontinent, with a 1961 census recording more than 1,600 of them. There is no legal 'national language' in India but the main official language is Hindi, which is spoken by well over 400 million people, largely across the so-called 'Hindi belt' in north India. English is the commonest non-native official tongue. Persian has also played an important historical role as a lingua franca.

The following table, arranged in descending order of number of speakers (as of 2001), is the latest official list (2008).

Hindi	422 million speakers
	Spoken mainly in the Hindi belt, north India
Bengali	83 million speakers
	Spoken mainly in West Bengal, Assam, Jharkhand, Tripura
Telugu	74 million speakers
	Spoken mainly in Andhra Pradesh, Karnataka, Tamil Nadu, Maharashtra, Orissa
Marathi	72 million speakers
	Spoken mainly in Maharashtra, Karnataka, Madhya Pradesh, Gujarat, Andhra Pradesh, Goa
Tamil	61 million speakers
	Spoken mainly in Tamil Nadu, Karnataka, Puducherry, Andhra Pradesh, Kerala, Maharashtra

Urdu	52 million speakers
	Spoken mainly in Jammu and Kashmir, Andhra Pradesh, Delhi, Bihar, Uttar Pradesh, Uttarakhand
Gujarati	46 million speakers
	Spoken mainly in Gujarat, Maharashtra, Tamil Nadu
Kannada	38 million speakers
	Spoken mainly in Karnataka, Maharashtra, Tamil Nadu, Goa
Malayalam	33 million speakers
	Spoken mainly in Kerala, Lakshadweep, Mahé, Puducherry
Oriya	33 million speakers
	Spoken mainly in Orissa
Punjabi	29 million speakers
	Spoken mainly in Punjab, Chandigarh, Delhi, Haryana
Assamese or Axomiya	13 million speakers
	Spoken mainly in Assam
Maithili	12 million speakers
	Spoken mainly in Bihar
Santali	6.5 million speakers
	Spoken mainly in Santal tribals of the Chota Nagpur Plateau (comprising states of Bihar, Chhattisgarh, Jharkhand, Orissa)
Kashmiri	5.5 million speakers
	Spoken mainly in Jammu and Kashmir
Konkani	2.5 million speakers
	Spoken mainly in Konkan (Goa, Karnataka, Maharashtra, Kerala)
Nepali	2.5 million speakers
	Spoken mainly in Sikkim, West Bengal, Assam
Sindhi	2.5 million speakers
	Spoken mainly in Gujarat, Maharashtra, Rajasthan, Madhya Pradesh
Manipuri (also called Meitei or Meithei)	1.5 million speakers
	Spoken mainly in Manipur
Bodo	1.2 million speakers
	Spoken mainly in Assam
Dogri	0.1 million speakers
	Spoken mainly in Jammu and Kashmir
Sanskrit	0.05 million speakers
	Spoken mainly in Mattur

95 An international swearing and insult dictionary

So-called 'agglutinative' languages, such as Finnish, have an almost infinite number of words because you can stick together great long strings of short ones and end up with new ones of indefinite length. If you ignore this cheating – which is typical of foreigners – you will find that, with at least a quarter of a million distinct words, English boasts a much larger vocabulary than related tongues, including the Germanic languages such as Dutch, Norwegian and Yiddish, and the Romance languages such as French, Italian, Portuguese and Spanish. This is because English started off as a Germanic language, sharing much of its grammar and basic vocabulary with German and Dutch, but, after 1066 when the 'Frogs' invaded, English became greatly influenced by Latin, which was the language of the universities and the Church, and Norman French (which sounds like the name of a used-car salesman).

The point is that, with this large vocabulary, we are now the most fecund insulters and richest swearers of all Europe, and possibly the world. The following helpful list of rude words and phrases contains examples from several of the languages that you are most likely to encounter in your travels. In many cases, owing to the dearth of foreign vocabulary, a free translation has been necessary, but the emotional impact should remain the same.

- Shit: *Schweiße* (German), *Chraa* (Arabic), *Merde* (French), *Skata* (Greek)
- Push off, fatso!: *Despacha-tegorducho!* (Portuguese), *Bouge de la gros porc!* (French)
- Bollocks/balls: *Testicoli* (Italian), *Bolas* (Portuguese), *Couilles* (French)
- Don't you speak English?: *Vous parlez pas anglais?* (French), *¿Usted no hablainglés?* (Spanish), *Sprichst du kein Englisch?* (German)
- Shut your gob!: *Ta guele toi!* (French), *Calatuaboca!* (Portuguese), *Chiuda la vostrafaccia!* (Italian)

- All right darlin'!: *Oyetia!* (Spanish)
- Has your nose always been like that?: *Ton pif, tul'as de naissance?* (French), *War deine Naseschonimmer so?* (German)
- How much did you say?: *Quanto o que você disse?* (Portuguese), *Vous avez dit combien?!* (French)
- I shit on *or* in/the milk/the sea/a prostitute/your mother: *Me cago en/la leche/el mar/la puta/en tu madre* (Spanish – a pretty good all-purpose selection)
- Bum/arse: *Cul* (French), *Rabo* (Portuguese), *Arsch* (German)
- I shit on the prostitute of a mother that gave birth to you: *Me cago en la puta madre que te pario* (Spanish again – and so eloquent)
- Do you mind! I'm British: *Un peu de respect! Je suis Anglais!* (French), *Você importa?! Sou britânico!* (Portuguese)
- Keep your hands to yourself: *Tenga la mani a posto* (Italian), *Borta fingarna!* (Swedish)
- Get that towel off my deckchair!: *Nimm das Handtuch von meiner Liege!* (German. This, the most useful phrase for use with Germans, may be too subtle for them. Either of the following pleasantries, *Blöde Fotze!* or *Mutterficker!*, can be used to emphasize your objection)
- Wanker!: *Branleur!* (French), *Wichser!* (German), *Cabrão!* (Portuguese), *Rukker!* (Dutch)
- Do you have lavatories in your country?: *Há privadas no seupaís?* (Portuguese), *Y-a-t-il des toilettes dans ce pays?!* (French)
- Fuck off!: *Va te faire foutre!* (French), *Vá por caralho!* (Portuguese), *Verpiss Dich!* (German), *¡Vete a t mar por culo!* (Spanish); *Vaffangulo!* (an euphonious Italian variation of the above, meaning, 'Go fuck yourself!')

Have a good trip.

NUGACIOUS DEVIATION

Big Stuff

96 Tyrannosaurus rex

In Piccadilly Circus one day I was stopped by a chap in a fuzzy Tyrannosaurus rex suit who was giving out leaflets for 'free' garlic bread at some nearby restaurant. Through the dark mesh behind his rubber teeth I glimpsed the haunted features of the out-of-work actor whose dream it had once been to play Hamlet. From the great Dane to Barney – what a comedown – just one short stagger from Ronald McDonald and the bottle.

Tyrannosaurus rex, one of the largest carnivorous dinosaurs, was around from the end of the Cretaceous (Latin for 'chalky') Period, between 14.5 and 65.5 million years ago – give or take a few million years. Its fearsome size and power are reflected in its name, which is Latin for 'tyrant lizard king'. A T. rex was up to 20 ft (6 m) tall, and if one had been passing by your house, its five-foot-long head could easily have looked in at you through your bedroom window and seen your girlfriend in bed. Your typical T. rex was up to 40 ft (12 m) long, the size of a bus, and weighed some 7 tons (again, about the same as a bus).

T. rex inhabited forested river valleys on the North American continent, where many fossils have been dug up, some of which are nearly complete skeletons. The first was discovered in 1902 by Barnum Brown in southeastern Montana. Most of the other thirty-plus T. rex fossils were also found here but some have been found in Canada and parts of Asia.

Tyrannosaurus rex became extinct with other dinosaurs about 65 million years ago in the Cretaceous–Tertiary (Cretaceous–Paleogene) mass extinction, which was probably the result of a 10 mile (16 km) wide lump of space rock hurtling into the Earth and causing mega-tsunamis, huge dust clouds, acid rain, deadly infrared radiation and panic-buying at Tesco. The impact released more than a thousand-million times more energy than that released by the bombs dropped on Nagasaki and Hiroshima.

Tyrannosaurus rex walked on two legs and ate meat. Its back legs were huge, with very strong thighs and large toes (three per foot) that gave it the power to move quickly – about 20 mph (32 km/h) – but its front 'arms', though tiny, were also powerful for their size. They couldn't reach its mouth but were equipped with two claws that would do you a mischief if you played slapsies with one.

The skull of the T. rex was massive and needed to be to provide the requisite piercing, gripping, tearing force that it used to eat other dinosaurs. Its bone-crushing teeth were up to a foot long, with those at the front of the upper jaw packed together like commuters, the tips pointing backwards like sharp chisels. Other teeth were wider apart and blunter, like deadly bananas. One bite was capable of tearing off about half a cow's weight of Triceratops.

The popular Victorian idea was that T. rex stood upright, and this is how you will see it in many illustrations. However, more recent research has revealed that it would have broken its bones if it had done this. The theory now is that the T. rex moved with its body roughly parallel to the ground, its long, heavy tail extending behind as a counterweight to the massive head, which was supported by a thick, rugby-player-type neck.

The largest, most complete and best-preserved T. rex fossil ever discovered is called 'Sue'. Sue was found in 1990 by paleontologist Sue Hendrickson in South Dakota, and named after her. The discovery led to unseemly wrangles with the owner of the land where Sue was found, before the 80-per-cent-complete skeleton was sold by auction to the Field Museum of Natural History, in Chicago, for a record $8,362,500. Minus gavel-wielder's commission, of course.

97 All about submarines

When I was a boy, my Uncle Roy explained to me that it is impossible to lick your elbow – it just can't be done. He was a fount of information, Uncle Roy. He knew how to navigate by the stars and how to tie a sailor's splice, which he'd learnt to do in his bunk when he worked on submarines.

Although the word 'submarine' dates from 1648, the first underwater boats weren't called submarines – 'eel boat' and 'plunging boat' were two of the English names that they tried out first. But ever since Leonardo da Vinci (1452–1519) sketched out an experimental design for a sub, the possibility of a real underwater boat has been the dream of men with nothing better to do.

A proposal for the first true underwater craft was written in 1578 by William Bourne, a British mathematician and naval nut. Bourne suggested a completely enclosed vessel, looking rather like two rowing boats glued together, that could be rowed underwater.

The first submarine to be successfully navigated underwater was built in 1620 by a Dutch chappie called Cornelius van Drebbel. It was made of wood and had oars, resembling Bourne's design in the use of greased leather to waterproof its wooden hull. The oars poked out through holes in the side, sealed with tight leather gasket-like flaps. For four years, between 1620 and 1624, Drebbel's submarine was rowed around blindly, 15 ft (5 m) below the surface of the Thames. Float-supported snorkels allowed the sub to stay underwater for hours.

Submarines have caught the imagination of novelists and film-makers too. Jules Verne created a great submariner anti-hero in Captain Nemo of the *Nautilus*, who used his submarine's stealth and power to subdue his perceived enemies. Subs continue to be used mainly for purposes of warfare – the first one to sink a ship being a Confederate sub in the American Civil War. But what with water being a better conductor of sound than air, the earliest ones could easily be heard by the enemy. Sound can travel more than 3,000 nautical miles through water, so you didn't need to be close to them to find them, either. (A nautical mile is about 1.1 miles.)

Even by the First World War, submarines were still not all that brilliant. They had no periscope and had to keep coming up to the top to see where they were – not exactly invisible then. Nowadays submarines are painted black to blend in with the dark of the deep ocean, but a submarine 100 feet (30 m) down in clear water can still be seen from the air.

Nevertheless, modern submarines are hugely sophisticated vessels and are now as quiet as the ocean itself, even though they are huge. They can submerge in less than a minute and stay down for six months at a time, using ballast tanks to control their depth. The nuclear-powered ones (that's most of them) can dive to a depth of more than 800 feet (244 m). This is equivalent to floating in the air two-and-a-half times as high as Big Ben. Even so, they still use a large snorkel-sort-of-effort to suck fresh air from the surface, rather like a fat holiday-maker exploring the Barrier Reef.

The submarines of today are very fast, indeed they are faster underwater than on the surface, and a nuclear one can go 60,000 miles (97,000km) on just one lump of uranium the size of a walnut. They are pushed through the water by a propeller or a pump jet, and steered by fins – usually. In 1921 an American sub ran out of fuel and had to put up sails made out of sailors' blankets and curtain rods. Nonetheless, it managed to sail 100 miles (160 km) to port at a speed of 2 knots (2 nautical miles per hour).

The most astonishing speed record was established on 17 August 1958, when the USS *Skate* made a circumnavigation of the globe in just fifty minutes. Well, OK, it was only 2 miles (3.2 km) off the North Pole and the distance around the world at that point was only 12 miles (19km), but still. Another weird polar thing happened around that time, when the crew of the nuclear submarine USS *Seadragon* got out at the North Pole and played a game of baseball. Whenever a batter hit a particularly long one, it landed either in tomorrow or yesterday, owing to the lines of longitude meeting at the Pole and making a nonsense of time zones. In any case, it was daytime all night at the North Pole at that time of year.

Most people who read this page will have tried to lick their elbow.

241

98 Twelve things you didn't know about Hoover Dam

In September 2005, Frank Clewer, of Warrnambool in Australia, went for a job interview wearing a nylon jacket over a wool sweater. As he walked into the building, 40,000 volts of static electricity that had built up on his clothes discharged themselves into the carpet, which caught fire and began to melt. 'We could hear a cracking noise, a bit like a whip, both inside and outside the building,' a fire officer told the BBC. That wouldn't have happened on concrete.

Once called the Boulder Dam, Hoover Dam is a concrete arch-gravity dam in the Black Canyon of the Colorado River, on the border between the Arizona and Nevada. It was begun in 1931 and when completed in 1936 was the world's largest concrete structure. The dam is named not after the vacuum cleaner company, nor the FBI man, but after President Herbert Hoover, who played a major role in its construction. Hoover Dam is now a National Historic Landmark. Here are twelve things you didn't know about it:

1 Hoover Dam height: 726.4 ft (221 m) – more than twice the height of Big Ben.

2 Length: 1244 ft (379 m) – 7.5 Olympic swimming pools.

3 Hoover Dam contains enough concrete to build a dual carriageway from the Statue of Liberty in New York to the Hollywood sign in California.

4 If it hadn't been poured in sections and cooled by pumping refrigerated water through it in tubes, the dam's concrete would still not have set. Indeed, it wouldn't have set until 2061: a 125-year curing time.

5 When Franklin D. Roosevelt took office in 1933, his Secretary of the Interior Harold Ickes smartly removed Hoover's name from the dam project. In 1947, President Truman put it back again. Big egos, these chaps.

6 Officially, ninety-six workers died building the dam. The first was reportedly J.G. Tierney, a surveyor who drowned looking for a good

spot to build. His son, Patrick, was the last man to die on the project, thirteen years later to the day.

7 Lake Mead, created by the dam, is the largest reservoir in the United States. Its surface area is 247 square miles (640 km²). It extends 112 miles (180 km) behind the dam wall and is 500 ft (165 m) deep. A B-29 Superfortress bomber that crashed into the lake in 1948 is still on the bottom.

8 Water flowing through the turbines in Lake Mead is going at about 85 mph (137 km/h). Don't try swimming in that.

9 Alfred Hitchcock's film *Saboteur* (1942) features a plan to blow up the dam.

10 Along with a white mineral 'bathtub ring' around the shore, the ruins of the town of St Thomas, Nevada, are visible when Lake Mead's water level drops.

11 Hoover Dam has its own police force, the imaginatively named Hoover Dam Police.

12 The dam spans two time zones, Pacific and Mountain Time. The clocks on Los Angeles-based architect Gordon B. Kaufmann's Art Deco dam turrets show the time in Nevada and Arizona, which is only polite.

99 The man who invented pyramids

'Imhotep', funny name – it looks like an anagram, and, in fact, it is. It's an anagram of 'Me pot hi'. Now, the record fails to show whether Imhotep (2650–2600 BCE) was drug-fuzzled, but, being a poet ('him poet' – there's another one) and a philosopher, it wouldn't be very surprising – you know what that Allen Ginsberg was like. On the other hand, Imhotep may not have had time for all that because his official job title was, stand by: Chancellor of the King of Egypt (the Pharaoh), First in line after the King of Upper Egypt, Administrator of the Great Palace, Hereditary nobleman, High Priest of Heliopolis (Sun City), Chief Carpenter, Builder, Chief Sculptor, Doctor and Maker of Vases in Chief.

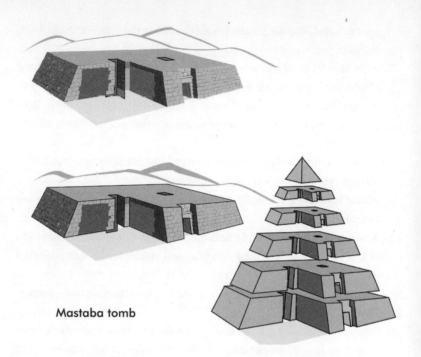

Mastaba tomb

Blimey, imagine if your maker of vases in chief was also your builder and your doctor. I wonder if he put scaffolding up to look in your ear.

Imhotep was the best jack-of-all-trades of all time and must have had a really good parking space. He was also one of the select few commoners to be made a god after his death. Stephen Fry will probably be the next one. The centre of his cult was Memphis – not Tennessee, but the ancient capital of the first nome (administrative division) of Lower Egypt. Imhotep may well have been the first chap to use architectural columns and seems also to have invented the stone-dressed building method. He designed the earliest known Egyptian pyramid, the Step Pyramid (Pyramid of Djoser), at Saqqara in 2630 BCE, the first stone building ever to be constructed to this huge size. Before this, pharaohs had customarily been buried in mastaba tombs (see illustration). While the pyramid is clearly a development of the mastaba – sloping sides, tapering profile, four sides, etc. – no one had thought of piling them up

244

before, and this leap of the imagination effectively made Imhotep the pyramid's inventor.

After Imhotep died in 2600 BCE, pyramids got even bigger, becoming some of the largest structures ever to be built. Indeed, the Great Pyramid of Giza (also known as the Pyramid of Cheops or Khufu) is, along with the Hanging Baskets of Babylon, one of the Seven Wonders of the Ancient World. (Sorry, not basket*s*, *gardens*.) The Great Pyramid of Giza remained the tallest human-made structure on the planet for thousands of years, until they got the top on Lincoln Cathedral in 1300, and is the only one of the Seven Wonders still in existence.

Building a pyramid with your bare hands in the toasting sunshine was a pretty enormous challenge for those Egyptian chaps back then. Construction firm DMJM recently did a detailed 'critical path analysis' to see what would be needed to get a job like that done, using only the inclined plane, the lever and the other tools possessed by the Ancient Egyptians. They looked at everything from the gravel required for ramps to the logistics of baking the bread for the crews' lunch, and worked out that, using stone that was dug up locally, except for the smooth dressing stones and the burial chamber granite, which came from elsewhere, 4,000 to 5,000 men could have built the Great Pyramid within 20 to 40 years.

There have been many nerdish theories over the years about how the pyramids were built by aliens, but graffiti hidden on foundations below the floor level of the pyramids, and in other places, reveals that the workmen were not Martians. Nor indeed were they slaves, as had been suggested.

The scrawls reveal that, to build these monster structures, gangs of workmen were organized into two crews, subdivided into five *phyles*, the Greek word for 'tribe'. These *phyles* were then split into divisions, each identified by a single hieroglyph representing such qualities as endurance, perfection and strength. The men seemed to have been perfectly cheerful and often competitive in their work, and the gang names have a modern ring to them: 'The Friends of Khufu' and 'The Menkaure Boozers' could be darts teams. The typical age of death for these guys was between 30 and 35, so Imhotep's big idea didn't do much to prolong their life, which seems odd, what with his being a doctor and everything. You'd have thought he would have worked out a way to improve longevity. Maybe he was too busy making vases.

100 The Harrier Jump Jet

There's no space for long words in newspaper headlines, so infant children are always 'tots', disagreements are 'rows', and helicopters, 'choppers'. In the 1960s, on the unveiling of a revolutionary military plane capable of Vertical/Short Takeoff and Landing (V/STOL) via thrust vectoring, headline writers under pressure called it the 'Jump Jet'.

The Harrier Jump Jet combines the advantages of the helicopter with those of the fighter jet. Like a helicopter, the Harrier can land or take off from a small area, including small seaborne aircraft carriers, and while a helicopter's maximum speed is about 250 mph (402 km/h), a Harrier can do 730 mph (1,175 km/h) without singeing the pilot's aerofoils.

The Harrier began its genesis during the Cold War, in 1957, when the Bristol Engine Company said they were planning a 'directed thrust' engine. NATO were interested and supplied Hawker Aircraft with money to design a 'Light Tactical Support Fighter', whose novel feature was its ability to take off and land vertically, using just one Rolls-Royce Pegasus jet engine. The way it did this was to direct the engine's thrust downwards through four nozzles so as to provide lift, like a space rocket. Once the plane was up, it could hover for a time, the pilot directing some of the thrust through 'puffer ducts' at the wingtips, nose and tail, so he could manoeuvre the plane backwards and forwards, and left and right. It was possible then to move forwards at speed, like a conventional plane, by the very simple technique of rotating the nozzles to point backwards – it wasn't exactly rocket science. Actually, it *was* rocket science.

One of the challenges, however, was the enormous amount of fuel required to overcome gravity in this way. No lift was being supplied by the air under the Harrier's wings, as happens with other aeroplanes during take off. All its weight had to be supported by the thrust of the engine. And it wasn't just fuel either: the jump jet could hover for a minute-and-a-half, but in this time it used 150 gallons of water to cool the engine.

Between 1969 and 2003, 824 varieties of Harrier were produced, but manufacture finished in 1997, the last 'rebuilt' Harrier being delivered in December 2003.

The Harrier's two main problems were its inability to go faster than the speed of sound, and the large amount of work the pilot had to do to keep it in the air. This did not mean the jump jet was finished though. In March 2010 the F-35B Joint Strike Fighter, which is a supersonic stealth jump jet, performed its first test-hover, when test pilot Graham Tomlinson held the aircraft almost motionless 150 ft (46 m) above the ground. In the F-35B, the pilot's commands are now converted into movement of the technically advanced plane by a new onboard computer – the epitome, like all computers, of reliability. Hang on – why has my screen frozen?

Potpourri

101 Bed warmers since Aristotle

There's an old practice that has dropped out of favour, but which has a lot to be said for it, and I think I shall try to bring it back. It is called shunamitism and it is the custom of introducing a naked virgin into the bed of an old man so as to rejuvenate him sexually and recover some of the potency of his youth.

The name for the treatment comes from the biblical story of King David (1040–970 BCE), who in his dotage could not keep warm in bed. A young virgin called Abishag(!), who lived in Shunem, a small village south of Mount Gilboa, and who was known for her great beauty, was chosen by David's servants to sleep with him. That is to say, she would lie next to the old codger and keep him warm but he would not have sexual relations with her (pull the other one). This was said to be partly because he already had eighteen wives. No wonder the poor fellow was so frail and knackered.

The ancient thinking behind the practice of shunamitism was that the heat and moisture of the virgin would radiate to the old man and revitalize him. If I'm honest, which I am, I must say that the science supporting this treatment looks a bit doubtful under the laser beam of modern inquiry. So, in the spirit of empiricism, I have decided to put the theory to the test, and even if it doesn't warm me up and rejuvenate me it sounds as if it might well be fun. By the way, where does one find 'virgins' these days? Are they listed in *Yellow Pages*? Perhaps it would be easier to try an ordinary bed warmer.

The likelihood is that bed warmers have been around ever since human beings began sleeping in beds. Aristotle himself wrote three great tomes on the subject of snoozing, including *De Somno et Vigilia* (*On Sleep and Dreams*), but since my Latin isn't all that brilliant, and since I haven't read them anyway, I don't know if he mentions bed warmers. Aristotle was, famously, straight as a lamppost but you can bet that many of his Ancient Greek friends will have heated things up by putting a warm boy between the sheets.

Vessels full of hot stuff were certainly in use as bed warmers at least as early as the sixteenth century and were a common item of domestic equipment in the cold countries of northern Europe, where the earliest were probably pottery, with metal becoming more common over time.

Your typical bed warmer looked like a giant banjo, consisting of a sealable metal frying-pan-type thing attached to a long handle turned from wood. The way they worked was that some poor fool shovelled hot embers from the kitchen fire into the metal pan, and closed the lid, which sometimes had decorative perforations in it to prevent lack of oxygen from extinguishing the embers. Once the bed warmer was full of smouldering coals the metal became extremely hot and the thing had to be carried by its handle to the bed, where it could be slid under the covers. It was not uncommon in damp climes for steam to result.

The main thing with metal bed warmers was to remember, after an evening of malmsey and roistering, when you staggered up the wooden hill to Bedfordshire with the flickering wick of your tallow-candle throwing hideous shadows across the portraits of your ancestors, not to climb into bed with the red hot copper banjo. This was likely to result in colourful ejaculations such as ''Sblood!', 'Gadzooks!' and 'Zounds!'

Before long a variety of contraptions, made from zinc, glass, earthenware and even wood, were manufactured to hold hot water. These were the first proper hot water bottles – and for the first time, the metal ones could now be put inside a newly devised cloth bag. The huge advantage of hot water bottles over metal pans full of red hot coals was that you could get into bed without setting your jimjams on fire or melting your foot off. Pottery soon became the material of choice and designs began to look more alike, finally assuming the appearance of a cider flagon on its side. Once filled, these could be securely closed with a stoneware screw cap. Rubber washers prevented leakage. A slight variation was to have the opening in the long side, with a knob on one of the short ends to ease carrying. These were known as 'pigs'.

Hot water bottle design remained unchanged for well over a hundred years and you can still find examples of the things in antique shops. It was the invention of heat-resistant rubber that put paid to them in the end.

The modern hot water bottle design – the one that looks like a colourful rubber flask that's been flattened by a tractor – was patented by a Croatian inventor named Eduard Penkala, though it is not recorded who holds the patent on the distinctive hot-water-bottle smell, which, once sniffed, is never forgotten. Penkala called his invention the 'Termofor', a name under which it is still sold. Despite the advent of 'heating pads', electric blankets and central heating across much of the developed world, hot water bottles are still widely used, especially in Chile and in Japan, where they are regarded as environmentally friendly and money saving. If you decide to go this way, bear in mind that hot water bottle rubber is a highly efficient conductor of heat, so it's a good idea to buy one with a furry cover. Or, in an emergency, use your girlfriend's muff.

102 Find your remote control

Once upon a not very long time ago a chap watching the TV who wanted to change channels would have to lift his fat bum off the sofa, walk the three paces to the set and press a button or turn a dial. These days, of course, you just lie there like Jabba the Hutt and squeeze the remote control.

But something has gone wrong, because it now seems to require at least three channel changers to get anything to work, especially if you are trying to watch a DVD. I get them all confused, and the other day I found myself trying to change channels with an old mobile phone.

There are millions of these devices around now and Carlos has kindly illustrated a collection of them. See if you can spot yours.

A. The Captain Kirk. The schizoid buttons on this one can give you the heebie-jeebies, but a hard one to drop, because of the 'waist'.

B. The Darth Vader. Also sometimes known as the Nosferatu, this remote is full of omen and Gothic horror. Lovely clear numbers though.

C. The King Dong. The name says it all: longer, harder, with more staying power. You can change channels all night with this hummer.

D. The Paxman. A bit of a terrier, this one. Short tempered. Will snap at your ankles and turn the sound up too loud during *Question Time*.

E. The Ironing Board. Don't be fooled by those effeminate lines, this one means business. Especially good for 'red button' functions.

F. The Rockford. Good-natured, but easily mistaken for your phone, this remote would rather talk its way out of trouble than fight.

103 The story of the Gettysburg Address

Everyone loves a good speech, especially if it's nice and short. The shortest speech I ever heard was uttered by a friend of mine at a wedding at which he was best man. He stood up, wobbled slightly, squeaked, 'Wendy', and sat down again, on somebody's hat. A chap at a nearby table saved the day by springing up and delivering a beautiful impromptu oration that brought a tear to every eye. He told me later it was one he had given at his brother's wedding, the previous weekend, with the names changed on the fly.

The Gettysburg Address is the name for the very brief speech delivered by Abraham Lincoln at the dedication of the Soldiers' National Cemetery in Gettysburg, Pennsylvania, on a November afternoon in 1863. This was the middle of the American Civil War, only months after Union soldiers had beaten the armies of the southern slave states at the Battle of Gettysburg.

Lincoln's three-minute (or thereabouts) speech was intended as a half-page footnote to a two-hour declamation by Edward Everett, the governor of Massachusetts, but despite his judgment that 'The world will little note, nor long remember what we say here', Lincoln's potent rhetoric led to the opposite happening. Everett's monster contribution, in contrast, is now largely forgotten. Of course, bums being as numb as they must have been by the time Lincoln stood up to say hello, the brevity of his remarks was doubtless a factor in their popularity. Here is the address in a version prepared by Lincoln after the occasion.

Four score and seven years ago our fathers brought forth on this continent a new nation, conceived in liberty, and dedicated to the proposition that all men are created equal.

Now we are engaged in a great civil war, testing whether that nation, or any nation, so conceived and so dedicated, can long endure. We are met on a great battle-field of that war. We have come to dedicate a portion of that field, as a final resting place for those who here gave their lives that that nation might live. It is altogether fitting and proper that we should do this.

But, in a larger sense, we can not dedicate – we can not consecrate – we can not hallow – this ground. The brave men, living and dead, who struggled here, have consecrated it, far above our poor power to add or detract. The world will little note, nor long remember what we say here, but it can never forget what they did here. It is for us the living, rather, to be dedicated here to the unfinished work which they who fought here have thus far so nobly advanced. It is rather for us to be here dedicated to the great task remaining before us – that from these honored dead we take increased devotion to that cause for which they gave the last full measure of devotion – that we here highly resolve that these dead shall not have died in vain – that this nation, under God, shall have a new birth of freedom – and that government of the people, by the people, for the people, shall not perish from the earth.

As an example of good speech writing in a nutshell, this is hard to beat. I commend it to the House.

BEAUFORT NUMBER	SPEED IN KNOTS	DESCRIPTION
0	Less than 1	Calm
1	1–3	Light air
2	4–6	Light breeze
3	7–10	Gentle breeze
4	11–16	Moderate breeze
5	17–21	Fresh breeze
6	22–27	Strong breeze

104 The Beaufort wind scale

The Beaufort scale was devised in 1806 by Admiral Sir Francis Beaufort (1774–1857) for estimating wind force at sea, without instruments. Its emphasis is on the observable effects of the wind, rather than its speed. The scale runs from 0 (calm) to 12 (hurricane). It is still in use today and has been adapted several times, most notably being modified to include descriptions of wind effects on land features. Crazy name, crazy scale.

STATE	LAND SIGNS
like a mirror	Smoke rises vertically
ples with the appearance of scales are ned, but without foam crests	Direction of wind shown by smoke drift but not by wind vanes
all wavelets, still short but more pronounced. sts have glassy appearance and do not eak	Wind felt on face, leaves rustle, ordinary wind vanes moved by wind
je wavelets. Crests begin to break. Foam of ssy appearance. Perhaps scattered white ses	Leaves and small twigs in constant motion, wind extends light flags
all waves, becoming longer, fairly frequent e horses	Wind raises dust and loose paper, small branches move
derate waves, taking a more pronounced n, many white horses are formed. Chance ome spray	Small trees in leaf start to sway, crested wavelets on inland waters
e waves begin to form, the white foam ts are more extensive everywhere. ably some spray	Large branches in motion, whistling in telegraph wires, umbrellas used with difficulty

BEAUFORT NUMBER	SPEED IN KNOTS	DESCRIPTION
7	28–33	Near gale
8	34–40	Gale
9	41–47	Strong gale
10	48–55	Storm
11	56–63	Violent storm
12	64	Hurricane

EA STATE	LAND SIGNS
ea heaps up and white foam from breaking aves begins to be blown in streaks along the irection of the wind	Whole trees in motion, inconvenient to walk against the wind
loderately high waves of greater length; dges of crests begin to break into spindrift. he foam is blown in well marked streaks along e direction of the wind	Twigs break from trees, difficult to walk
igh waves. Dense streaks of foam along the irection of the wind. Crests of waves begin to pple, tumble and roll over. Spray may affect sibility	Slight structural damage occurs, chimney pots and slates removed
ery high waves with long over hanging crests. e resulting foam in great patches is blown in ense white streaks along the direction of the wind. n the whole, the surface of the sea takes on a ite appearance. The 'tumbling' of the sea comes heavy and shock-like. Visibility fected	Trees uprooted, considerable structural damage occurs
ceptionally high waves (small and medium ed ships might be lost for a time behind e waves). The sea is completely covered with ng white patches of foam lying along the rection of the wind. Everywhere, the edges of e waves are blown into froth. Visibility ected	Widespread damage
e air is filled with foam and spray. Sea mpletely white with driving spray. Visibility very iously affected	Widespread damage

105 Historic dumb predictions

Did you hear about the fortune-teller who was also a contortionist? She was able to foresee her own end. I do not know who made up this joke, so I shall assume it was Barry Cryer. The point is, though, that looking into your crystal ball for portent is fraught with trouble, and anyone rash enough to try predicting the future is liable to find his hostages to fortune coming back home and biting him on the bum. Check this lot out for wildness of inaccuracy.

- 'Heavier-than-air flying machines are impossible.' Lord Kelvin, president, Royal Society, 1895.
- 'Radio has no future.' Lord Kelvin (again), 1897.
- 'The abdomen, the chest, and the brain will forever be shut from the intrusion of the wise and humane surgeon.' Sir John Eric Eriksen, Queen Victoria's Surgeon-Extraordinary, 1873.
- 'If excessive smoking actually plays a role in the production of lung cancer, it seems to be a minor one.' US National Cancer Institute, 1954.
- 'Who would ever want to use one?' US President Rutherford Hayes, speaking about the telephone, 1876.
- 'The cinema is little more than a fad ... It will never catch on.' Charlie Chaplin, 1914.
- 'Who the hell wants to hear actors talk?' Harry M. Warner, Warner Brothers, 1927.
- 'Can't act. Can't sing. Balding. Can dance a little.' Fred Astaire's MGM screen test, 1928.
- 'Stocks have reached what looks like a permanently high plateau.' Irving Fisher, Professor of Economics, Yale University, 1929.
- 'This is the biggest fool thing we have ever done. The bomb will never go off, and I speak as an expert in explosives.' Admiral William D. Leahy, speaking to President Harry S. Truman about the atomic bomb.
- 'Nuclear powered vacuum cleaners will probably be a reality within

ten years.' Alex Lewyt, President, Lewyt (Vacuum Cleaner) Corp., 1955.

- 'I think there is a world market for about five computers.' Thomas J. Watson, IBM Chairman, 1943.
- 'Computers in the future may have only 1,000 vacuum tubes and only weigh one and a half tons.' *Popular Mechanics*, 1949.
- 'There is no reason for any individual to have a computer in their home.' Ken Olson, Founder, Digital Equipment Corporation, 1977.
- 'We don't like their sound. Groups of guitars are on the way out.' Decca record executive dismissing the Beatles, 1962.
- 'A man-made voyage [to the moon] will never occur regardless of all future advances.' Dr Lee De Forest, inventor, 1926.

Oddball Gentlemen
(and a Lady)

106 John Harvey Kellogg, a natural flake

John Harvey Kellogg (1852–1943) was an American doctor and holistic-health expert who ran a sanatorium focusing on the salubrious benefits of cornflakes and exercise, and the hideous dangers of wanking.

John Kellogg was a bright boy who, after school in Battle Creek, Michigan, went on to New York University Medical College, graduating in 1875. Four years later he got married and, together with his wife, fostered more than forty children (over time, obviously) and adopted seven of them. The words 'glutton' and 'for punishment' leap to mind.

Kellogg became chief medical officer of the Battle Creek Sanitarium, which was run on the somewhat stern health principles of the Seventh-day Adventist Church. Exercise and abstinence were compulsory. Meat and alcoholic drinks were forbidden in the belief that this would aid digestion and suppress sexual stimulation. Who knows what depraved things a chap might do after eating a sausage?

Prisoners, I mean 'clients', of the Battle Creek Sanitarium were not allowed tobacco either, and were made to do breathing exercises while marching all over the blimmin' place, so that their food would be properly digested.

Kellogg seems to have had an obsession with the nether regions, especially what doctors call 'the bum'. He designed an enema machine that could pump gallons of water into patients, and would follow up this delightful treatment with a pint of yoghurt, half of which entered the body through the mouth, the rest going up the South Circular.

Notable figures travelled thousands of miles to submit to Kellogg's

therapies. They included sometime president William Howard Taft, vegetarian author George Bernard Shaw and Australian pianist Percy Grainger, who, although *The Oxford Dictionary of Music* doesn't say so, may well have composed his delightful arrangement of 'Country Gardens' with half a pint of banana Yoplait up his jacksie.

You could not imagine a more boring product than breakfast cereals, but the humble cornflake was to become the source of protracted wranglings and punch-ups in the Kellogg family. Together with his brother Will, John Kellogg first began making prophylactic cornflakes as the nineteenth century was drawing to its close. But the brothers argued over the amount of sugar that should go in and Will set up his own firm, Battle Creek Toasted Corn Flake Company, which eventually became the Kellogg's we know today.

John Harvey Kellogg wasted much of his life trying to discourage all kinds of sexual activity, but especially 'self-abuse'. His extremely dreary anti-wanking volume, *Plain Facts about Sexual Life*, which he drafted during his honeymoon(!), advocates the avoidance of 'sexually stimulating' food, giving over plenty of space to his second-favourite subject, yoghurt enemas.

Kellogg was something of an over-achiever in the field of anti-masturbation, which he regarded as the cause not only of epilepsy and 'dimness of vision', but as literally deadly. On the cheerful topic of 'masturbation-related death', he said, 'Such a victim literally dies by his own hand.' I wonder whether Dignitas have thought of introducing this as an alternative to the plastic bag. It might be a pleasanter way to go. As a treatment for a boy suffering from the 'solitary vice', cornflake-man recommended bandaging his hands, putting a wire cage over his genitals, sewing up his member, electric shock and circumcision. Of this latter, he said: 'The operation should be performed by a surgeon without administering an anaesthetic, as the brief pain attending the operation will have a salutary effect upon the mind, especially if it be connected with the idea of punishment . . .' Modern child psychologists might take issue with this approach, and possibly also wonder whether Dr Kellogg wasn't unleashing some sort of repressed sexual sadism.

The Battle Creek Sanitarium was sold during the Great Depression, but Kellogg bounced back, for the rest of his life running a successful operation in Florida, and turning his attention to racial segregation and eugenics – theories about as sensible as the idea that roping the pony, sanding the pole, tipping the waiter, whittling the dibber or pulling the one-eyed burping trouser-gecko makes you blind.

What a weirdo.

107 'La Goulue', inventor of the cancan

On 13 July 1866, in the northwestern suburb of Clichy, Hauts-de-Seine, 4 miles (6.4 km) from the centre of Paris, a baby was born to a poor Jewish mother, Mme Weber, originally from Alsace on the border with Germany and Switzerland. She named her daughter Louise.

As a young girl, Louise Weber loved to dance and by the age of sixteen, when she was meant to be working alongside her mother in a laundry, she would regularly sneak off to the dance hall dressed up in the customers' most glamorous and expensive outfits.

Soon she was dancing in small clubs around the city and, though not a beauty, she had in her younger years an elfin quality that, along with her vivacious personality, led her to become a popular character. Louise's saucy dance routines were also a big hit with the men. She had developed a characteristic lifting and swirling of the hem of her dress that revealed the embroidery on her underwear, and she was known for playfully flipping a gentleman's hat off with her toe during her high kicks. Her habit of swallowing the contents of a customer's glass while dancing past his table led journalist and impresario Gabriel Astruc to nickname her 'La Goulue' (the glutton). Unfortunately, over the years, her liking for the falling-down-liquid would come to make her nickname more and more appropriate.

Before long La Goulue was mingling with the glitterati, including artists such as Pierre-Auguste Renoir, through whose introductions she began modelling, being photographed many times by Achille Delmaet in the nude (not him – her). One day in the park she encountered Joseph Oller, one of the owners of the Moulin Rouge, who took an immediate shine to her cheeky personality and hired her as a dancer. From 1889 until 1895 she performed nightly at the Moulin Rouge, her outrageous flirting earning her more than twice as much in tips as she got for dancing, and making her the highest paid entertainer in Paris. She was now '*La reine de la sensualité Parisienne*' – the queen of Parisian sensuality.

A frequent visitor to the Moulin Rouge was Toulouse Lautrec, who immortalized her dancing the cancan in a series of posters. The cancan had long been a respectable, working-class dance, but La Goulue adapted it to her own style, with the purpose of 'entertaining' the male clientele. In its typical form, the cancan was performed in frilly bloomers by dancers whose energetic high kicks, splits and cartwheels were accompanied by squeals, leading to the uplifting of their ruched skirt hems to reveal their legs and underwear. Often La Goulue and her friends dispensed with the underwear altogether, so that the high kicks exposed bare bottoms and other geographical features which I will leave to the reader's imagination. *The Oxford Companion to Music* called the cancan: 'A boisterous and latterly indecorous dance of the quadrille order, exploited in Paris for the benefit of such British and American tourists as will pay well to be well shocked. Its exact nature is unknown to anyone connected with this Companion.'

But though La Goulue was a superb performer, she was no businesswoman. Having become rich and famous she decided to leave the Moulin Rouge in 1895. She developed an animal-taming act and poured her savings into a touring fairground show. These expensive efforts were unmitigated failures.

Six years after leaving the Moulin Rouge and ruining herself, Louise Weber married a man named José Droxler, setting up home with him in poverty until his death. Finally, in 1928, La Goulue returned to Montmartre, where, alcoholic, fat, toothless and destitute, she sold nuts, cigarettes and matches on a corner by the Moulin Rouge. Now looking exactly like her nickname, the sometime Queen of Montmartre went unrecognized by passers-by.

A year later, on 29 January 1929, Louise Weber died and was buried in an out-of-the-way cemetery in the suburb of Pantin. But she had left an indelible mark, and at the end of the twentieth century her remains were transferred to the Cimetière de Montmartre, where her headstone reads, *'Ici repose Louise Weber, dite "La Goulue" . . . Créatrice du French Cancan.'*

108 Matthew Robinson, lord of the water

Matthew Robinson, second Baron Rokeby (1712 –1800), was an English eccentric of the old school. Shunned by many men for his oddness, women were said to find him 'uncanny'. To his sister, Mrs Elizabeth Montagu, socialite and bluestocking friend of Dr Johnson, he was an embarrassment.

After taking his degree at Trinity Hall Cambridge, and being made a fellow, Robinson travelled abroad, visiting, among other places, the German spa town of Aix-la-Chapelle (Aachen). On his return, he fell in love with fresh air and refused to have a fire in the house, even on the bitterest day. He detested doctors, depending instead on pints of water and restraint. In his *A Journey Round the Coast of Kent* (1818), L. Fussell noted that Robinson 'studiously avoided every species of ostentation', and 'pursued a course of temperance so rigid that it amounted to austerity . . . a mode of life which every person besides himself would have thought a mortification'. Though wealthy, Robinson hoarded vast sums of gold in his wardrobe, not out of meanness, but because he was anxious about putting his money in the Bank of England.

Robinson was a shy man and his life was that of the bachelor-hermit. Though polite, he seemed to have what Fussell called, 'too much phlegm of the philosopher about him to appear amiable'. His rare visitors had to put up with listening to him recite long poems of exquisite dullness and, when alone, he spent his time painstakingly copying the paintings of Rubens and van Dyke, becoming all the while an ever more enthusiastic supporter of baths, bathing and water in general.

In 1754, Robinson inherited the family estate, Mount-Morris, a house designed by Christopher Wren in a rather lonely bit of Kent. Causing a hut to be built on the beach at Hythe, Robinson made daily trips to the ocean to swim, heedless of the British weather. His servant often had to drag him unconscious on to dry land when he had spent too long in the sea. Obsessed with getting enough water inside, as well as outside, himself, Robinson had a series of drinking fountains put along the way to sustain him on his long walk, his man following behind in a liveried carriage. If he found locals drinking from his fountains, he did not charge them, but instead gave them half a crown, about £25 in today's money.

Indifferent to eighteenth-century fashion, Robinson grew an enormous patriarchal beard that hung down to his waist. It stuck out beneath his arms and could be seen from behind. When he stayed at the Chequers Inn at Lenham, on his way to vote in a general election, the locals mistook him for a 'Mohammedan'.

In 1794, on the death of his cousin, who was the Bishop of Armagh and Primate of Ireland, Robinson inherited the title of Lord Rokeby and converted his estate's greenhouse into a bath, which was supplied by a spring. He had a glass mounted overhead to warm the bath in winter, and in summer would lie for hours, drinking copious amounts of water, his silver beard spreading over the surface like pondweed.

All Rokeby's meals were taken in this bath, his diet consisting chiefly of beef tea and venison, but when Prince William 'Silly Billy' Frederick (later the Duke of Gloucester) came to dinner, Rokeby did manage to serve up three courses of perfectly normal food, along with wines from his cellar. He himself drank no wine or spirits, no tea and no coffee: just water. He would eat nothing foreign, substituting local honey for sugar.

Lord Rokeby sat for a brief time as Member of Parliament for Canterbury. He was a radical politician who supported freedom of religion, thought, behaviour, trade and animals. He allowed horses, bulls, cows, sheep, goats and dogs to wander freely around his estate, and liked to traipse about in the early hours before sunrise, dressed up in a farmer's outfit.

Lord Rokeby lived to be eighty-eight, spending much of his life drinking water in the bath. He died in December 1800, not underwater, but in his bed.

He never married.

109 Rector of Stiffkey, 'Prostitutes' Padre' eaten by a lion

God help American tourists visiting Britain's old towns. Godmanchester, Ravenstruther and Stiffkey may all look easy enough for an English speaker to say but they are actually pronounced something like 'Gumster', 'Renstray' and 'Stewky'. And it is with the sometime rector of the last of these places that our story is concerned.

Harold Francis Davidson (1875–1937) was an Anglican clergyman known by his parishioners as 'Little Jimmy' because he was only 5 ft 3 in.

high. After taking a degree at Oxford University, Davidson toured Britain with comic-monologues act, subsequently becoming a curate of St Martin-in-the-Fields in Trafalgar Square, London.

In 1906, he was made rector of the parish of Stiffkey-with-Morston, on the Norfolk coast, where he and his wife Moyra raised a family of four children. He served as a navy chaplain in the First World War, and then began spending much of his time in London, away from his increasingly deaf, mad and adulterous wife. Every week, for more than a decade, he would leave the rectory before dawn and take the first train up to London, where he would trawl the West End and the City on the lookout for girls to 'rescue' from vice. If he drew a blank he would befriend waitresses, particularly those of the colourful Lyons Corner Houses, returning to Stiffkey just in time to deliver his weekend sermon, shake his wife's hand and hop back on the train to his good works in London. Recording his activities in later years he noted, 'I was picking up roughly . . . 150 or 200 girls a year' – an unfortunate choice or words.

In November 1930, Davidson missed his train back from the capital and was visibly absent from the annual Stiffkey Remembrance Day service. Major Philip Hamond, who was a big cheese locally and had harboured a dislike for the rector ever since he had turned him down as churchwarden a decade earlier, was apparently 'incandescent with rage' at the rector's absence. He complained to the Bishop of Norwich, accusing Davidson of 'immorality' because of his activities in the Big Smoke.

The Arrows Detective Agency, which had been hired by the Church of England in December 1931 to look into the rector's doings, finally discovered one Rose Ellis, a sometime prostitute, who produced an extremely tasty oral testimony (no pun intended), after eight generous ports in the Strand Palace Hotel. Following this, Davidson was smartly charged on several counts under Church law: immoral conduct with Ellis, immoral conduct 'in embracing a girl in a Chinese restaurant in Bloomsbury', immoral conduct 'towards a woman in a café in Walbrook' and 'the immoral habit of associating with ladies of loose character'.

Davidson's trial began on 29 March 1932 at Church House,

Westminster. Large crowds attended the hearing, which lasted twenty-six days. The newspapers, of course, revelled in reporting the jaunty parade of waitresses, jugglers, publicans and tarts who gave evidence for the prosecution. Seventeen-year-old Gwendoline (aka Barbara) Harris told how the rector had pretended to be her uncle, paid her rent and invited her to live at his London home. He had missed his Remembrance Day train, she said, because he was 'trying to kiss me all the time'.

The big torpedo finally struck Davidson's defence when a photograph was produced of the dog-collared rector staring into the eyes of a fifteen-year-old nude girl, Estelle Douglas. The girl had her back to the camera and the rector's left hand was on her naked shoulder, his right just a 16th of an inch from her rather choice bum. Apart from a black shawl that was literally falling off her, Estelle was as nude as you like. Davidson told the court that he had been offered money for posing, in order to help his case. Estelle said that two Fleet Street photographers had asked her to remove her clothes to get a better shot. She might have been merely naive, but he, surely, ought to have smelt a rat – only a blind man with no feeling in his hands could have failed to appreciate the young lady's nudity. Nonetheless, the picture does look very posed.

In July 1932 Davidson was convicted on all charges, the picture proving his guilt in the eyes of many. After the failure of his appeal to the Archbishop of Canterbury, the rector had to find a way to make ends meet and decided to start a naturist colony (what else?), also taking the opportunity to pose on Hampstead Heath beside a dead whale. In September he appeared inside a barrel on Blackpool promenade, next to a flea circus and a three-legged boy, in an act which featured him starving himself almost to death, or being 'roasted' in an oven while being poked with a pitchfork. In October of the same year, Davidson was formally defrocked in Norwich Cathedral. He missed much of the action by turning up late.

Now described as 'an ex-clergyman of no fixed abode' he appeared for the 1937 summer season as 'A modern Daniel in the lion's den' at Thompson's Amusement Park in Skegness, where he preached from the Bible inside a cage beside a lion and lioness, Freddie and Toto. It was while performing his act on 28 July that he accidentally trod on Toto's tail and was seriously mauled by Freddie. The ex-rector of Stiffkey was taken to the local hospital, where he rapidly died, after, somewhat curiously, being injected with insulin. A coroner recorded a verdict of death by misadventure, which must have been a contender for the understatement of 1937.

But the Prostitutes' Padre wasn't finished causing trouble yet. In true style, police had to be called to manage the surging crowd of 3,000 enthusiastic mourners and press who stuffed the village of Stiffkey for the laying to rest of this delightfully turbulent priest.

110 Le Pétomane

On 1 June 1875, Joseph Pujol was born at 13 Rue des Incurables in Marseille. One of five children, Joseph led an uneventful childhood until one day he made a momentous discovery. As he was bathing in the sea, he put his head under water and held his breath. Suddenly, he was aware that water was entering his body through the opening in his fundament for which there is a common 'street' term that I am avoiding. Joseph now found he could squirt the water out again in a powerful jet, and over a considerable distance. Being a child of scientific curiosity he soon taught himself how to do a similar thing with air. This had the benefit of musicality.

On beginning his military service Pujol became the talk of the barracks with his flatulent imitations of everything from the demure tootling of a young girl to a full 21-gun salute. Friends, who found his little demonstrations hilarious, suggested that when he had completed his soldiering he should build his repertoire into a proper act.

Pujol was already a good trombonist and comic turn and he found he could draw a crowd in Marseille with his novel show. Paris seemed the next step but, cautious by nature, he decided to take his act to the provinces first. So, with the wind at his back, he set off.

Pujol boasted that he was one of the few musical performers to pay no authors' royalties, but, despite his broad repertoire, he produced only four notes: the *do*, *mi*, *sol* and *do* of the octave. Nonetheless, the act was a hit and in 1892 he headed for Paris where, he said, the sails of the Moulin Rouge would provide a marvellous fan for his routine.

Le Pétomane ('the fart maniac'), as he now styled himself, received a warm hand on his opening and was an instantaneous success with the Moulin Rouge audience. He was soon earning a fortune despite only doing what we can all do. But, as Plato said, 'It ain't what you do, it's the way that you do it', and Pujol farted with more panache and brio than anybody in the world.

He came on dressed in an impressive costume of red coat, black satin breeches ruched at the knee, white tie, stockings, patent leather shoes and his trademark black handlebar moustache. Le Pétomane began with a reassuring remark to his audience, many of whom were not sure quite what was about to happen and were anxious for their noses. 'My parents ruined themselves perfuming my rectum,' he would announce, and would then begin. His repertoire included some old favourites including 'The Little Girl', 'The Mother-in-Law' and 'The Mason', as well as 'The Bride on Her Wedding Night' (very quiet) and the morning after (very loud), and 'The Dressmaker Tearing Two Yards of Calico'. This one lasted ten seconds and reportedly possessed great aural verisimilitude. It was followed by 'Cannons' and 'Thunder'.

Pujol would then disappear behind the scenes to insert a 3 ft (1 m) rubber tube, through which he would puff on a cigarette, finally blowing out the smoke in a great nimbus. Keeping up the variety, he would next play a little flute with six stops, using the same tube, his party piece being 'Au clair de la lune'. The man was a true *fartiste* and the act finished with his removing the tube to blow out a candle from the distance of a foot or so, as well as several of the gas footlights, which must have required eye-watering force.

The crowds went wild and, convulsed with mirth, helpless audience members, especially women, staggered into the aisles, crying with laughter.

But Pujol was aware that he needed to prove the absence of trickery so he initiated a series of private men-only performances in which, dressed in a bathing costume equipped with a rear opening, he would lower himself into a basin and then discharge two litres of water in a glittering arc.

Le Pétomane made several phonographic recordings during the good years but the wind of change was blowing, and, after some arguments with the management, Pujol left the Moulin Rouge in 1895. He performed with his own touring theatre until the outbreak of the First World War and shortly thereafter retired as a performer to run bakeries.

As it happened, his wife quite often had a bun in the oven, too. Over his long life, Joseph Pujol fathered ten children, and in time had several grandchildren. He died in 1945, aged eighty-eight. The Faculty of Medicine had offered 25,000 francs to examine his body but, though he had happily agreed, his family refused to authorize a post mortem on his famous bum.

The street in Marseille where he first worked as a baker is now named Rue Pujol in honour of his rare gift.

RELATIONSHIPS
AND THAT

Love, Romance and 'Horizontal Refreshment'

111 The ten habits of the highly effective Lothario

When I was an art student I would often see girls I thought would make good portrait subjects, but I was shy at first about asking them if they would pose for me. As soon as I did ask, though, I found there was nothing to it. The next step was to find out if they would pose nude. To my great astonishment they nearly always said yes, which goes to show that if you don't ask, you don't get. You've got to do this kind of thing properly, though. Imagine you've just approached a woman leaning against the mantelpiece at a party. All you need do now is copy the technique of those chaps who annoyingly walk off with a lady after two minutes' chat.

1. Get straight to the point: imagine that tonight is your last night on earth. No beating about the bush, *get in there*.
2. Persistence: keep up the pressure. Unless she walks away in a huff, you must persist. Confidence and sexual assertiveness are the keys to success. There's absolutely no need to look like Brad Pitt. Being handsome has little to do with it.
3. Body language: the way you stand, where you look and what you do with your hands are all important. Look straight into her eyes, but also at her mouth. Point your body directly towards hers and stand with your feet wide apart with your fingers in your belt, like a swaggering cowboy, thumbs pointing towards your 'gentleman's area'. These are primitive courtship signals that save on words.
4. Touch: take every opportunity to touch her. Don't grab; instead brush

lint off her shirt, playfully squeeze her arm, blow confetti off her neck or helpfully tuck a stray curl of hair behind her ear.

5 Compliments: don't go mad; save your tongue for later and show her what you think by looking at her. As a girl once said to me, 'How can you respect a man who kisses your arse?'

6 Humour: if you can laugh her into bed, so much the better. But, if you are not naturally funny, steer clear.

7 Ask questions: don't talk about yourself, ask about her. 'Have you ever been unfaithful to your boyfriend?' is an excellent start.

8 Flowers: always a success, if you've got some to hand. I knew a chap who'd lift a dripping handful out of a hotel vase and present them with a kiss. Women thought this was so daring and masculine. Never buy flowers from a petrol station.

9 Don't pay without a promise: pay for meals and tickets only if you have had a genuine promise of horizontal refreshment in return. A golden commandment.

10 Get used to the turndown: I had friend who used to say to girls, quite bluntly, 'Why don't you take your clothes off!' I asked him if he didn't get a lot of rejection. 'Naturally,' he said, 'but I also get a lot of screwing.'

112 Classic sleeping positions and what they say about you

Nobody ever accused Lyndon B. Johnson of being Oscar Wilde, and the coarseness of his wit is illustrated by his famous description of Gerald Ford as 'so dumb that he can't fart and chew gum at the same time', and, more piquantly, 'so dumb he couldn't tip shit out of a boot if the instructions were written on the heel'. Ford did seem a bit ungainly, falling down the steps of Air Force One, skiing into chairlifts, and getting married wearing one brown shoe and one black, but he was certainly lucky, being the only US vice-president and the only president to be elected to neither office. After watching President Nixon resign on television and realizing he was now in charge, Ford went to bed. 'My feeling is that you might as well get to sleep,' he said. His favoured sleeping position is not recorded, but it may well be one of the following. Perhaps yours is also here.

1 The Animal: position adopted by chaps who have no current bed-partner, except for Rover. Fine so long as the animal isn't under the covers with you, which is known as the 'I don't like Uncle Vivian, he smells funny' position.

2 The Snorer: this position is not so much adopted, as naturally occurring. Its cause is a curry, five pints of beer and several large scotches. When the snoring starts, the woman (absent from illustration because she's gone to sleep in the spare room) makes a hasty retreat. Related to 'The Guffer' (see illustration, position 6).

3   The Duvet Thief: this position is one of the most common. Like the Snorer, the Duvet Thief position is often denied by the duvet thief until the bed-partner takes a picture on his iPhone and shows the perpetrator, at which point it is still denied.

4   The Parachute Accident: this is what happens when a parachute jump you are doing while tethered to your instructor goes wrong and you encounter the concrete-hard earth face first at 80 mph (130 km/h). In bed it's more relaxed, and you are less dead.

5 The Lovey-dovey: this is tolerable only in the early days (nights) of a bed-sharing relationship, when it is used briefly to interrupt the vigorous, repeated and heroic intercourse sessions. However, after a while it gets a bit annoying; you don't want someone leeching on to you every night, breathing down your neck. A position for young lovers, not middle-aged farts.

6 The Writing on the Wall: self explanatory. The opposite of the Lovey-dovey. It's all over bar the conversations with the flying plates and the fights over custody of the computer and the Persian rug. Ring solicitors in the morning.

7   The Starfish: Laurence Stern in *Tristram Shandy* (1761) has this exchange – '"My brother Toby," quoth she, "is going to be married to Mrs Wadman." "Then he will never," quoth my father, "be able to lie diagonally in his bed again, as long as he lives."' The Starfish is a common position for the chap who has been unattached for some time, a kind of reversion to default setting. Bodes unwell for the continuing relationship.

8   The Neurotic Weirdo: anybody who sleeps with another person who does this with their legs deserves some kind of bed-sharing Nobel Prize. Never camp on a sheer mountain ledge with a woman who sleeps this way. You are likely to be launched into the void.

113 Really bad chat-up lines

Have you noticed how some chaps effortlessly chat up women and seem to have a magnetic attraction for them no matter what they do or say? We can leave them to it; this page is a guide to how *not* to do it, for those other fellows who couldn't attract a woman if they were the last man on earth. Of course, it doesn't help to have greasy hair, an anorak and a copy of *The Collins Book of Train Spotting Stories*, but neither will any of the following chat-up lines get you anywhere. They are a hopeless mixture of the offensive, the gushing, the sad and the much-too-blunt. See what you reckon. I'm sure you couldn't do worse.

- Right. You'll do.
- You don't sweat much for a fat lass.
- Would you like to see a trick I learned in prison?
- What the hell are you looking at?
- Your eyes are like a golden gateway into a world of which I wish to be a part.
- Wow! Are those real?
- You're ugly, but so intriguing.
- Hey, Toots, if beauty was an animal, you'd be an elephant.
- Would you like to see my train timetables?
- Why are your arms so hairy?
- My first two girlfriends died from eating poison mushrooms; my last girlfriend died of a head injury. (She wouldn't eat her mushrooms.)
- Are you in heat?
- How was paradise when you left it, Angel?
- Christ, your eyebrows are thick.
- Sorry about my breath, my gums are crawling with disease.
- May I buy you a drink? Or d'you just want the money?
- Hey gorgeous, can you suck a golf ball through a garden hose?
- Mind if I take my trousers off?
- I bet you £10 you're going to reject me.
- Can I kiss your face?

- Nice jewellery. It would look good on my bedside table.
- Do you like being hit?
- I love older women.
- What colour is your toothbrush?
- I sometimes crap my pants.
- You look exactly like my mum.
- So then, do you like fat guys with no money?
- Come on – we're leaving.
- God, what short legs you've got.
- Hey, I like spotty women.
- Buy me a pint, will you, sweetheart?
- My stools are soft, what are yours like?
- I'm gay. Like to try curing me?
- You remind me of a prostitute I used to use.
- Would you like to come home and tie me up?
- Hello, can I have some sex, in exchange for sex?
- Women adore me. I'm impotent.
- I'll bet you £10 my willy can't fit in your mouth.
- What's a slapper like you doing in a posh place like this?
- My teeth are bad because of all the sweets what I eat.
- Hey girl, you ever played nude leapfrog?
- You smell wet. Let's party.

114 Three great lovers

Errol Flynn (1909–59)

Errol Leslie Flynn was a swashbuckling Australian-American actor who combined romantic Hollywood leads with a wine-women-and-cigarettes-and-brawling-and-cocaine-and-prison-and-song lifestyle, making himself a bad-boy woman-magnet. Flynn's distant antecedents were Tasmanian convicts and he was, himself, repeatedly expelled from school for fighting and reportedly for having it off with a school laundress.

Before becoming a famous sex symbol, Flynn had been an unfamous ditch-digger and a ranch 'hogget-dagger', whose job was to de-testicle rams. He moved to England as a young man, where he began acting, after a time being signed to Warner Brothers. He then moved to the US and became a citizen in 1942, just in time to get into serious trouble when two underage girls, with the homely names of Betty and Peggy, accused him of rape. Flynn was publicly defended by a group known as American Boys' Club for the Defense of Errol Flynn (ABCDEF). He was cleared of the charges.

Errol Flynn was married three times but seemed to have a particular penchant for very young ladies. In the late 1950s he met fifteen-year-old Beverly Aadland and cast her in his last film, *Cuban Rebel Girls* (1959). His interest appeared to be not entirely professional. Indeed, Beverly Aadland was in the car with Flynn shortly before he died of a heart attack in Vancouver on 14 October 1959. As he was being driven to the airport he started to feel ill so he was taken to a friend's apartment, where, naturally enough, a party started. Flynn, who didn't realize he was in the middle of a heart attack, told stories and larked about. Then, retiring for a lie down, he died. The coroner later reported that his body was so ravaged by hard living that it looked like that of a much older man. He was buried with six bottles of whisky, a gift from 'friends'.

In Charles Higham's *Errol Flynn: The Untold Story* (1980), the author alleged, controversially, that Flynn was a bisexual fascist-sympathizer who had spied for the Nazis and had affairs with Howard Hughes, Tyrone Power and Truman Capote. None of them denied it – Power and Hughes being rather dead, and Capote having started the rumour himself.

The best story I know about Errol Flynn concerns a prank he played during the filming of *The Adventures of Don Juan* (1948), when he asked makeup artist Perc Westmore to make him a huge fake penis. Putting this on, he reclined nude on a couch, draped a silk square over the monster, and waited for his actor-sidekick Alan Hale to come into his dressing room. When Hale appeared, Flynn blew on the silk, causing it to slip to the floor. Without missing a beat, Hale said, 'I'll take a pound and a half.'

Casanova (1725-98)

Giacomo Girolamo Casanova de Seingalt was a right Casanova. His name translates as Jim Newhouse, which doesn't sound romantic enough for this legendary seducer, amateur scholar, actor and, briefly, abbot. An extraordinary workaholic, with a penchant for getting into trouble with girls, the Church and everybody else, Casanova nonetheless counted as chums Louis XV, various popes and Mozart. He was himself a writer and his *Histoire de ma vie* (*My Life Story*) endlessly reports how brilliant he was in the seduction department. Indeed, without his own boasts he might now be forgotten.

Casanova was born in Venice, where he suffered juvenile nosebleeds that were cured by a witch. In 1744 he became a secretary to a cardinal in Rome and then travelled to Corfu, Naples and Constantinople, working his way back to Venice, where he tried to settle down but, instead, caught VD for the first time. The pox (syphilis), gonorrhoea and other venereal diseases were to dog him throughout his life. By 1750 his CV included jobs as a clergyman, secretary, soldier and (bad) violinist, in countries around the world.

In 1749 Casanova met a young Frenchwoman, Henriette, who seems to have been the love of his life, but she left him and he fled to Lyons, becoming a Freemason. But the Inquisition didn't like the cut of his jib and in 1755 he was arrested and his literary assets seized – which must have made his eyes water. Books on magic and sexual positions were impounded and he was sentenced to five years in the Venice Piombi, a lead-roofed prison in the Doge's Palace. He was just twenty-one and things were going badly.

However, on the night of 31 October 1756 Casanova escaped from his cell and was let out by a guard who mistook him for a politician. He moved to Paris, where he was now a celebrity, and in 1757 persuaded the French government to let him start a lottery. This became a huge success, making him a millionaire, but three years later he had to flee his creditors and travelled around Europe again. Between 1774 and 1782 he worked as a spy for the Venetians, squeezing in girls wherever he could.

In later life Casanova sometimes dressed as a woman – what is it with these people? – but by 1789 he was feeling bored and decided to write his sexual memoirs, *Histoire de ma vie*, is the work for which he is best remembered, but its stories are probably hugely exaggerated. As Casanova said himself, 'The same principle which forbids me to lie does not allow me to tell the truth.' He would have made a good politician. How he had any time for seducing women beats me.

Casanova died in bed – on his own – in 1798.

Rudolph Valentino (1895–1926)

Known as the 'Latin Lover', Rudolph Valentino was one of the best recognized and most popular Italian silent-film actors of the 1920s. Women found him, as one contemporaneously put it, 'triumphantly seductive'. Boxing heavyweight Jack Dempsey said of him, 'He was the most virile and masculine of men. The women were like flies to a honeypot.' H.L. Mencken, who knew and liked Valentino, said he was 'catnip to women'.

However, his exotic good looks and dandified clothes drew suspicion from some journalists that his true sexual proclivities might lie in a different quarter and his pomaded hairstyle soon became known as the 'Vaselino'. In 1926, when a talcum-powder machine appeared in a posh Chicago hotel, Rudolph Valentino and his films were blamed for turning American men into sissies. Valentino challenged the author of one of these stories to a duel. Though stylish, this was a bit camp, let's be honest.

In 1919, shortly before becoming a superstar, Valentino married an actress named Jean Acker, who, for some unguessable reason, locked him out of the bedroom on their wedding night. They shortly separated, without consummating their union, and not long afterwards Acker struck up a relationship with a former Ziegfeld Follies girl named Chloe Carter, with whom she would remain 'best friends' for the rest of her life.

In 1921, during the production of *Camille*, Valentino met Natacha Rambova, a costume designer, whose 'career' had been 'assisted' by Alla Nazimova, a well-known lesbian. Valentino and Rambova married in Mexico, but he was soon arrested for bigamy under California law, having been divorced less than a year. Something wasn't quite right about the relationship anyway, and they sort of went off each other. Valentino petulantly left Rambova just one dollar in his will.

Pola Negri was the last woman in Valentino's life, though never his wife. Strangely, just like the other girls, there were rumours of lesbianism, based on little more than her extremely close friendship with a vaudeville performer called Margaret West, who was her 'best friend', with whom she lived.

Despite the tittle-tattle, women continued to find Valentino magnetically attractive, just like Rock Hudson, and spent a fortune going to his films. Before reaching the age of thirty-two, however, Valentino died from complications of appendicitis. At his New York funeral in 1926, 100,000 people caused a day-long riot.

There remains no evidence that the great Latin Lover Valentino was a homosexual actor indulging in well-publicized 'marriages' of a lavender tinge for 'image purposes'. The very idea is ludicrous and totally unheard of in Hollywood.

115 The top twenty-five things women hate about men

There's a whole long list of things which women do that drive men up the wall. There's the shopping thing, then there's the million-shoes thing, the scented-candles business and the cushions-everywhere problem. But since there is only so much space in this book I cannot do the subject justice. Instead, here's a list of things women hate about men. It is the result of a consultation programme with my own research committee (all my girlfriends) and is comprehensive – though not exhaustive. Anyway, forewarned is four-armed, as the Hindu Goddess Kali might say. (The views expressed are not necessarily those of the management.)

1   Not listening to vital information ('selective deafness'): a woman will say, 'Now listen, Geoff, *don't* come home after work because we are going to Bill and Sandra's tonight – remember? Pick me up at the

station at 6.' At 6.30, the man drives up to his house as usual and wonders why all the lights are off. His wife, standing outside the freezing cold station, has left nine messages on his phone, but the battery is flat. Let us cast a veil over the heartache to come . . .

2 High resistance to advice – especially in-car: when men are lost, they will not ask directions, and if suggestions are made, they will not accept them. This is allied to the 'crap-passenger' problem. Well, at least we don't rotate the map as we travel, to make sure it's pointing the way we are going.

3 Talking in grunts: wha'?

4 Crepuscular penile tumescence: otherwise known as the Morning Glory, Dawn Boner or EMBV (Early Morning Blue-Veiner). I understand that it is the inconvenient time of day that is the problem here. At least it stops you rolling out of bed.

5 Literal-mindedness: when a woman says, 'I tried to fix that tap washer but water sprayed everywhere and I couldn't get the top back on and spent the whole day mopping up – and the washer's still not replaced,' the man will say, 'You should have turned the water off first.' Women do not require a technical solution to a problem like this; what they want is a response such as, 'Oh you poor thing. Here, have a glass of wine and a big hug.' Frankly, any man who did respond in this way would be extremely strange. Furthermore, it should work both ways; for example, women need to understand that when they say to a man something like, 'The grass is really long. It looks untidy,' they have *not* given an explicit instruction to the man to mow the lawn – as they seem to think they have.

6 Assumption by the man of PMT when the woman disagrees with him: I have a friend who, at one time, had a wife and two teenage daughters in his house. He really had no idea what he had done wrong, ever.

7 Sport obsession: this one is hardly enough to balance out the shoes, the shopping, the scented candles and the fancy photo frames. Learn to live with it ladies.

8   Lack of shopping skills: if she wanted Gok Wan she should have said so.

9   Staring at a lady's embonpoint: all men are aware that a lady's cleavage, the breasts and the general bosomal zone comprise an area of high danger. It's rather like the sun – you must never look directly at it; it will harm you. As soon as you see the area, look away or you will end up with damaged eyes (black ones). T-shirts with slogans saying things like 'You are a naughty boy – go to my room!', tight-striped sweaters, dangling jewellery and 1950s-style conical, or 'uplifting', bras are absolutely no help, girls. We do our best in the circumstances.

10 Birthday/anniversary-forgetting: remembering ancient football results or the exact number of bolts in the Forth Bridge but forgetting the birthday is a combustible mixture.

11 Daughter by proxy: men are said to make it their wife/girlfriend's responsibility to phone their mum, buy her presents etc. Well, why have a dog and bark yourself?

12 Delegation of project management (related to the above): women complain that they have to organize everything – holidays, Christmas and so on. Trouble is that if you *do* try to organize Christmas (i.e. put on paper hat, turn on telly and get the beers in) women are not satisfied. You can't win.

13 Chronic eructation and flatus: otherwise known as burping and leg-lifting farting, all the time and everywhere. Leg-lifting is important for tone control. A high-pitched squeak creates the unwanted impression that you have hidden a hamster.

14 Looking for things with their mouth: 'Where are my car keys?' Look, things get found, don't they?

15 Sissy 'mummy's-boy' behaviour: now this is one I can go along with. Those chaps who scream when a wasp flies past or who run away from cows – that's not right. Not to be confused with a manly moistening of the eye at the funeral of your mother, which women find attractive.

16 Hands down pants: apparently the absent-minded rearrangement of the trouser-furniture annoys the ladies. Related to pocket-juggling.

17 Tidiness/cleanliness confusion: women cannot understand how a man can wash his car but be indifferent to a grimy kitchen or bathroom. Rearranging things is apparently not the same as cleaning. Curious.

18 Snoring: so long as you don't snore while you are listening to her tell you about her day I don't see the problem. That's what the spare room is for.

19 Tit-and-toilet-humour obsession: if it's funny why not laugh?

20 Hanging on to old rubbish, e.g. socks with holes: thrift is good.

21 Huffing and puffing during sentimental films and women's TV programmes: if you demand silence from her during documentaries about Spitfire pilots it probably is unfair to eat crisps loudly and complain during her chick flicks.

22 Cheap presents: petrol station flowers, crappy chocolates or joke presents such as a sleeping bag in the shape of a human being are all bad. Avoid.

23 Mistaken beliefs: such as that the telephone is for conveying information and not having conversations, or that you can get in a quick pint thirty seconds before time is called. Ladies, these are both *true* beliefs.

24 Competitiveness: who can drink the pint fastest, eat the hottest curry, etc. What's wrong with it?

25 Inability to read a Sunday newspaper without muddling the sections and taking them off to the bog (which men use as their office) and reading them for hours. Related toilet problems: not replacing empty toilet rolls (I thought they replaced themselves), not picking up bath mats and poor lavatorial aim. What is this? Are we expecting the blimmin' Queen?

New Man Skills

116 Are babies dangerous?

Spaced Out: The Very Best of Leonard Nimoy and William Shatner is a 1996 album containing some very upsetting 'singing' by these two *Star Trek* legends. Shatner, who played Captain Kirk, 'speaks' his songs, sounding like Sir John Gielgud after several large ones, while Nimoy, who played Spock, at least makes the odd effort to squeeze out a tune. It's a highly illogical listening experience, Captain, and one that music lovers should avoid.

It's important, of course, not to confuse *Mr* Spock with *Dr* Spock (1903–1998), the paediatrician whose 1946 book, *The Common Sense Book of Baby and Child Care*, has sold more than fifty million copies, making it one of the best bestsellers in the history of bestsellers. Its basic message, 'You know more than you think you do', reassured nervous mothers.

If you've ever seen a new father holding his newborn baby, like a carboy of nuclear poison, you will realize that men probably know less than they think they do, which wasn't much to start out with. The main thing to remember, chaps, is that babies are not intrinsically dangerous, though they can get you into trouble. Here's a top-ten advice checklist.

1 Babies cry a lot. This does not mean they are broken. They may need food (hot dogs, pickled onions and leftover chilli are not recommended) or they may require their nappy changing (see below).
2 Never attempt to change a baby's nappy. Ever. It is like trying to shovel a storm-swept Somme trench during an unusually fierce pounding by the Hun.

3   Baby sick will not hurt you. This is worth knowing because you will be meeting a lot of it.

4   Do not imagine that any intimacy will occur between yourself and your lady for decades after your baby is born. Babies are nature's contraceptives and the minute you get into your stride the yelling will start. Eighteen years is the typical contraceptive half-life of a new infant.

5   Do not put a wet baby in a microwave to dry it off. They go bang.

6   Health visitors can harm you. They are often repellently patronizing and man-averse. Get a few beers in if one of these horrors is expected when you are around.

7   Babies are mother-in-law magnets. Make sure you have a few beers in.

8   Research shows that new babies make men tired and irritable. Not exactly brain surgery, then. Our old friend beer is the answer.

9   Babies do not bounce – even the plumpest. Try not to drop them.

10 If your lady is breastfeeding be aware that a baby will take complete ownership of its mother's breasts – for months. No matter that her shirt puppies are in optimum condition; you are not going to get a look-in mate.

117 A look at washing machines

My seafaring Uncle Roy used to say, 'Women and seamen don't mix,' which always made my mother blanche, for some reason. My own motto would be: 'Men and washing machines don't mix.' I mean, do *you* understand all those wretched pictograms on the labels inside your clothes? What's the difference between a crossed out triangle and a crossed out square with a circle in the middle? And what if the circle has a dot in the centre – or two dots? I mean, it's enough to drive a man mad – if he ever bothered to think about it.

Fortunately, some labels spell things out for you in old-fashioned words and sentences, often in a variety of languages. The most amusing label ever may be the one first noticed in 2004 sewn into the backpacks and laptop cases made by the Tom Bihn company of Washington State, US, which contained care instructions in English, with French translations. These were along the lines of: 'Do not machine dry. Ne pas secher a la machine.' However, the following extra two sentences appeared at the foot of the label in French only: 'Nous sommes desoles que notre president soit un idiot. Nous n'avons pas vote pour lui.' Which means roughly: 'We are sorry our president is an idiot. We didn't vote for him.' Tom Bihn says he doesn't know which waggish employee of his small company inserted the rude addition but has offered him or her a pay rise for what has become a brilliant aid to marketing. Whether the president in question was intended to be Mr George W. Bush, M. Jacques Chirac or Mr Tom Bihn himself remains a tantalizing mystery.

Anyway, here's a straightforward explanation of the ordinary non-seditious symbols and legends that you'll find on your clothes, for the next time you find yourself alone with a washing machine. Best of luck, old chap.

General classification

When you first examine the symbols below, only the meanings of the iron and the water tub are immediately guessable, but it will help if you understand, before you start, that the symbols are classified into groups.

- The water tub is washing
- The circle in a square is drying
- The iron is ironing
- The triangle is bleaching
- The circle (usually containing a letter) is dry cleaning

The general principle on all the symbols is that the more dots there are, the hotter the temperature should be. A cross through a symbol means 'don't'.

118 Putting the remote down and other new man behaviours

Writing in the *Journal of Neuroscience* not so long ago, researchers from somewhere or the other said that if you squirt oxytocin – the so-called 'cuddle hormone' – up a man's nose it will make him 'empathetic', to the extent that, when shown pictures of a girl hugging a cat, he will become as 'tuned in' to the girl's feelings as a woman would be.

Now, while I have no objection to pussy-cuddling, I don't see the point of this nonsense. I mean, are we supposed to carry a nasal spray around with us and squirt it up our noses like invalids whenever someone wants a cuddle? My trouser pockets are bulgy enough, what with my hipflask and little black book. No, intranasal cuddle-hormone therapy is a silly idea that I think could well cause a chap to grow breasts and actually turn into a woman. What's more, it's unnecessary if you just follow these simple steps towards becoming a 'new man'. With any luck it will help you overcome some of the female objections set out on preceding pages.

New man behaviours

1   Once your programme is on the television, there's really no need to cling on to that remote control for dear life. If the lady of the house wants to watch something else, just explain to her that you are watching *your* programme. Don't worry, she'll soon settle down.

2   If your bacon and eggs are not up to scratch there's no need to blow your top. She might find a sheet of instructions useful, though.

3   Always lift your legs when a lady is hoovering around you. Good manners cost nothing.

4   If there's a story about science or politics or sport in the paper, don't let her trouble her head over it. A simple drawing in bright colours

will do wonders to explain things. If she keeps on asking, just say that these are not matters for her. She'll soon recognize your intellectual superiority and put the kettle on.

5 If you are going to break wind, it's only polite to give a lady plenty of notice.

6 Make sure you keep the broom cupboard properly supplied with new brooms, dusters and whatnot. If she runs out you'll never hear the end of it.

7 If she's spoiling for an argument over nothing – you know what they are like – remember the sage motto: 'Never wrestle with a chimney sweep.' Don't sink to her level, that's the point.

8 Don't forget to compliment her if she's taken trouble with her appearance. There's no reason she can't go shopping, do the housework and cook your dinner without taking a moment to look attractive for you when you get home.

9 Coffee mornings with her girlfriends are perfectly all right, so long as you aren't around, but night classes and so forth smack alarmingly of education. Put your foot down – with a firm hand.

10 She should adopt an NSN (Never Say No) policy in the bedroom. It's your right to insist on this.

11 A new man always lifts his hat before breaking wind in front of a lady.

SCHOOL FOR SCOUNDRELS

Showmanship

119 Sword-swallowing for fun and profit

Like fire-eating and walking across a bed of red-hot coals, sword-swallowing is a dangerous feat, whereby some street performer in front of a crowd of cheering urchins sticks one or more long sharp swords down his gullet, leaving the quillon, hilt and pommel (the handle bits), and sometimes also part of the blade, sticking out of his mouth. He finally slides the sword/s out again without, apparently, hurting himself. It seems impossible and, as Sherlock Holmes said, 'It is impossible as I state it, and therefore I must in some respect have stated it wrong.'

Sword-swallowing is not a trick in the usual sense, but the above description is stated wrong in the following respect. The sword is not a sharp weapon but a special prop with blunt edges. Using a sharp sword would have immediate, very noticeable and highly scarlet results. It is properly swallowed insofar as it does actually go down the food tube (oesophagus). However, it is not propelled from the mouth to the stomach by neuromuscular contraction, as a cheese sandwich would be. Instead, it is simply slid down the gullet. Nonetheless, the trick requires practice and skill, and is not something a novice is capable of performing.

For example, a lot of training is required just to overcome the gag reflex and stop yourself retching all over the place – an act not known for its ability to fill the hat with coin. According to Dan Meyer, Chief Executive Director of the Sword Swallowers Association International (SSAI), the pharynx is inured to touch by having fingers, spoons and knitting needles repeatedly put into the throat, with the performer graduating finally to a wire coathanger. Oh, the romance of it.

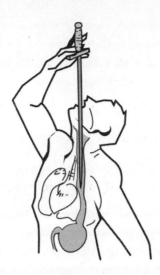

Sword-swallowing is said to have originated in India around 2000 BCE, spreading to China, Ancient Greece and throughout the Roman Empire into Japan and medieval Europe, where it was popularized amongst the public by jongleurs and other silly fakirs. In the modern age, George M. Gould AM, MD and Walter L. Pyle AM, MD described the process, along with sexual sneezing and other oddities, in their 1898 volume, *Anomalies and Curiosities of Medicine*, which has the longest subtitle I have ever seen: *being an encyclopaedic collection of rare and extraordinary cases, and of the most striking instances of abnormality in all branches of medicine and surgery, derived from an exhaustive research of medical literature from its origin to the present day, abstracted, classified, annotated, and indexed.* In this book they say:

The instrument enters the mouth and pharynx, then the oesophagus, traverses the cardiac end of the stomach, and enters the latter as far as the antrum of the pylorus, the small cul-de-sac of the stomach. In their normal state in the adult these organs are not in a straight line, but are so placed by the passage of the sword. In the first place they head is thrown back, so that the mouth is in the direction of the oesophagus, the curves of which disappear or become less as the sword proceeds; the angle that the oesophagus makes with the stomach is obliterated, and finally the stomach is distended in the vertical diameter and its internal curve disappears, thus permitting the blade to traverse the greater diameter of the stomach.

So there you have it. I wonder if it gives you a sword throat. Sorry.

120 Harry Houdini: small man, big mouth

The films of Hollywood director George Marshall are not much remembered today, except perhaps for *Destry Rides Again* (1939) and his 1953 non-masterpiece, *Houdini*, which starred Tony Curtis as the dashing, popular and charming escapologist. Of the various gigantic inaccuracies in this allegedly biographical fairytale, the biggest is the depiction of Houdini himself. In contrast to Curtis's witty, smiling sex-god, the real Harry Houdini was an unprepossessing, boastful, shrimp-like creature, with bowlegs, a squeaky eunuchoid voice and filthy manners, who was so big-headed that he was heartily loathed by fellow magicians. The only thing they got right in the film was his muscle-bound thighs.

This small magician with a big mouth was born Ehrich Weiss in Budapest on 24 March 1874, though he always told people he was born in Appleton, Wisconsin. Four years after Ehrich's birth the family moved to the US, where his father served as a rabbi, settling finally in New York City.

Ehrich started performing as a trapeze artist at the age of nine, in due course taking up magic and adopting the name 'Harry Houdini' in honour of his hero, the distinguished French magician Jean Eugène Robert-Houdin (1805–71). This name-thing was a crass error on Ehrich's part, since the Frenchman's surname was Robert-Houdin *not* Houdin. Presumably Ehrich thought his first name was Bob. On the other hand, of course, Harry Robert-Houdini would have been a bit of a mouthful.

Houdini started, as most performers do, at the very bottom, going round the dime museums doing card tricks. He billed himself as the 'King of Cards', which was a bit of a cheek since, by all accounts, his sleight of hand was less than invisible. In later years Houdini would boast to other magicians that he could work out any card trick that he saw three times. A brilliant young magician, Dai Vernon, took him up on the challenge, showing him a trick whereby he very plainly pushed the top card of the deck into the middle. With Houdini staring aggressively at his hands, he caused the card to appear back on the top, without any funny business. Indeed, Vernon did it seven times, Houdini repeatedly insisting that he 'do it again'. At last he was told by the surrounding group, 'Face it Houdini, you're fooled.' For years Vernon used the title 'The Man Who Fooled Houdini' in his publicity material.

Harry concentrated increasingly on escapes, which particularly suited his uncouth, bombastic performance style, and in 1899, at the age of 25, he was booked on the vaudeville circuit, where he became a huge hit. In 1900, billed as 'The Handcuff King', he took his act to Europe, where he was equally popular, at one point escaping, to much excitement, from Scotland Yard.

Houdini had an uncannily sophisticated understanding of the value of publicity, knowing just what would draw the press. His assiduous courting of the newspapers was the real secret of his success. Better to jump manacled from a famous bridge surrounded by photographers, or be tossed into the East River handcuffed inside a weighted, roped and nailed-up packing crate, than wriggle unannounced out of a sack in some dingy dime museum. He realized that a 'challenge' would bring the press running, so why not involve the press themselves? It would benefit both parties. Take the *Daily Mirror* handcuff challenge, for example, which involved Houdini surreptitiously inviting a challenge from the newspaper, and sneakily specifying the props – for so we may call them – before the challenge was issued, to great fanfare, and the feat performed.

The press, the public and Houdini were happy, and the money poured in. Houdini was now earning a fortune, doing much the same act as the one he had used in the dime museums. He bought a brownstone house at 278 W. 113th Street in Harlem, New York, for $25,000, which is little changed today – except for the number of zeroes at the end of the price.

As the twentieth century got into its stride, Houdini escaped from handcuffs, underwater packing cases, jails and – while dangling from a rope high above the street – from straitjackets. He got out of a padlocked milk can overflowing with water, and he escaped from wet sheets, mailbags and once from a huge paper envelope sealed with wax by members of the audience. He made an elephant disappear, he walked through a solid wall built by bricklayers in front of the audience and he was nightly manacled upside-down inside his 'Chinese Water Torture Cell'. Despite what happens in George Marshall's *Houdini*, this trick had nothing to do with his death, which was, as it turned out, more pedestrian.

But he couldn't escape from everywhere. In magic circles the tale has long been told of Houdini's making a call from an American hotel telephone booth. Seizing his opportunity, a waggish young chap locked the door to the booth, shutting Houdini securely inside, and causing him to rattle the handle in fury while releasing clouds of blood-curdling and strongly accented invective. He was finally let out, but didn't seem at all amused.

The new century provided Houdini with great backdrops and props: new skyscrapers, aeroplanes – which he learnt to fly – and moving pictures. Houdini himself made a few silent films, but watching him being tied to a chair with a long piece of rope and then charmlessly wriggling out, or enduring the *longueurs* as he writhes around on the floor in a straitjacket for minutes at a time, you can't help wondering what people saw in it. There were no porn channels in those days, of course.

In 1926, Houdini was planning his act for the following season, which would feature him being buried alive and then escaping to great tumult. A bronze coffin had already been made. But in October, after a lecture at Montreal's McGill University, a student called J. Gordon Whitehead came with two friends to Houdini's dressing room and, so as to test his claim that he could take a blow without injury, hit him repeatedly, without warning, in the abdomen.

Although in severe pain from his injury, Houdini continued to perform. On 24 October, in Detroit, Michigan he gave his last show, in considerable distress. He was taken to hospital where a ruptured appendix was removed, but he died of peritonitis a week later, on 31 October – Halloween. He was just fifty-two.

More than 2,000 mourners came to Houdini's funeral on 4 November, his body carried in the bronze coffin he'd had built for his Buried Alive act. This time, to nobody's amazement, he failed to escape.

121 A bedtime coin trick

If you've ever tried to move a washing machine or stop the Earth rotating with your foot, you will understand the basic principle of inertia, which is that things that are moving tend to go on moving (think planets), and things that are still tend to stay still unless you push on them hard (think broken-down car). Here's a nifty little trick that uses the principle of inertia. It is educational, fun and doable at bedtime. All you need is one or more coins of the same denomination, a bed and an elbow.

Method

1   Take your clothes off and drop them on the floor or hang them up, depending on your style. Put on pyjamas, if you wear them, and brush your teeth. The latter is not a requirement and will not affect the trick, but good oral hygiene is important in a gentleman.
2   If there is a woman (or anyone) in the bed, ask her to hide under the covers or go and make a milky drink, or something.
3   Take a coin or coins from your pocket and stand facing the bed. Larger coins are better for this trick because they are heavier and therefore less likely to fly around. It's best to begin learning this with a single coin and build up, a coin at a time, as you become more accomplished.
4   Lift your dominant arm into the position shown in the illustration, and, with your other hand, place a coin on your extended elbow about an inch or two from the sharp end.

5   Now quickly straighten your arm, at the same time cupping your hand. Because of inertia the coin/s will try to stay where it/they are even though the supporting elbow has disappeared from beneath it/them. And, before the force of gravity can attract it/them towards the centre of the planet, your hand has time enough to catch it/them. I wish I hadn't started this wretched 'it/them' business.

6   Practice is the key to success here, but it shouldn't take you too long to become proficient. Try ten goes a night and you'll be an expert within the month. In the early days you will have to put up with the occasional coin flying out of your hand at speed and breaking your girlfriend's mirror or knocking nail varnish and mascara bottles all over the place, but art requires sacrifice. Usually though, the bed will catch dropped coins for you, which is why bedtime is a good time to learn this little number.

7   As soon as you catch more often than you miss, you can begin to add coins. Before long you will be impressing the hell out of your wife/mistresses/bedfellow, etc. with your ability to catch a whole pile of them. What's more, next time you are feeling romantic you'll be able to ask the girl at the bar, 'Would you like to see me do an incredible miracle with money?' How can she say no?

Great Hoaxes and Swindles

122 'Find the Lady' explained

'Find the Lady', also known as 'Chase the Ace' and 'Three-card Monte', is a famous but nowadays little-seen con trick, in which a player shows a punter two indifferent black suit cards and a red queen, which he then throws face-down on a table and moves slowly about. Punters who correctly identify the queen's position win double their money. Except that they never do, because the card thrower secretly manipulates the cards so that he remains in total control of the queen's position.

I was chatting to a magician called Bobby Bernard not so long ago and he told me that when he was a young fellow, in the 1950s, he was watching a man entertaining a crowd with 'Find the Lady' on a stack of milk crates in Oxford Street. Being a magician, Bobby knew what chicanery was going on and he made a bet. Then, instead of allowing the card tosser to pick up the card he had identified as the queen, he went to do it himself. Before he could touch it, a large man next to him put a burning cigar in his ear and said menacingly, 'You've had your bet, son. Now eff off!' which, valuing his face more than his fiver, he did.

This cigar-man was what is known in the argot of the 'Monte men' as a 'shill', a confederate who encourages others to bet and occasionally 'wins' large sums himself. The team running a 'Find the Lady' con often consists of three or more men, all working together, one on the lookout for the police. At the slightest sign of a blue light, the lookout shouts 'Grub's up!' and they vanish, leaving the cards, the milk crates and a lot of bemused punters with light wallets.

The whole 'Find the Lady' setup is designed first to lure unsuspecting punters and then – like all con tricks – to reel them in using their desire to believe that they can beat the house. You can see how the psychology works: the crowd is happy, two punters (shills) keep 'winning,' and the game looks so simple as to be winnable by chance one time out of three. Unlucky punters who take the plunge sometimes 'win' their first bet, often 'going halves' on the bet with a 'nice man' in the crowd (a shill), who offers to share any winnings with them. And there's nothing like winning to get you hooked. Subsequent larger bets have a tendency to haemorrhage the punter's cash.

The patter of the Monte dealer, known in the trade as 'spieling the broads', is an important part of the act. 'Broad tossers', such as the famous Mississippi Monte man 'Umbrella Jim', used to begin with something sentimental, along the following lines: 'Gentlemen, I take no bets from paupers, cripples or orphans.' Sometimes they work in amusing and fair-sounding verse (doggerel):

> Hey diddle diddle, the queen's in the middle;
> When the money goes down, the queen can't be found.
> Five will get you ten, ten will get you twenty:
> *Cherchez la femme*. Find the lady.

Or you might hear:

> Here's a game of hanky-poo:
> The blacks for me, the queen for you.
> Maybe you win, and maybe you lose,
> It all depends on what you choose.

This sounds like a fair bet, but it is less than the full truth. As he speaks, the broad tosser flashes the faces of the cards – or 'tickets' as they are known – towards the punter and throws them down. When you see this done there is no doubt where the queen is. But in the act of throwing, the broad tosser is able to change their positions at will, even removing the queen and 'ringing in' a 'stranger' card that will always lose. With three indifferent cards on the table the punter can never win.

I won't explain the precise chicanery involved as it would require a lot of technical drawings and, anyway, even if you knew exactly what was going on and the way the con was being worked you could never win. With 'Find the Lady' even when you win, you lose, often to the tune of several teeth. No, the secret to avoid losing is this: do not bet. You are welcome to ignore this advice, of course, and try your luck, but there's a word for this and it is 'Sucker!'

123 Operation Mincemeat

In late 1942, the Allies were planning to invade Sicily, a strategic objective so obvious that Winston Churchill remarked, 'Everyone but a bloody fool would know that it's Sicily.' A plan was clearly needed to disguise the place of intended invasion, and cause the Germans to take their resources out of Sicily and put them in the wrong place.

Royal Navy intelligence officer Lt Cmdr Ewen Montagu developed an idea of Flight Lt Charles Cholmondeley's, of the RAF, to trick the Germans into thinking that, by good luck, they had intercepted highly secret documents containing the details of the Allied invasion plans. Together with Cholmondeley, who was another intelligence man, Montagu planned to fake several documents full of disinformation and attach them to the body of an apparently drowned man, which they would cause to wash up on a beach in Spain, where the supposedly neutral government was known to cooperate with German military intelligence, the Abwehr.

Montagu decided to make the dead man the apparent victim of a plane crash at sea in an area where the tides were likely to wash the body ashore. He was confident that the Spanish would pass on to local German agents any useful information they picked up from the corpse. The plan was approved and given the code name 'Operation Mincemeat'.

Renowned pathologist Sir Bernard Spilsbury helped Montagu to decide what kind of body they would need. The corpse, when discovered, would have to appear to be that of a man who had died at sea and drifted ashore after days. The coroner of St Pancras found them a suitable cadaver, that of thirty-four-year-old Glyndwr Michael, a vagrant Welshman who had killed himself by eating rat poison. He had died on 28 January 1943 at St Pancras Hospital, leaving few clues in his body as to the cause of death.

Now that he had a body, Montagu began to create a plausible identity for his courier, making him 'Captain (Acting Major) William Martin, Royal Marines'. He chose the name 'Martin' because there were several other similarly ranked Martins in the Royal Marines at the time. He gave Major Martin a birthday in 1907, thus making him a couple of years older than his own corpse. Montagu also kept him Welsh, lending him Cardiff as his town of birth.

The contents of the cadaver's pockets were contrived to reveal something of the living character. A bunch of keys, a letter from his father and theatre ticket stubs indicated a life beyond work. There was a photograph of his fiancée 'Pam' (actually an MI5 girl named Jean Leslie), together with two of her love letters. There was also the bill for four nights' lodging at his club, a bill for an engagement ring and a terse letter from the manager of Lloyds Bank, demanding payment of his overdraft. Major Martin seemed to be a chap living on tick.

Major Martin was also assigned a briefcase containing several carefully faked documents, including a personal letter from Lt Gen. Sir Archibald Nye, Vice Chief of the Imperial General Staff, to Sir Harold Alexander, commander of 18th Army Group in Algeria and Tunisia. Amongst the persuasively 'touchy' subjects covered in the letter was a highly misleading reference to Operation Husky (the planned invasion of Sicily) as the invasion of Greece, and to an intended attack on Sardinia for which the cover target was Sicily.

Major Martin also carried a letter to Admiral Cunningham, Allied naval commander in the Mediterranean, from Admiral of the Fleet The Right Honourable The Earl Mountbatten of Burma KG, GCB, OM, GCSI, GCIE, GCVO, DSO, KJStJ, PC, FRS. If they were trying to impress the Germans with post-nominal letters of the alphabet, they had picked the right man. Mountbatten's letter included a joke about 'sardines', devised by Montagu as a supposed reference to the fake invasion of Sardinia.

But how to make sure none of these letters came adrift of the corpse in the water? The team decided to attach Major Martin to his briefcase with a long chain, such as are used by bank couriers to prevent the theft of cash. Although officer couriers never used such chains, this seemed a trifling point.

On 15 April 1943, the ruse was explained to Winston Churchill while he was in bed smoking a cigar. It piqued his interest. So, with approval from the highest levels, with the documents inside the bag, and the letters and whatnot in the pockets, the body of the unfortunate tramp was taken out of the fridge, tidied up, given a military haircut and dressed. He was then sealed inside a steel canister full of solid carbon dioxide (dry ice). This produced enough carbon dioxide gas to drive out the oxygen and inhibit further deterioration of the corpse. Cholmondeley and Montagu took the canister, with 'Major Martin' inside it, to Holy Loch in Scotland, where they put it aboard a submarine, HMS *Seraph*. It set sail on 19 April, with its commander Lt Bill Jewell telling his men that the canister contained a secret weather forecasting instrument.

On 30 April, eleven days later, the sub surfaced at a point a mile off the coast of southwest Spain, near the town of Huelva. The canister was brought up and all crew but the officers were then sent below. Commander Jewell swiftly briefed the three officers on the interesting, and actual, contents of the tin and explained their job. They opened the canister, put a lifejacket on the corpse and attached the briefcase. Since it seemed unlikely that the Major would keep the bag on his wrist during a long flight from Britain, the chain was looped around the belt of his trench coat. After a swift psalm (number 39), the four sailors rolled Glyndwr Michael off a blanket into the sea. The canister was sunk.

At about 9.30 the next morning the body was found by a local fisherman, José Antonio Rey Maria, and a few days later the corpse, its intact briefcase and unopened letters were handed over to the British Vice-Consul. The briefcase was returned to the intelligence people, and on 4 May 'Major Martin' was buried in Huelva with full military honours. Had the scheme failed?

In fact, Operation Mincemeat was going exactly to plan and the Spanish had been busy. They had quickly realized the likely importance of their find and had reported it pretty smartly to the Abwehr agent in Huelva. They had then set about investigating the contents of the briefcase. They cleverly removed the wet letters from their wax-sealed envelopes by inserting a long double-pronged pincer, winding them around it and pulling them out through the gap at the top of the envelope. The letters were dried under a lamp and the Abwehr chief in Madrid was given an hour to make copies. He immediately radioed the contents to Berlin.

The documents were carefully put back in their envelopes, soaked in seawater for a while and returned to the British. When the intelligence johnnies examined them, they found that they had clearly been tampered with and assumed they had been read. Winston Churchill, who was in the US, received an interesting message: 'Mincemeat Swallowed Whole'.

Not only had the letters been read, they had got as far as Hitler himself, who, persuaded of their genuineness, immediately ordered that 'Actions regarding Sardinia and the Peloponnese take priority over all else.' German military forces were diverted from Sicily into Greece, Sardinia and Corsica, allowing the Allies a much easier time of it when they eventually invaded Sicily on 9 July. Indeed, the Germans remained poised two weeks later to repel the imminent attacks they still expected in Sardinia and Greece, leaving their vital forces with nothing to do but twiddle their thumbs.

By a combination of fine planning, care, cleverness, brass neck and several dollops of good luck, Operation Mincemeat had been a triumphant success and much back-patting was gone in for. However, recognition for the unconscious role of the late Glyndwr Michael in this great success story was a long time coming. For years afterwards Montagu maintained that the body he had used had been given willingly by the parents of the dead man on the understanding that his name would never be revealed. In fact the Welsh vagrant's parents had both died before him and he had no known relations. It was not until 1996, more than half century after the event, that Roger Morgan, an amateur historian, uncovered Glyndwr Michael's true identity.

Two years later, in January 1998, the Commonwealth War Graves Commission quietly appended an inscription to the gravestone of 'Major Martin' at his burial place in Huelva. It reads simply, 'Glyndwr Michael served as Major William Martin RM'.

124 The Society for Indecency to Naked Animals

In 1999 an HBO documentary called *Private Dicks: Men Exposed* was shown on US television. It featured a plump middle-aged man called Bruce, who, sitting in just his underpants, talked about his penis, which, he admitted, was smaller than a cigar stub – 'when it's *erect*'. After transmission it emerged that 'Bruce' was the notorious hoaxer Alan Abel, a man deeply feared by the media for his uncanny ability to devise hoaxes so seductive that journalists would hug the knife as it stabbed them.

Take Jim Rogers, from the campaign group Citizens Against Breastfeeding, who was interviewed hundreds of times in 2000, arguing that breastfeeding should be banned because it was 'incestuous' and led to 'smoking, drinking, and, in one instance, Monica Lewinski, who was breastfed until she was four years old'. A lot of po-faced journalists shook their heads at Rogers' medieval attitudes, but Mr Rogers was, of course, Alan Abel who, even after exposing his hoax, continued to receive requests to appear on TV.

Abel was born in 1930 and took a degree in education before becoming a writer, film-maker and jazz percussionist; his forte was, however, the media prank. Angered by hypocrisy and the mindless pap that TV and newspapers poured over their somnolent consumers, Abel understood which hoaxes would best work, such as launching the popular Topless String Quartet, or, under the auspices of 'Taxpayers Anonymous', demanding to see the government's books, ordering them to bring all their cancelled cheques to his house. He also ran for Congress, insisting on the installation of a lie detector in the White House and the addition of 'truth serum' to the Senate's drinking-fountain water. In later years Abel formed a gift-wrapped-urine company, whose spokesman was Mr Stoidi Puekaw. Read backwards this is 'wake up idiots', a slogan that put some of his underlying attitudes in a nutshell.

Alan Abel died in 1979 after suffering a heart attack on a skiing holiday. When his widow contacted the *New York Times* to announce his death, journalists went to great lengths to make sure he was really dead before daring to write up the story. One reporter even surreptitiously rang the funeral home where his body was being held. The paper published its obituary on 2 January 1980. The following day Abel held a news conference to announce that reports of his death had been greatly exaggerated. The funeral home number, absently supplied to the *New York Times* by his distracted 'widow', was that of an accomplice.

But Alan Abel's longest running hoax was one of his first. In May 1959 the *Today Show* ran a story about the Society for Indecency to Naked Animals (SINA), whose slogan was: 'A nude horse is a rude horse'. Anyone who bothered to think about the organization's name would have noticed that something funny was going on – it is worse than meaningless – although this didn't stop the hoax galloping away with itself. In more than one sense, the story had 'legs'.

SINA's entirely imaginary leader, G. Clifford Prout Jr (played by the then unknown Buck Henry), pointed out that grazing cows were 'hanging their heads in shame because they are forced to be nudists in a clothed society'. He explained that all horses, cows, dogs, cats and other domestic animals that stand higher than four inches or are longer than six inches should wear clothing for the sake of decency. Many people sent in money, which was always returned. Five long years after SINA's launch, *Time* magazine finally exposed the hoax. Abel explained that his aim had been to attack censorship, poke fun at people's foibles and fears, and mock 'the humorless, misguided, pathetic, self-proclaimed champions of democracy'.

Alan Abel claims to be still alive, but how could anyone be sure? In case he is, I take my hat off to him. Actually, I take all my clothes off to him. He deserves a medal.